PORNOGRAPHY AND THE PULPIT:
Understanding the Sins of the Shepherd as a Means of Restoration

RICHARD NEVARD

PublishAmerica
Baltimore

ISBN: 1-4241-1911-1
PUBLISHED BY PUBLISHAMERICA, LLLP
www.publishamerica.com
Baltimore

Printed in the United States of America

Pornography and the Pulpit

ACKNOWLEDGMENTS:

To my wife Christi:
You taught me new depths to grace
so I could find new heights to love.
Thank you.

Testimony of the Recovering Pastor

Therefore, since through God's mercy we have this ministry, we do not lose heart. Rather, we have renounced secret and shameful ways; we do not use deception, nor do we distort the word of God. On the contrary, by setting forth the truth plainly we commend ourselves to every man's conscience in the sight of God But we have this treasure in jars of clay to show that this all-surpassing power is from God and not from us. We are hard pressed on every side, but not crushed; perplexed, but not in despair; persecuted, but not abandoned; struck down, but not destroyed. We always carry around in our body the death of Jesus, so that the life of Jesus may also be revealed in our body. For we who are alive are always being given over to death for Jesus' sake, so that his life may be revealed in our mortal body. So then, death is at work in us, but life is at work in you.

2 Corinthians 4:1-2, 7-12

INTRODUCTION

Of all sin's deadly vices, none is as insidious as sexual addiction, and of the varied offspring of sexual sin, pornography addiction is surely a favored child. Pornography addiction has been defined as a continued pattern of compulsive sexual behavior which has a negative impact on the individual's personal, social and/or economic standing. While pornography use has been generally viewed solely as an act of the will, overwhelming research in the past two decades has found pornography to be an addictive substance which adversely alters the chemicals in the human brain, is cognitively connected to past childhood trauma, and socially induced by outside stressors; pornography is a sin that affects body, mind and spirit.

While for much of human history, pornography was generally viewed as a sinful behavior that existed outside of the Church, with the inception of the Internet, pornography use has since burst through the walls of virtually every church in the United States. Every congregation, regardless of size, has someone in it that is sexually addicted.[1] More than 50% of all Christian pastors are reportedly addicted to pornography and among church laity, the numbers are significantly higher.[2] While these staggering figures are brought out in anonymous surveys, far to few of these clandestine confessions make their way outside of the ecclesiastical closet in order to find healing and restoration. Moreover, today's denominations are stalemated on how to deal with this moral collapse and so are ill-prepared to stem this raging flood. Because of this churches today are under the leadership of spiritually fragmented men and women and the life and work of the Church is grievously suffering for it. This epidemic threatens both the family and the Church, causing untold numbers of spiritual casualties. Refusing to deal with pornography addiction in the Church will destroy lives, tear apart families, deeply wound congregations, and destroy the witness of Christ in our world.

Pornography addiction is a spiritual sickness, infecting the nature of human sexuality and forever altering the human psyche. Remarkably, pastoral ministry has not only shown itself susceptible to sexual addiction, but pornography addiction has shown itself to be the "drug of choice" among clergy. The same personality traits that compel an individual toward pastoral ministry are found in persons most inclined to sexual addiction, and the pastoral office itself is set up in such a manner as to influence clergy toward pornography. Further, pornography addiction is a generational sin, perpetuating itself through the damaged spiritual and emotional experiences of dysfunctional life, a "sin of the fathers to the third and fourth generation" (Exodus 34:7b; 20:5).

This book is an interdisciplinary method, integrating biblical-theological foundations with social science research and pastoral concerns related to pornography. It addresses the nature and purpose of human sexuality and shows how sin has distorted this image; it exposes the unique pathological characteristics of sexual sin and the pattern of its destruction. We will explore the effects of pornography on Western society as a whole as well as focus on the damage caused to societal and spiritual structures, such as the family and the local church. It explores more closely what causal factors are at work in the fall of these persons called of God and how the office of pastoral ministry lends itself to pornographic vulnerability. We will look at the path of perdition in which the clergyperson denigrates spiritually to the point of forfeiting God's saving grace in their lives and the process of recovery he or she must pass through to recover their faith and spiritual footing. Finally, the book addresses from a biblical perspective the issue of restoration for the fallen minister, first understanding the Church's role in reconciling the individual to relationship with God and then constructing a workable plan for restoring the person to the office and work of pastoral ministry.

My hope and prayer is that this book will serve as a catalyst for recovery for pastors, families and churches so that we may once again be in the world but not infected by the world.

Rick Nevard

My Story:

There is an old saying: "Let's confess our sins to each other — you go first!" When it comes to discussing something as personal as sexual addictions, people are interested in the topic, but not particularly in getting personal with their own history. It's the nature of the beast. In the same way, most people are not interested in reading a book about sexual addictions and dealing with their own monsters until they know the person writing the book has been where they are. You have to earn the right to be heard. For that reason I've included My Story, my personal testimony of how I entered into and found deliverance from pornography addiction. For the sake of those still struggling I have decided not to be too descriptive with the details. I've provided some of the environmental issues as backdrop to help you see some of the causes for my personal struggles, many of which show up in the principles we will discuss in the book. I think it's also beneficial for you to know that my research and writing took place *during the process* of my recovery. The ideas presented are not the work of someone straining to recall a journey long since passed, but are lessons hammered hard upon the crucible of my daily struggles. While much of what I write is mirrored in my own experiences, I was determined not to write with a particular bias in any direction. I have prayerfully sought to let the experts speak from their own proficiency and to let Scripture do the same. My hope is that countless numbers of people, pastors and laity alike will find deliverance from sexual addiction, that families and congregations will find healing, that the integrity of Christ's Church may be restored.

As best as I can remember, I was nine-years-old when I first encountered pornography. Like poison injected into the bloodstream, it coursed throughout my soul long before I knew anything about God or his grace. I wasn't raised in a Christian home — oh, we would make our yearly Easter pilgrimage — that is, unless we could convincingly fake an illness. My sisters and I grew up in a rural town in New Jersey. The youngest of six and the only male, I was my father's last hope of carrying on the family name. Unfortunately, as appealing a notion as leaving a legacy seemed, dad never did see the need to invest himself in his progeny. For me, life in the Nevard home consisted of an alcoholic father, the typical crisis experiences that accompany multiple teenagers and preteens in the home, and a working mother who tried her best to hold it all together. They say necessity is the mother of invention and necessity dictated that the older three siblings in the family care for the rest of us. A good plan in theory, but the self-obsession of adolescence makes for a lousy babysitter and an even worse surrogate mother. Needless to say, the younger three, as with the older ones, were on their own.

As with most young boys, I idolized my father. A building contractor by trade, dad was the epitome of manhood to me: driving trucks, work boots covered in cement, constructing buildings with his own bare hands. He was a man's man: a gun collector and hunter, requiring red meat at every meal, I don't believe I ever saw my dad eat a piece of lettuce. Rarely would he eat dinner with the family, instead, mom would bring his meals to the living room, where he would spend his nights lying on the couch, watching old WWII movies. Even his vices were manly: he smoked his Camels and drank his booze, swearing obscenities that would make his old Navy buddies blush. I was soon to find that he had another, darker, more sinister vice — Dad was addicted to pornography.

Looking back, I now see dad was just a man, his victories overshadowed by his failures. He was self-absorbed and neglectful of his family, verbally and, at times, physically abusive. Unable to express affection, words like, "I love you," or, "I'm proud of you" were rarely spoken if ever. In fact, our family as a whole was never very demonstrative in their expressions of love and praise. Words said and unsaid leave indelible marks on the soul of a child. Because of his alcoholism, dad found himself frequently in and out of rehab. My earliest memories were of my sneaking to the refrigerator to water down his bottle of gin and vivid memories of my helping mom pick him off the ground after falling in a drunken stupor or helping to drag him into the psyche hospital after dad attempted suicide. My father had made many mistakes and lost many battles, but seeing him through the eyes of a nine-year-old boy, desperate for a male role model, he could do no wrong. He was my dad and I was going to make him proud, I was going to be just like him.

Dad had an office downstairs in the house. How cool was that to a young boy! Being left alone (or, at least unsupervised) much of the time, dad's office was a wonderful escape, a place to explore his world, and so, connect with him emotionally.

When I think back, I'm amazed that I survived childhood at all. Many times I would pull his rifles down from the gun racks on the wall. With careful eye, I would imagine myself as a big game hunter in Africa. Against the wall to the right of my father's desk was one of those old safes that you see in the movies. I always thought it was funny, watching the safecrackers on television. The tumblers on that old steel box were so loud that a small child could (and often did) easily break in. Inside was a magical world of intrigue and excitement. Stacked on top of one another was an assortment of handguns, including a loaded .45 cal revolver, complete with belt and holster. I remember, I would strap that belt around my waist and in my mind I bested the toughest hombres in the old West. But still there was more to discover, more secrets to unearth. Underneath the guns and bullets was a small stack of magazines more lethal than anything I could shoot.

The magazines were different: No glossy photos, the paper was more like the supermarket tabloids today. The contents of the pages bordered on the bizarre. Oddities that can best be described as exhibits from an adult *Ripley's Believe it or Not*. I vividly remember a picture of a woman with three breasts and advertisements for very unusual toys. These were my first experiences with pornography. More than thirty years later those images still haunt me. It was a generational sin that my father probably inherited from his father and which was now being passed down to me, and, like Harry Chapin's song, *Cats in the Cradle*, I was growing up to be just like him.

It didn't take long before the pictures under the guns became more interesting than the guns themselves. I would borrow a few of the rags to share with my friends. Before long those friends were bringing family collections of their own. Dad had built a barn in the back yard to house all of his tools and lumber and I was given the top portion as a fort (real men have forts, not club houses!). That upstairs hideaway became the neighborhood adult library for my friends and me. Centerfolds were taped to the walls and a growing stack of Penthouse magazines sat on the makeshift table. The older boys taught those of us who were younger how to masturbate. Soon the walls that separated each of us from the rest of our world began to close in. What more did we need? We would play baseball or go fishing and then climb the ladder to our reading room for a couple hours of escape. I didn't need my father's stash any longer. In fact, I began to discover I really didn't need my dad any longer either. Family influence began to fade and the only thing that mattered was my collection.

This behavior continued off and on until I was fifteen and dad decided to sell the house and move us all to Florida. Looking back, I'm amazed that I didn't begin craving my porn. Was it just a childhood interest that passed as I got older? I was soon to find out that it wasn't. I didn't like Florida at first. It was hard starting over. At that time our next door neighbor was an old woman, named Dot, who was a little fireball. She loved football and was a member of the Quarterback Club, traveling around the country to follow her favorite teams. Dot lived alone and so she loaned me her house and pool when she was out of town. It wasn't long before my curious nature took me to exploring her house and, low and behold, I found a new set of Penthouse and Playboy magazines. Immediately I took up where I had left off and very quickly Dot's empty house became my new place of escape.

A year later we had moved to a new home in that town. Dad and I had built a set of townhouses and finance rates forced us to move into one of them. Again, giving up the porn didn't pose a problem for me. I began to make friends at school and a couple of those friends (female!) invited me to go to church with them. Now, I've studied experts in evangelism techniques, but common sense still proves that when three girls invite a sixteen-year-old boy to go to church, that boy goes to church! It was a little Nazarene church on the other side of town - much different from the Easter services at our old Episcopal Church! It was a small life-giving church and I soon found Christ and invited him to be my Savior and Lord. Again, looking back, I'm not sure if I was even aware then that pornography was wrong. It was at this point I began to discover that real girls are a whole lot more fun than pictures in a magazine and dating became a big part of my life. It is only by God's grace and my emotionally arrested state of development that kept me from actual sex. God was there, but he wasn't Someone I gave much credence to back then.

After graduation I joined the Air Force. During basic training I experienced a true spiritual awakening that I can best describe as a sanctifying experience. It was during this time also that I led my first person to the Lord. God was real and I began to grow. After training I was stationed at Minot, North Dakota, or, as they say in the Air Force: "Why not Minot?"

There were plenty of reasons to that question. The long dark nights, the bitter cold winters, the lonely days of small hometown life yet no place to call home. I lived on base in the barracks, isolated from church and any Christian contact. On that base of several thousand people, I found myself desperately lonely and unusually anxious. Something within me compelled me to search through my roommate's dresser, and there I discovered his small stack of Playboy magazines. Immediately my pulse began to race and blood was fiercely pumping in my chest and my head. My mind recalled those euphoric rushes and my entire body fevered. I wasn't prepared emotionally or spiritually for what I was experiencing, I didn't know what was happening. All I knew was that there was this insatiable need to pick up those magazines and drink in those images. For the first time I knew what it really meant to have a war rage against my soul (1 Peter 2:11). I knew, somehow, that life for me was being forever altered. "We know that the law is spiritual but I am unspiritual, sold as a slave to sin. I do not understand what I do. For what I want to do I do not do, but what I hate to do…I have the desire to do what is good, but I cannot carry it out…When I want to do good, evil is right there with me…What a wretched man I am!"

(Romans 7:14b-15, 18b, 21b, 24a).

I discovered, as Paul did, that sin doesn't lose its influence over you, even when you give yourself to Christ. All things become new, except for the old sin nature. I wrestled for several months until I was finally able to get on the other side of this addiction and find enough strength to be free for a time. But, as is true with all things fought in our own strength, victories are hollow and short-lived. It returned a time or two over the next couple of years, but then I met Christi. Beautiful, vivacious, I was hooked. Love had won over lust. My compulsive nature wasted no time and three months later we were married. In my mind I thought, certainly, there would be no need for pornography and masturbation now. I have the real thing lying right beside me! But sin's reprieve would soon give way and pornography would again exact its due. I hated lying to Christi about my addiction, but how could I tell her? How could she possibly understand? She had her own negative experiences with men from her youth to contend with. One of her more routine expressions was (and is), "Men are pigs!" I knew that if the truth ever came to light that our marriage would be over, yet, because of my shameful secret, there was always a barrier between Christi and me. I could never express genuine love for her because, in truth, I was too focused on me. Pornography addiction, as with most addictions brings a preoccupation with self. It's hard to love others when you are too busy loving yourself. For seventeen years Christi languished emotionally, desperately needing me to love her but always doubtful that I did. Pornography continued to be an addiction that would overwhelm me for a time until I was able to gain control over it again. I became a periodic user, commanding every bit of strength I had within me to break free for a time. But after a few years, my attentiveness diminished and my resistance down, the serpent would strike another fatal blow to my spirit. It held me even when I was working in youth ministry. Warning teenagers about sin's deadly snare, yet, trapped in one myself.

When I received my call to pastoral ministry, my hope, albeit faint, was that finally I would be released from this affliction. And for a good many years I was able to hold back the great tide of sexual sin. I pastored a small church and watched God bless both the work and me. With a compulsive inner drive, I gave every ounce of strength I had to ministry. I dealt with gossipers and backbiting and betrayal. I watched as those closest to me turned their anger in on me. I realize now that those same emotional issues of neglect and abuse that I experienced as a child were being visited upon me in the pastorate. Afraid, overwhelmed, hurt, and tired, I checked my e-mails one morning to find an explicit picture of a naked woman and an invitation to view more by following their link. The trap was set, the bait in place. Every neurotransmitter in my brain sprang to life and those same euphoric feelings from my past were once again gathered around for a reunion celebration. Even as the picture file was still opening, I knew that I had lost. I followed that link which led me to a hundred more. Several hours went by and by the time I logged off I was intoxicated by lust, my body and mind soothed from the chemical releases in my brain, my spirit overwhelmed with grief. Oh, what have I done?

Now what do I do? Do I confess my sins? The stakes are so much higher now. I faced the real threat of losing my family, my ministry, my home, my employment — my future. Who do I turn to? Could anyone understand? Would they extend mercy to me or pass harsh judgment? People wonder how an addict could let things get so far out of hand and wonder why someone would risk so much for something so small. Such persons demonstrate that they have either never been given over to a destructive addiction or they have neatly kept from applying these questions to their own set of circumstances. I hope and pray it's the former, but I suspect it's more the latter.

For the next several months I lived life as a double-minded person, unstable in all my ways (James 1:6-7). Every day was another emotional roller coaster ride, working at the church during the day, edgy throughout the evening, overcome with temptation through the night and indulging my lust until the wee hours of the morning. Immediately after the sting of death had injected its poison (1 Corinthians 15:56), after masturbatory release had been achieved, I would fall to my knees, earnestly pouring my heart out to God, asking forgiveness and begging for deliverance. Yet, even as I prayed, I knew in the back of my mind that tomorrow would bring more of the same. I know now that the reason I asked God to take lust from me was because I was unwilling to give it up. Deliverance requires human surrender to enact the Divine Authority. When the father brought his son, who was demon possessed, to the disciples, they were unable to help (Mark 9:14-29). After Jesus healed the child, the disciples ask why they were ineffective. Jesus' response to his friends was "This kind can come out only by prayer and fasting" (v. 29). Prayer and fasting: enacting God's power and enabling his authority through denying self. Miraculous healing from such sin is not always instantaneous. Many times it's a battle to the death. And it is, in fact, in death that victory is achieved. It took Jesus' death to purchase our release from sin and it took my death to self to enact his authority over sin in my life as well.

My dumbest mistake became my vessel of hope. You see, the only place that I had Internet access was at the church, in the Sunday school office. It was here that I was reintroduced to sexual sin and here that I fed my addiction. I thought I had covered my tracks pretty well, deleting all files of a sexual nature. But when you have a board member with a Masters degree in computer engineering, you find that there are places somewhere in that computer where those files can still be accessed. I thought cookies were kept in cookie jars, not computers! One morning I received a phone call from the Church Treasurer. She asked if she and this computer-genius board member could come to the church and talk with me about some things they found on the computer. I was had. I was caught and I knew it. After hanging up the phone I began to panic. My heart raced and my breathing became erratic. "What do I do?" In desperation I began to pray that God would help me get out of this, that I may think up something that will get me off the hook. Then it dawned on me: I was asking the God of all Truth to help me fabricate a lie. Something broke within me. Years of sin's torment and masquerading righteousness had been severed in one fell swoop. I breathed deep and prayed, "Alright Lord. Just give me the strength. I admitted my sin to these two ladies and promised to get help.

I'd like to say that I immediately walked the steps of recovery, disclosing my sin to my wife and District Superintendent, but, in truth, I was still calling the shots. I set up an accountability partner outside the church who would come by each week to ask if I was "behaving myself." And I had, for a time. But this serpent's head would not be crushed so easily. A second time I gave into my lusts and a second time these ladies called me on the carpet. This time confession to my wife and my District Superintendent was no longer my choice. My D.S., David, was very kind. There were times that I didn't like the way he handled things, but in retrospect, I was defensive and even argumentative at times. He set me up with a counselor and gave me a week to tell my wife. The counselor suggested that I bring Christi to my next counseling session in order to break the news. I assured him that the guilt upon me was so strong that I would not be able to wait. I tried desperately that night to soften the blow, hinting to the nature of the issue at hand, but I couldn't do it. I just couldn't get my mouth to form the words.

In the counselor's office, I found the strength to give voice to those very painful issues. I will never forget the heartrending look of betrayal that swept across her face. Eighteen years of marriage, three children together, she sacrificed and struggled beside me, supporting me and helping me in fulfilling my dreams and I had, in one brief statement, crushed her spirit. Needless to say, the drive home was in absolute silence. Once home, though, words poured out like a busted reservoir. We fought and consoled, we talked of divorce and leaving ministry, we prayed and then argued some more. But, by the end of a very long evening, Christi had accepted the truth and offered to me very tender words of forgiveness. Christi gave me mercy.

This isn't to say that feelings of anger and betrayal didn't erupt. Those feelings swept over Christi, seemingly every hour — how could they not? What could I do? I didn't defend myself. I had no right to defend myself. I let Christi express her feelings with whatever amount of intensity she needed and I stayed right there taking every angry word of it. Christi had biblical rights to divorce me; she didn't have to stay in this mess. But one anchor held her fast: Christi had already decided in her heart to forgive me. In her mind every other option was now off the table. She didn't deny or repress her emotions; she walked through each of them until she came out the other side. I never knew such depths of grace existed, I learned new levels of God's grace by seeing it displayed through Christi.

Was everything magically better? Not by a long shot. I submitted to the District Superintendent's terms for voluntary suspension. I filed my credentials and stepped out of ministry for two years. I went through counseling during that time and made monthly reports of my progress. Since we lived in the church's parsonage, we had to abruptly move, relocating and uprooting the kids. Christi suggested I go back to seminary for my Masters, which not only gave us a good excuse for leaving, but also provided me with purpose and direction. We were twice blessed to find that the seminary offered free counseling to students and their families. I had to find a job, which wasn't easy. I had a Bachelors degree so low paying employers didn't think I would stay around and, because my degree is in Theology, no high paying job would give me a chance either. Three months had passed and I practically had to beg for a job that paid starvation wages. We moved from a five-bedroom parsonage to a two-bedroom apartment that would have fit in its garage. Guilt and humiliation were my close companions during that time, but closer still were my God and my family.

Through the counseling and my twelve-step work I was able to not only deal with my pornography addiction, but I was able to look deeper within myself and see the underlying issues of why I was given over to this compulsive behavior. In the same way an archeologist carefully digs into the earth, one layer at a time, to unearth important truths from the past, I began to dig down and discover certain truths about my past. I discovered things such as issues of insecurity and a strong need for approval stemming from my childhood. I discovered that, along with my addiction to porn, I was also addicted to food, needless spending, and overworking. But the deeper I went the more I needed to know where these issues originated and why they manifested themselves in such deplorable ways. Just as the archeologist, after he or she has unearthed several artifacts, wishes to piece together the context of the period to understand the narrative, so I needed to know the context for my story as well. The two-year journey has been hard, but now, having gone through it, I'm grateful for the expedition. I am twice blessed, because God has allowed me to help other sexual addicts to step on the path of recovery and self-discovery. My deepest hope is that this book will help you to begin this journey too.

Rick Nevard

CHAPTER 1
PRIMARY THEOLOGICAL QUESTIONS

Creation Theology

"The Splitting of the Adam"[3]

"For you created my inmost being; you knit me together in my mother's womb. I praise you because I am fearfully and wonderfully made; your works are wonderful, I know that full well."
Psalm 139:13-14

From the very moment the expectant parents decide on the color paint for the nursery walls gender distinctions are being introduced. Throughout the maturation process, gender differences are being taught to little boys and girls. Not necessarily the anatomic distinctions, but rather the distinct gender roles. These distinctions are reinforced as we mature and become more pronounced as we get older. Throughout the many millennia of humankind's existence, we have enforced these distinctions and ascribed them to be the natural order of things.

In truth, there is more common ground between the sexes than we have allowed ourselves to believe and nowhere are these similarities more pronounced than in the basic biological structure of the "man." Travel back in time, farther and farther, all the way back to the first trimester of pregnancy. The only noticeable difference between the male-female structures is a single chromosome. The mother's egg carries two X-chromosomes while the father's sperm normally carries an X and a Y chromosome. We have, at this point, dared venture into "no man's land," to "boldly go where **no man** has ever gone before," back to the point where the only existing gender is female. The mother's chromosomes carry the basic body structure of the child, which is female. This means that all babies are initially created female, with breasts, ovaries and a vagina. If the father's sperm carries the Y-chromosomes it will overpower the female's X decision and "modify" the basic model of the baby to male. This all takes place as early as the first trimester of pregnancy, but it is important to recognize that we all start out female. "The penis is actually the clitoris transformed and enlarged by androgens. As the vaginal lips enfold the penis, the urinary tract is extended and enclosed."[4] All males were first female, all females could have been born male; it is all in the hands of that one tiny Y chromosome — and God.

In addition, just as the male body is a modified version of the female, the same can be said of the male brain. That same Y chromosome that transformed our bodies also does a number on our brains. The left and right hemispheres of the brain are conjoined by several million neurological fibers. The hormonal chemicals in the male, such as testosterone, are at work modifying those fibers, forming us into distinct male and female individuals. These brain modifications have an impact in how we think, feel, process information, reason and react.

Here is another example of science elucidating Scripture. Notice the name Adam gives to his new partner: "woman." The word woman in the Hebrew language means "life," or "life-giver." It is through the woman that all human life springs (this understanding ties well with the curse placed upon Eve after the Fall: "I will greatly increase your pains in childbearing..." (Genesis 3:16a). Sin diminished the joy of childbirth, woman's chief role and greatest satisfaction). All life flows from the woman — all life begins as woman. If the entire human race, then, begins as female, what does this say about the first created human called "man?"

"God created man...male and female he created them."

Then God said, "Let us make *man* in our image, in our likeness, and let *them* rule... So God created *man* in his own image in the image of God he created him; *male and female* he created *them*.

Genesis 1:26-27 (italicized mine)

Humankind is from the very beginning a "duality in unity," first in relation to God and earth and also between male and female. As part of creation, humanity's being is derived from God, yet he is fashioned from the dust of the earth. He is formed from earthly materials but then filled with the immortal breath of heaven. The duality of humankind is further asserted as "man" (a neuter-gendered term, used for both male and female) is created with sexual differentiation and sexual interrelation; *Adam*, commonly translated as "man," is from the very beginning created male and female.[5] While the term "man" was ascribed to the first male, it was not used for the male in isolation. There is no man without the interrelation of male and female; both are needed to complete the species.[6] God creates Adam both male and female, and then he "split the Adam,"[7] sexually differentiating the human species. The original Adam was incomplete; it took "the scalpel of God in a surgical separation"[8] in order to make "man" whole.

In Genesis 1:26 God creates man (singular) and then refers to him as "them" (plural). In the very next verse, the author notes that God did indeed create "him" (singular) and then designated two unique sexes (plural) for that one distinct creation known as "man." Throughout history, the plural usage in this text has been attributed to both Adam and Eve and to the future human race that would come into being because of them. The term "man," *ha'adam*, is a collective term, incorporating both male and female together. Similar to today's usage of the term "humanity," it is a generic reference that incorporates both genders, used within the context of community.[9] Collectively we are the whole of man; isolated we are fragmented. God created a solitary human, called "man," and yet, while perfectly made, God considered his creation incomplete because the human was alone. God had in mind to create community and continuity by forming male and female from the same *man*. When he stood back to inspect his handiwork, God declared this new species "very good" (Genesis 1:31).

Can you see the implications? Human beings apart from one another are incomplete: "It is not good for 'man' (Adam) to be alone." God created them to be joined as one (including sexually) in order that they may be whole, or, once again be made "one flesh." The thing that makes sexual sin so diabolical is that it tears the person, body and soul apart. "All sin is done outside the body, *but he who sins sexually sins against his own body*" (I Corinthians 6:18, italicized mine). It causes the person to withdraw from their partner and their God into a state of isolation and desolation. Pornography is a counterfeit of God's design, a selfish form of *eros* love, done simply for our own gratification. Worse, it causes us to compare those airbrushed glossy photos to our spouses, which causes us to "lurk at our neighbor's door" (Job 31:9b) to see if the grass is indeed greener. The isolation becomes even more pronounced as the sin causes such shame that the person pulls further away, covering their sin with lies, their shame engulfs them in despair.

Patriarchy has caused us to see the male as the dominant person and thus conferred on the female secondary status and in many cases blame for the anthropological mess we have made of things. We have, at times, carried this assertion beyond reason and beyond Scripture to the false conclusion that man would be better off disconnected from woman, celibate and chaste. But the duality of man shows a need to be connected both with heaven and earth, God and community, male with female. The Triune Godhead was creating for himself a form of "triune creation," joining God with humanity, male with female. Even when the male, Adam, walked in relationship with God, he was seen as incomplete. Thus, completion of human sexuality can only occur when joined in a community of three: male, female, and the God who made them both.[10]

Mankind was made for community; to find completion in unity with one another and wholeness in unity with God. Therefore, the blessings of God are those things that draw persons together in unity with God; the ultimate curse, then, would be those things that break unity.

Nature and Purpose of Human Sexuality

The Legend of Eros

In Greek mythology, Eros is the god of sexual passion, the son of Aphrodite the goddess of desire. Eros is extremely beautiful but also extremely immature, irresponsible and the cause of much trouble. (Eros is the Greek word for passion, ecstasy, madness and irrationality – it is not long into puberty before we begin to experience all four of these dimensions!) In Apuleius' play *The Golden Ass*, the beautiful Psyche (the soul) is tricked into believing that Eros is repulsive and must never look at him. But finally curiosity gets the better of her and she wakes Eros to look upon his face. Immediately Psyche falls in love with Eros but Eros is frightened and runs away. Obsession grabs hold of Psyche. With uncontrolled passion and in a complete state of madness, Psyche searches throughout the earth and even the underworld in search of her lost love.[11]

Here is a dramatic example of art imitating life. Immediately our minds can recall episodes in our own past dating experiences that parallel this Greek tragedy. Just as Psyche was falsely led to believe that Eros was ugly, our parents rightly teach us as children that private bodies stay private and mistakenly taught that sexual stimulation is a bad thing ("Don't touch that or you'll go blind!" "If you play with it, it will fall off!" – by my calculations, we should have long since witnessed the formation of a new variety of the human species known as the blind eunuchs). Lessons in human sexuality are marked with shame and ignorance. In the Garden Adam and Eve were unashamedly sexual animals. It was not until deception led to desire and desire led to sin that shame was introduced to humankind: "Who told you that you were naked" (Genesis 3:11)?

But, as with Psyche, we are restless, sexual, curious creatures; we are drawn to sex, we were born for Eros. In addition, like Psyche, curiosity gets the better of us and we must take a peak. "The woman saw that the fruit of the tree was good for food and pleasing to the eye…" We imagined how the experience would enhance who we are: "and also desirable for gaining wisdom…" We must sample a taste: "she took some and ate it." Immediately we look for someone to share this experience with: "She also gave some to her husband who was with her, and he ate it." After the experience has passed, we realize our mistake: "Then the eyes of both were opened, and they realized they were naked." We make vain attempts to try to contain this rage of emotions: "so they sewed fig leaves together and made coverings for themselves." Sexual sin brings shame and separation: "Then the man and his wife heard the sound of the LORD God… and they hid from the LORD God." (Genesis 3:6-8).

For Psyche her senses were completely given over to Eros and with the same speed the sensation escapes and she is cursed to search the world and even descend into the depths of Hell itself to recapture Eros. Likewise, a small sampling of sexual sin is all that is required to bring such a rush of adrenaline to our brains that immediately we are hooked. Sometimes the obsession begins subtly, for others it is with a rage: Pandora's Box is not just opened, the lid has been ripped off the hinges! But the experience is short-lived and the same level of intensity is never reached again. The experience of sexual addiction has been compared to addiction to crack cocaine. The first experience causes a sense of euphoria unmatched by any other experience. But no matter how many times you use your drug, the same level of emotional ecstasy is never reached, and, when the person comes back down from the drug, the lows sink farther down than ever. This is why drug users move to harder drugs and why sexual addicts move to harder pornography or more dangerous sexual experiences. They literally start "looking for love in all the wrong places," at times reaching down to the depths of their own personal hell.

Eros and the Sacred[12]

Let us take a short look at the characters of Apuleius' play and see if we can discover what it is that God had originally designed sex to be. Eros is the Greek word for sexual love and in the Bible is to be viewed only in the context of a marriage between a man and woman. In Scripture all other sexual relationships are viewed as sinful and therefore derive a different word and interpretation altogether. Psyche is the Greek word for soul, or the self, complete with emotions, appetites and volition. It is the very essence of one's being, derived by God.[13]

While *eros* is a Greek New Testament word, its Old Testament counterpart is all the more compelling. The word synonymous with *eros* in the Hebrew is *hasaq, aheb,* which denotes both a human and divine love, but in both cases it still carries a sexual connotation.[14] There is this understanding that spiritual dimensions are at play in the physical realm, even in sexual love.[15] There is something deeply spiritual about the sexual experience both positively when engaged within God's set pattern and negatively when deviated from God's plan.

Old Testament Jewish thought was overwhelmingly positive toward sexual love in marriage. Marriage was viewed as a joining of the whole of the persons, body, mind and spirit together, honoring God in marriage, bringing God's creative blessing upon such union in the conception of a child. Marriage and sex were seen as the continuing and flourishing of God's nation, strengthening the bonds of community and, thus, was to be celebrated.[16] This idea of human sexuality as a mortal/divine communion is carried over from the Old Testament to the New Testament. W Thimme, in his work, *Verbum Dei Manet in Aeternum,* depicts a synthesis in the New Testament between *agape* and *eros* as they relate to God and humankind. *Eros* is the expression of adoration by creation to their Creator and ecstasy in God's fulfilled love with his children.[17]

Interestingly, while early Christianity brought higher levels of love and respect to the marriage relationship, the celebration of human sexuality had become more associated with pagan worship rather than the God who created it. First century Christianity, on the surface, practiced a strict code of sexual morality, including total abstinence by a small number. This was the stand presented to outsiders, especially those considering Christ. Lacking the strict Judaic boundaries of circumcision and dietary laws, Christians made sexual discipline one of the chief differentiations of who was to be considered Christian and who were considered pagan.[18] The Apostle Paul, in 1 Corinthians 7, sought to offer a moderate approach to human sexuality in marriage, but his faint praise for marriage seems to set the stage for centuries of Christian asceticism toward sex. Paul's strong contention for remaining celibate is best understood in the light of the church's expectation of an imminent *parousia*.[19] In other words, if you're thinking that Jesus is returning to earth any day now (literally), then it makes no sense wasting time on marriages that will have no time to deepen and having children that will not have time to grow. When time is short, every activity is detracting us from telling the world about Christ. While Paul never intended to establish asceticism, the assertion that followed throughout the early centuries was that the "true followers of Christ" were to cast their eyes on the end of the age and the inauguration of the age to come and not focus on the futile worries of continuing the human species.[20]

Hellenistic philosophy played a significant role in influencing the Gnostics of the first few centuries, especially Plato's dualistic teaching of the spiritual as being good and the material as being bad. The notion of "a more nobler way" coupled with the Platonic influence of dualism served to further cloud theological understandings. Paul in his epistles seemed to back-peddle a bit from his recognition of celibacy to the point of making marriage a requirement for ecclesiastical office (1 Timothy 3:2, 12; Titus 1:6). The new identity in Christ honored marriage and celibacy and became a major proponent against sexual immorality.[21] But following the first century, Gnostic influence and Hellenistic philosophy began to infiltrate the church, advocating *all* sexual intimacy as contrary to the will of God. As early as St. Ignatius of Antioch (ca. 107) in his letter to Polycarp, people were encouraged to embrace chastity. We see that the expression sexual love began to move from a place of honor and a source of celebration to a place of being seen as a "necessary evil."[22] Soon sexual renunciation became a prerequisite for the highest spiritual graces and became expected of those who would be leaders in the Christian community.

Likewise, the Council of Carthage in 390 AD set forth dictates concerning clergy celibacy. The first doctrinal statements show that human sexuality was beginning to take a back seat to the "true ways of God."[23] This ideal was perpetuated throughout the centuries through the spiritual writings of the monastics.[24] In the fourth-century, John Chrysostom's homilies appealed to his congregation's sense of shame over their own sexuality, inspiring some to seek a higher level of spiritual honor and achievement through abstinence and mental ascetics. He writes that monks who have slain such passions receive some of the eternal blessings in this life and are comparable to the angels in heaven.[25] While celibacy was considered the positive way for the Christian, interestingly, marriage continued to be promoted as holy and right in the eyes of the Church. Some Christian leaders, such as Clement of Alexandria, commended marriage as even more virtuous than celibacy, but only as couples rose to the challenge of abstaining from sex except in the necessary coarse of producing children. For the early church fathers, sexual intercourse was to be viewed for nothing more than reproduction. In the words of Athenagoras in *Plea for Christians*, "Each of us thinks of his wife with a view to nothing more than procreation. For as the farmer casts the seed into the ground and waits for the harvest without further planting, so also procreation is the limit we set on desire."[26] The Christian Church laments at the view of sex devoid of love, yet, at one point in time, the Church was a major proponent of this view, denigrating human sexuality as a "necessary evil for seasonal planting."

Agape love, sacrificial love, has been exclusively defined as "God's love," leaving *eros* completely to matters of the flesh. In order to cultivate the spirit above the flesh, the Church has disregarded a very essential part of humanity's being. Thomas a' Kempis was a strong proponent of this notion as he warned Christians: "You must surrender all other loves for his love…the love of creatures is deceptive and unstable; the love of Jesus is faithful and enduring. Whoever clings to any creature will fall into falling; but he who holds to Jesus shall stand firm forever."[27]

All love is an extension of the God whose very nature is love. If God is the source of all love then he is the source from which we draw sexual love. God created sexual beings and without reductionism or prudity, declared them very good. It was God who gave the orders: "Be fruitful and multiply" (Genesis 1:28b).

To deny *eros* is to diminish *agape*. In the Hebrew language there is no linguistic distinction between *eros* and *agape*. Judaism held to the ideal that sex and birth were great blessings from God. They were consistently opposed to celibacy and asceticism.[28] To speak of *agape* as a God-type of love is a misnomer because it causes us to see *phileos* (love for friends and brothers) as secondary, and *eros* as completely separate from God. While *agape* is the type of love God has for his creation, all three find their origin in the Author of all love and his divine graces run throughout them all. Thomas a'Kempis is right in that God's love is faithful and enduring and that we have allowed sin to diminish love of one another to something deceptive and unstable, but God can use *eros* as a means of redemption just as he uses *agape*.

Eros as a Sacrament

"It is vital that Christian *agape* should enable *eros* to be integrated in the sacred union."[29] If *agape* and *eros* are indeed two branches from the same tree, or, two blessings from the same God, then perhaps the proper understanding of human sexuality will incorporate both dimensions of love, making this love sacramental. Philip Toynbee suggests it be "seen as a step toward God – not as a substitute for taking such a step – shared sexual joy may be a genuine act of worship."[30] To worship ('*abad*) is to revere, to celebrate, to serve, and to give thanks, the very same qualities involved in the sexual union of a husband and wife. Worship is the celebration of the Creator and procreation is the physical manifestation and celebration of the creation process. God designed life as a celebration. He could have made the process of procreation as simple, sterile, and unsatisfying as a firm handshake. Instead, he made it exciting, scary, messy, and wonderful. The Master Creator designed the sexual organs of both the male and female with a host of pleasure sensors, intending for sexual intercourse to be a pleasurable experience. "Such worship can be the most intense and powerful passion a person ever experienced: an ecstatic, joyful celebration of life and its divine source, cherishing the gift and fervently thanking the giver."[31] If God indeed views sex as a form of worship, how does this affect the way we understand human sexual expression?

Eros should be seen as sacramental (Lat. *sacrramentum*). A general understanding of sacrament is "an earthly sign with a heavenly meaning." The word's origin is found in the Greek rendering, *mysterion*, or "mystery," which "refers to the hidden things of God that cannot be known except as God discloses."[32] I believe the Greeks were on to something in their legend of Eros and Psyche in that there are dimensions of spirituality played out in the act of sex. Alen Ecclestone wrote: "The primitive impulse to deify sexual love was not wholly misguided; it has all the features of great mystical experience: abandon, ecstasy, polarity, dying, rebirth, and perfect union."[33]

"Submit to one another out of reverence for Christ. Wives, submit to your husbands as to the Lord. For the husband is the head of the wife as Christ is the head of the church, his body... Husbands, love your wives, just as Christ loved the church and gave himself up for her to make her holy...This is a great mystery, but I speak concerning Christ and the Church."
Ephesians 5:21-23, 25, 32

There is an inextricably interwoven relationship between a man and a woman and Christ and the Church. Inarguably Paul is explaining how the marital relationship should emulate Christ's love for the Church. Could it not also be offering us some parallels concerning sexual union as an expression of Christ and the Church? St. John of the Cross saw a direct correlation between the physical union of the man and woman as a sacrament, or a manifestation of the wonderful union the Church has with God in Christ. If this is even partly true, certainly we have missed some rich understandings in this passage. Here we see a mystical experience that takes place when two hearts are united and celebrated through sex. John of the Cross called it "a part of the genius of Christianity."

Here is the essence of Christian anthropology. Sexual union in the context of the marriage relationship now becomes a spiritual experience, a beautiful act of worship as God's creation explores and celebrates the wonders of his handiwork. It is through the consummation of this spiritual act that we are able to reenact the magnificent work of human creation. This marital union affirms who we are, both our personal identity and our sexual identity. It "brings reconciliation and hope for the future, expresses gratitude to one another, and as it does it sustains our personal being, heals old emotional wounds and elicits the growth of our personality...marriage impinges on the sacred; through it our school of love, our little church, our way of knowing God."[34] Human sexuality as God designed it to be then becomes an act of human/divine grace by which God is honored and we become more what He had created us to be.

With the creation of humankind, especially the completion of man found in the sexual differentiation of male and female, we see God's handiwork and blessing in human sexuality. God's intent for human meaning, therefore, is seen in the unity of the male-female sexes, and most poignantly in the merging of the two into "one flesh." The sexual encounter of the husband and wife fulfill God's call upon the two as they merge together as one, and is validated in the blessing of recreating life, allowing humanity to propagate and increase.[35] Name one other human activity that offers the creative miracle of human life! Human sexuality is a divine mystery, which carries with it both a physical and spiritual need to connect with another. It expresses God's intention that authentic humanness is to be found in relationship.[36] Sexual expression, within the context of marriage, is, therefore, an expression of love for one another that points the persons to God; its gift is a blessing from God, its expression is a blessing to God. Thus, human sexuality becomes a form of worship.

It is not blasphemous to think of proper sexual experiences in marriage as sacramental or worshipful. It is, in fact, blasphemous to lower such spiritual acts to something solely physical. It is a dangerous practice to separate *eros* from *agape*, casting the psyche into a state of denigration.

Immanuel Kant wrote:

Sexual love makes of the loved person an object of appetite; as soon as that appetite has been stilled, the person is cast aside as one casts away a lemon which has been sucked dry...taken by itself, it is a degradation of human nature; for as soon as a person becomes an object of appetite for another, all motives of moral relationship cease to function, because as an object of appetite another person becomes a thing and can be treated as such by everyone.[37]

God's design for sex is cheapened. Instead of sacrificially giving one's self to their spouse, celebrating this "one-flesh" that God has created, they begin to seek out ways to satisfy their own selfish appetites. Human sexuality becomes a means to its own end. The man or woman begins emotionally detaching from their spouse and attaching with others, engaging in surreptitious trysts with the person at work or clandestine drives through the red light district of the city. While sex in its proper context proliferates healing and wholeness, sexual sin diminishes the persons' sense of being and spiritual sensibilities; *Eros* stripped of *agape* can turn one of God's greatest blessings into sin's most insidious vices.

The Nature of Sin

"The Lord God planted a garden eastward in Eden, and there he put the man whom he had formed" (Genesis 2:8). God had designed a very special environment as a proper setting for humankind. Adam and Eve's will was holy and inclined toward God. Yet, they still possessed the power to chart their own course. The *Westminster Confession* states: "God created man male and female, with righteousness and true holiness, having the law of God written in their hearts, and power to fulfill it: and yet under a possibility of transgressing, being left to the liberty of their own will, which was subject to change."[38] Humanity by its very nature is self-conscious and self-determining, capable of choosing his or her own moral path. The consequence of that choice was to be cast out of the Garden and humanity has ever since been restlessly searching for such a place to which they can return. God allowed temptation to test our allegiance – evil was present even in the garden. Yielding to sin, evil had taken root inside of humankind. Evil is all around us *and now also* evil is within.

The result of humankind's test is summed up in one sentence: "She took the fruit thereof, and did eat, and gave also unto her husband with her; and he did eat" (Genesis 3:6 KJV). One of the key terms for sin is *harmartia*, which means to "miss a goal or way."[39] God's original design for human sexuality was to draw his creation to himself and to each other. Sin marred that image when Adam and Eve chose their own will over God's.

Sin as a State:

Sin started on the outside, but now it has also taken root inside. The nature or, predisposition of sin has become an inherited state for all humanity. It continues today to be a moral condition fueled by genetics and environment. Traducianism is the theological view that the soul as well as the body originates through the parents. Not only are gender differentiation and physical characteristics the direct result of our parentage, but the very essence of our spirituality has been designed by God to be passed on through the father and mother at the point of conception. Arminianism supports the idea that God created Adam immediately (*ex-nilio* — "out of nothing") but the rest of humanity are created mediately, or, are the direct result of human reproduction. Throughout Church history, Christian theology has been influenced by Platonic philosophy's teaching of the soul's preexistence.

However, in recent centuries a Poly-Partite Unitarian View has taught interconnectedness between both body and soul and that both are meted out at the time of reproduction.

God does not directly create a soul tainted by original sin, but rather it is passed on through generational lines dating back to the Garden.[40] Apply this truth to pornography and other sexual addictions and we begin to see the possibility of particular genetic characteristics of personality and sinful dispositions being passed on through the parents. With this new insight into humankind's sinful condition, questions begin to emerge: Are some people more prone to certain types of sins than others? Can certain sins be passed on generationally, similar to the way one inherits eye or hair color? What about the addiction to alcohol and the evidences of generational alcoholism? Are some people born with a proclivity to certain sinful lifestyles? What about those who claim to be born with homosexual tendencies? "Even from birth the wicked go astray; from the womb they are wayward and speak lies" (Psalm 58:3). The notion does not relinquish responsibility for our behavior, but, in fact, brings ownership into proper perspective. Instead of persons inclined to certain lifestyles claiming that this is the way God made them, they are forced to recognize that God's perfect image in us was marred at the time of conception. How is the state of sin passed on through the generations? Could it be found in the genetic codes of DNA? Can we simply discount those who claim a certain genetic predisposition or can we be open to the notion that Adamic sin has taken root inside of his offspring? "Oh, wretched man that I am! Who will deliver me from this body of death?" (Romans 7:24)

Because of Adam's sin, we are inwardly predisposed toward sin – its nature is implanted in each of us. The term coined by St. Augustine is "original sin" (Lat. *peccatum originale*),[41] yet its roots are patristic and biblical, most clearly expressed by the apostle Paul: "as all die in Adam, so all will be made alive in Christ" (I Corinthians 15:22); "By the offense of one, judgment came upon all men to condemnation" (Romans 5:18). This "native depravity"[42] implants a corrupted nature within the person, whereby they are utterly indisposed and wholly inclined toward evil.[43] Because of the Fall humanity inherits a nature disabled from that which is spiritually virtuous. We are now in a state of hopelessness, unwilling to pay our physical penalty and unable to pay our spiritual penalty. We are a damaged breed — angels with soiled robes and tarnished halos.

Where Sin Crosses Paths with Human Sexuality

What happens when God's blessing of sexual love (*eros*) crosses paths with this world's sin (*hamartia*)? Our bodies that were created by God and for God become cut off from God, unclean vessels, unfit for his Spirit's dwelling and heaven's eternity. Further, instead of the body becoming God's temple through which we offer worship and receive wholeness, it becomes an object of scorn, Satan's refuse through which we become disconnected from God, one another and from our very selves. God's blessing becomes the object of focus and sex becomes a form of idolatry. If sin is a deviation from God's plan then sexual sin is any involvement of *eros* apart from God's perfect design. God designed sex to draw a couple into perfect sacramental union and as a creative expression of worship. Sexual sin drives a wedge between husband and wife, it corrupts God's plan of human fulfillment and becomes a weapon that destroys the human soul and corrupts humanity as a whole. To list sexual sin under the umbrella of *eros* is a misnomer. If *eros* is sacramental love given to us by God for sacred union then "erotica" is idolatry and a diabolical trap to divide and conquer. *Eros* is physical love as a divine gift and expression of worship – neither of which are found in sexual sin.

All issues of sexual sin fall under the banner of fornication, or sexual immorality (*porneia*), and can generally be defined as any form of illicit sexual activity (Genesis 34:7; Leviticus 19:29; 21:9; Deuteronomy 22:13-21; 23:18; Matthew 15:19; Mark 7:21; I Corinthians 5:9-11; 7:2; 2 Corinthians 12:21; Galatians 15:19; Ephesians 5:3-5). Involved in this broad definition would be our description for the term pornography, the sexual and/ or emotional lusting after one who is not your spouse. (Numbers 15:39; Proverbs 6:25; Ezekiel 20:30; 23:5; Matthew 5:28; Romans 1:26; Colossians 3:5; 1 Thessalonians 4:5; 1 Peter 4:3; 1 John 2:16). Yet, the Bible makes clear distinctions of the various types of sexual immorality.

For example, adultery (Heb. *niupim* "harlotry") is the sin of sexual activity between a married or betrothed man or woman with anyone other than their spouse. There are a vast number of places where this sin is denounced in Scripture (Genesis 38:34; 39:9; Exodus 20:14; 21:12; Leviticus 20:10; Deuteronomy 5:18; 22:22; Proverbs 2:17; Deuteronomy 5:18; Matthew 5:28; Mark 7:22; 15:19; John 8:5; I Corinthians 6:9; Hebrews 13:4), and considered a capital punishment.[44] Another capital case of sexual sin is in the cases of rape (Genesis 34:31, Deuteronomy 22:25-27), and is, in fact, considered in the cuneiform law codes the same as adultery.[45] Another form of sexual immorality would include incest (Heb. *hurkel*), or, sexual activity between members of the same family (Genesis 11:31; 35:22; Leviticus 18:6-18; 20:11-14, 17, 19-21; Deuteronomy 27:23; Ezekiel 22:10; Matthew 14:4; Mark 6:18; 1 Corinthians 5:1). Tying closely with incest (including the use of the same Heb word, *hurkel*) would be homosexuality, sexual relations between two or more persons of the same gender (Leviticus 18:22; 20:13; Deuteronomy 23:18; Romans 1:27; 1 Co 6:9) and bestiality, sexual activity with an animal (Exodus 22:19; Leviticus 18:23; 20:15-16; Deuteronomy 27:21).

The strongest Scriptural rationale in considering these sexual behaviors sinful abominations and punishable crimes is that they were considered an assault on God's creation, that were made in his image (Leviticus 20:10-21; 1 Corinthians 6:20), an assault on the sanctity of the body, which is God's temple (1 Corinthians 6: 13b-20), and the family, which is God's ordered structure (Genesis 2:18, 24; Proverbs 18:22).[46] Further, it was an assault on God's established people (Leviticus 11:43-44; chapter 18). Human sexuality is a gift from God to draw persons together with one another and with God himself. Sexual sin is God's gift defiled: it isolates individuals, blocking them off from those around them and the very Source of life itself. These same areas assaulted in the pages of Scripture have been the same strategic areas of assault throughout history and continue to be the areas of threat today.

While many of the characteristics are the same for all sexual sins the primary focus of this book is the issue of pornography particularly as it affects members of the clergy.

Pathology of Sexual Sin

And the wild regrets, and the bloody sweats,
None knew so well as I:
Or he who lives more lives than one,
More deaths than one must die   Oscar Wilde

As the flirting progressed, I started thinking again that there was a Prince Charming out there who would make me feel whole. I progressed from flirting to having affairs. Every time I had an affair, I would fall madly in love. The excitement of the chase was often followed by the heartbreak of being used and then by obsessing about a person I couldn't have. Guilt, shame, and remorse were feelings I had to cope with every day. I would promise myself I would stop what I was doing, but I couldn't. I was searching constantly for the love I needed and hating myself for the men and the sex and not being able to stop. I prayed so hard, and then I would curse God because I couldn't stop; I thought God wasn't listening to me. I felt so hopeless I wanted to die.[47]

It is an inherent part of human nature to connect with others. Theologically, we believe that the whole process reflects the face-to-face nature of our being created for communion with God and each other. This is the foundation of both our sexuality and human community. If we accept the idea that we are created for communion with God and one another and that our psychological development is imbedded in this communion, then we begin to see that our spiritual life is enmeshed in our psychological development. "Divine purpose and the most powerful human drives encounter each other at the point of our capacity to love and be loved."[48] Love withheld or unrequited brings a hollow ache within the human heart. People will go to any lengths to try and fill this spiritual/emotional void. Many times the oversexed woman or the overworked man is emotionally arrested at a point in their childhood development when love was withheld, they are, in most cases, seeking to fill a void created by an emotionally detached parent.

Just as Adam was before God made Eve, we are unfinished people and we fear the very things needed to restore us. In isolation we become worse; when we come out of isolation through full disclosure, we get better. Our spiritual hunger is wrapped up in this, so sexual misconduct becomes a poor substitute for communion with God and others. Built inside of each of us is a missing God-shaped piece of the puzzle to our human existence, a void in self that can be satisfied by nothing less than a right relationship with God through Christ. If we were to find that large piece of the puzzle we would discover another, smaller piece inside the larger, a familiar piece in the shape of a person.

Characteristics of Pornography Addiction:

At this time I was in seminary studying theology and working as an assistant in a local church. Everything seemed to pile up on me all at once. For one thing, I couldn't stand living the lie anymore, preaching and teaching the "Answer," yet secretly living in total bondage.[49]

Addictions tend to follow a set emotional pattern, beginning with outside stressors and quickly moving within the person themselves. The pattern continues, impressing its compulsive cycle on the soul of the individual. The more the cycle continues the stronger it becomes enmeshed within the person, until, finally, they cannot catch sight of a way to break the pattern. It's the only way they know how to interact with life:

1. Cycle of Addiction

Outside Stresses

Self-resolve   *Restlessness*

Guilt   **Cycle of Addiction**   *Temptation*

Remorse   *Behavior*

Relief

Generally, that emptiness is not enough to drive a person to act out with their addiction, especially someone who has strong moral or religious beliefs. Coupled with the inward pain is an outward stressor. The outside stresses accumulate and because the person has languished for some time in his or her spirit, they find themselves ill prepared to deal with these stresses. Fixation on the problem and unresolved anger toward the individual places the person in a vulnerable state for temptation. When an opportunity to sin presents itself, the individual will be ripe for the picking. The very natural next step is to act out with the drug of choice, in this case, viewing pornographic images followed by chronic and compulsive masturbation. The neurotransmitters of the brain begin to charge and the person experiences euphoric sensations and relief from their pain. But the escape is short-lived and quickly followed by a deep sense of remorse and overwhelming sense of shame. The shame is accompanied with a strong sense of self-determination to never again succumb to the addiction. But just as short-lived as the relief is, so also is the self-resolve. The emptiness is still there, only now pressed by feelings of self-loathing. The stressful circumstances have not changed; instead self-confidence is diminished and the person feels less able to deal with life's trials. The pain becomes too much and the only way to escape is to once again give into the addiction, reinforcing the behavior and weakening resolve.

It cannot be stressed too emphatically how devastating are the emotional feelings of one who falls into the snare of pornographic addiction, especially if the individual is or becomes a Christian. Everything within their spirit tells them this is wrong; body and soul are torn apart as this war rages. Feelings of guilt and shame are multiplied as the person continues to live within the Church, a community that neither understands nor sympathizes with such behaviors. Because the addiction wreaks such havoc on their brains, they are unable to find the strength within them to give it up, but because of the overwhelming shame associated with sexual sin individuals cannot find the intestinal fortitude to voluntarily open up so as to find the help so desperately needed. This quandary forces the individual to emotionally withdraw further from their support system and the isolation causes the whole cycle of addiction to be repeated and reinforced. Despair turns to depression, depression to fatigue and fatigue to surrender.

Not only is the addiction cyclic but it is progressive. It is impossible to remain at the same level of your addiction and stay satisfied. Addiction is about crossing lines they never dreamed they would cross. "A magazine excites, a movie thrills, a live show really makes the blood run."[50] One person wrote: "As I fed my malady and it progressed, so did the pictures in the magazines. There was always that enticing revelation of more and better and wilder pulling me on. It was as though lust had to keep advancing, and never satisfied, had to resort to the ever-more explicit images on which to feed."[51] Swimsuit magazines and lingerie catalogues become open doors into human nature's more baser side. Like your very first potato chip or Hershey kiss, it is a taste that will never be satisfied with just one. "It's not that bad" is a very dangerous phrase when it comes to human sexuality. I remember the excitement I felt as a child when the Sunday paper would arrive because I knew there would be department store circulars with pictures of models in their underwear. Nursing bras were even more exciting because they demonstrated how the cup unhinges, revealing that half-inch of upper breast. As the various medias continue to push the envelope on what is appropriate and inappropriate, you can be sure that there is an eager crowd ready to progress along with them.

The selfishness of their sin nature has opened them up to thoughts and attitudes contrary to God's nature and design. Ignoring the Holy Spirit's direction and the leading of their own conscience they began allowing those toxic thoughts and behaviors to poison who they are. In order to protect their addiction and maintain any sort of sanity, they isolate themselves emotionally from the life-giving relationships of God and those they love; soon they find that they are being blocked off from their very selves. The void created by self-obsession becomes so painfully real that they sink deeper into their sinful lifestyle and with that they sink deeper into despair. They are left in such dire straights that the only relief from their torment is to act out again…it's all they have left.

The destructiveness of pornography addiction is vast, beginning in the very soul of the individual and spreading out, infecting every area of life. In chapter two we will see how pornography fits into the scope of sexual sin, defining what exactly pornography is and fully exploring how it transgresses God's intention for human sexuality. Further, as a sin that tears apart spiritual and relational unity, we will explore the effects pornography has had on culture, family, and the church.

CHAPTER 2
SOCIAL RAMIFICATIONS OF PORNOGRAPHY

Consequences of a World Gone Bad

If one were to scoff at the notion of a sin-stained planet with morally bankrupt inhabitants, certainly a sober look at the social state in which we live will remove all doubt. In chapter one, we grasped a picture of God's design for human sexuality and how sin marred that picture. In this chapter we will see just how far this distorted image has dragged creation away from God's original plan and purpose for sex. In the previous chapter we caught a glimpse of how human sin expelled mankind from the Garden into the dark shadows of sexual sin. In this chapter we will seek to understand how devastating sexual sin, particularly pornography addiction, can be.

What is Sexual Addiction?

Before we can focus in on pornographic addiction it is important to define sexual addiction as a whole and to better understand what sexual addiction is, we must first examine what it is not. First of all, sexual addiction is not a disease – at least not one yet recognized by the American Medical Association (AMA). Likewise, while it is not yet listed as an official mental disorder in the current DSM-IV (Diagnostic and Statistical Manual of Mental Disorders), it is slated to be included in the upcoming DSM-V. Sexual addiction is not an excuse for having marital affairs nor is it a viable defense in criminal proceedings involving sexual behavior. It is neither rare, nor incurable. Interestingly enough, sexual addiction is not found in the majority of rapists and stalkers and persons who struggle with sexual addictions are no more likely to engage in rape or child molestation than any randomly-selected stranger. Sexual addiction can best be described as a continued pattern of compulsive sexual behavior which has a negative impact on the individual's personal, social and/or economic standing:

The "Sexaholic" has taken himself or herself out of the whole context of what is right or wrong. He or she has lost control, no longer has the power of choice, and is not free to stop. Lust has become an addiction. Our situation is like that of the alcoholic who can no longer tolerate alcohol and must stop drinking altogether but is hooked and cannot stop. So it is with the Sexaholic, or sex drunk, who can no longer tolerate lust but cannot stop.[52]

A very close relative of sexual addiction is what has become known as love or relationship addiction which involves an inability to regulate one's emotions in relational settings. Love addiction is one of the more difficult addictions to identify since its destructive affect is stationed in the mind of the love addict, rather than their outward behavior and its influences are easily masked in today's culture.[53] While the sex addict craves sexual expression, including graphic sexual images, the love or relationship addict craves an unhealthy level of emotional attachment. Interestingly enough, viewed in the context of a loving relationship, love addiction is many times viewed and promoted as a positive thing. For a person to require a greater expression of love from their spouse is a far-sight more suitable than requiring they diet or undergo breast enhancement surgery. We will further differentiate between these two addictive behaviors when we discuss the particular behaviors that entice each gender.

Defining Pornography

Pornography is not a new phenomenon that arose with Hugh Hefner and Larry Flynt. History records that Tiberius Caesar (45 BC-37 AD) had purchased hand-drawn scrolls from Egypt depicting sexual acts and had young men and women trained in sexual practices who were brought to the palace to perform for him. The word pornography comes from the Greek word *pornographos*, which translates "writing of harlots." Webster defines it as "the depiction of erotic behavior (as in pictures or writing) intended to cause sexual excitement."[54] Some of the more popular forms of pornography would include magazines, movies and explicit Internet web sites. It is important to note that Webster's definition includes not only visual stimulation but also verbally printed materials. Fantasy involves the creative imagination which stimulates the mind. This includes not only the mental picture of the ideal body but also the ideal person and ideal relationship. The list of pornographic materials, then, must be expanded to include romance novels, some of the movies commonly referred to as "chick flicks," and many of the Internet chat rooms.

The addictive process of pornography thus becomes a desperate search for wholeness and happiness, an escape from our current state of crisis, it stems from a sense of deficiency in one's self.[55] One single mother explained, "I was seeking companionship... I learned of some Internet sites I could visit to make friends and have fun. At first, the sexual talk in these chat rooms seemed harmless and none threatening. My loneliness and craving to feel wanted drew me into relationships I really didn't want."[56] The alcoholic finds escape in a bottle, the food addict finds emotional fullness in the refrigerator, the out-of-control shopper finds emotive contentment with the swipe of the credit card, the addicted gambler finds exhilaration with the roll of the dice, and the workaholic finds emotional satisfaction by finishing one more task. Likewise, the "sexaholic" finds emotional release perusing pornographic websites or searching out like-minded addicts in chat rooms. And just like every other addiction, pornography proves to be nothing more than an insidious illusion.

Pornography addiction is a pathological relationship with any form of sexual media or activity. It is an obsessive preoccupation accompanied by compulsive acting-out that spirals out of control. It happens not in quest of pleasure but because, somewhere along the line, the psyche confused sex with love and the body interpreted a rush of adrenaline as a triumph over fear, loneliness and inadequacy. These are people without any sense of real intimacy in their lives. Pornography is a powerfully addictive substitute because, for a few seconds, it seems to fill the emptiness. And that fleeting comfort keeps them coming back for more.[57] Here is where the snake strikes and injects its deadly poison.

Virtual Reality:

We are half-hearted creatures, fooling about with drink and sex and ambition when infinite joy is offered us, like an ignorant child who wants to go on making mud pies in the slums because he cannot imagine what is meant by the offer of a holiday at the sea. We are far too easily pleased. (C.S. Lewis, *Mere Christianity*)

There are other factors that play a part in our personal profile and proclivities toward certain addictions, some of which we will cover throughout these pages. For now let it suffice to say we all carry our own set of mental, emotional and spiritual baggage. The saying a generation ago was: "When the going gets tough the tough get going." Today we would rephrase that to say, "When the going gets tough we find that the tough aren't as tough as they thought." Pornography, like all addictions, becomes an escape, a place to run to when circumstances become too tough to deal with. Our addiction helps us to transcend our lot for a time, to detach from reality; it creates a virtual reality of a spiritual experience — it seems real, but turns out to be only an illusion.[58]

"You belong to your father, the devil... He was a murderer from the beginning, not holding to the truth, for there is no truth in him. When he lies, he speaks his native language, for he is a liar and the father of lies" (John 8:4). Pornography is an escape from reality, an escape from the truth, a hiding out in fantasy; pornography is living a lie. Because this sexual addiction gives the illusion of spiritual transcendence we can conclude that addiction is a spiritual sickness, a spiritual counterfeit, promising freedom from pain, but in the end multiplying the bonds and deepening the anguish we feel. What we had once hoped would make us whole has instead emptied us of our hope and has begun to swallow us up. "Pornography promises something like intimacy and then cheats you of real intimacy twice. First it pushes a wedge between you and God – the only one who can know and love you completely. And secondly it gets you so focused on your own desires that you are unable to know and love anyone else in an intimate relationship."[59]

The National Coalition for the Protection of Children and Families conducted a survey of 857 young men at 5 different religiously affiliated colleges. Of those 857 students sixty-eight percent admitted to *intentionally* looking for porn online. Ten percent said they viewed porn regularly and five percent thought they had a problem with it. Compared to other national surveys these numbers seem significantly deflated. These same students agreed that porn was addictive, that it was a sin that damages our relationship with God, and destroys families. Many Christian colleges are working hard to begin programs to offer students a safe place to confess their struggles with sexual sin while others continue to bury their heads in the sand. One ministry student wrote a letter to the president of his seminary, admitting his own struggles with lust and asked that they instill a more modest dress code at the seminary pool. The president's response was that no problem exists on their campus and they must not restrict the types of bathing suits being worn for fear that pool membership may decrease and the pool begin to lose money. Time eventually showed that the student population on that campus is fraught with persons struggling with the addiction.

There are certain misconceptions about pornography addiction,[60] such as its rarity. Pornography addiction affects men and women of all ages, of all backgrounds, and of all walks of life. As for its prevalence, there are literally hundreds of hospitals, clinics, conferences and counseling offices helping many thousands of people through recovery.[61] Nationally, there are four major 12-step programs devoted to sex/pornography addictions (and countless other Christian programs) with more than 2,000 groups meeting every week, and numbers increasing daily. Another misconception is that pornography addiction is a harmless, victimless crime. One of the common jokes about sex/pornography addiction is, "If you're going to have an addiction, this is the one to have!" The perception is that pornography addiction is harmless and enjoyable. Mental and emotional breakdowns, suicide, unwanted pregnancies, abortion, child abuse, sexually transmitted diseases, physical destruction to one's own body, AIDS, family disintegration, increased health care costs, demoralization of society and spiritual alienation are all consequences of sex addictions. A further study that dispels the notion that pornography is a victimless crime was conducted by the Attorney General's Commission on Pornography, where it was discovered that **all** pornography is linked with organized crime. There is literally no aspect of the pornography business where organized crime does not have a stronghold. The commission further asserts that pornography has a direct link with such crimes as physical violence, fraud, money laundering, tax evasion, drug distribution, prostitution, sexual abuse and murder.[62]

Characteristics of Pornography Addiction

I can remember many, many, many times during withdrawal when I was crying and howling like a wounded animal in my condominium and I was lying prostrate on the floor in the living room pounding my fist into the carpeting and I would call someone up – usually my sponsor, but I would call other people, too. They would pick up the phone and say hello, and I would just start bawling, bawling uncontrollably. Those people loved me unconditionally. After the numbness wore off I started having a lot of feelings come up, as so many people do, feelings of rage, anger, hysteria at times...I realized what I was grieving for was that life as I had known it up until then was dying. I would no longer be able to do the things I had been doing in order to get the anesthesia I was so desperately looking for. That was a very mournful period for me. [63]

There are distinct characteristics found in pornography addiction that may or may not be involved in other types of addictive behaviors:[64] First of all, pornography addiction is secretive and progressive. In effect, the addict develops a double life: hiding magazines and videos or getting up in the middle of the night to check out explicit web sites. Because of the shame attached to this secret life, the principal fear of the addict is being found out; because the devastation to the individual's life is so great, the deepest need of the addict is being found out. Another characteristic of the person addicted to pornography is emotional isolation. Mentally and emotionally the addict detaches himself or herself from human relationship. Devoid of intimacy, pornography obsession is primarily a form of selfishness, something done exclusively for the individual's own sense of need or desires. Lustful fantasies take the place of human contact, replacing relationship with something completely impersonal. The deep sense of shame felt after acting out with their behavior causes the individual to retreat further inside them to protect the behavior from being exposed and to protect themselves from the pain of dealing with their addiction.

Pornography addiction is victimizing. The overwhelming obsession with self-gratification blinds the addict to the harmful effects his or her behavior is having on others. If achieving gratification means that persons are used or even victimized, the addict will conveniently block off all cognitive reasoning until satisfaction has been achieved. In the case of married individuals, the addict pours his or her emotional energy into feeding the addiction, while the spouse is left outside their partner's walled up heart. We will talk more about this later. While porn addicts may or may not involve themselves in rape or molestation, they cannot help leaving a host of casualties in their wake, themselves included. Pornographic addiction is progressive in the sense that the emotional highs experienced in the initial stages of acting out will eventually require more explicit images and eventually lead to baser types of sexual behaviors. Finally, pornography addiction, left to its own vices, always ends in despair. When married couples (properly) make love, they are more fulfilled for having had the experience. Addictive sexual sin leaves the participants feeling empty and guilty, despairing over the experience. In these dark moments of despondency the addict most likely feels abandoned by God. Often they think to themselves of how badly they want help to stop, but they do not know where to turn for that help.

Pornography Transgresses God's Plan

Pornography, as with all sexual sin, at its most elementary level is a sin of lust.

Lust, if seen in its most fundamental form, is the sin of idolatry, a giving of ourselves to something or someone other than God. Idolatry, in the Greek *eidololatria*, is defined as "whoredom," or "wanton disloyalty;" in the Hebrew, idolatry *zana* is defined as "having illicit intercourse,"[65] both showing a clear sexual connotation for this term. Deities of the non-Hebrew religions of the ancient Near East were made in the likeness of various animals who were seen as representations of the different attributes of the different gods. Through time, however, the attributes depicted in the image denigrated to the point where it was regarded as deity itself. In similar fashion it can be said that humanity's appreciation and attraction to the human creation and the worshipful expression of human sexuality became maligned to the point of worshipping the human body apart from the person and the act of sex devoid of intimate personal unity. Concrete representations of God, such as the bronze serpent Moses fashioned in the wilderness (Numbers 21:9) were common among ancient Hebrew culture. However, it was when the objects that represent God's goodness began to be viewed as a god in its own right that boundaries are crossed and God's wonderful gifts become the enemy's greatest weapons.

According to Micah 1:7, idolatry is a form of sexual prostitution, a giving of ourselves, that which rightfully belongs to God, to a god of our own making. Isaiah 44:18-20 identifies the source of idolatry to spiritual blindness and self-delusion. Similarly, we have seen that pornography is usually introduced and takes hold at times when a person is spiritually blind to the things of God. The vast majority of people who are hooked on pornography were introduced to it at a very early age and they are most vulnerable to be reintroduced to it as an adult when they are lax in their relationship with God. Disassociation with the Light means associating with darkness. The dramatic changes in brain chemistry perpetuate the behavior as persons unwittingly lie to themselves as a form of self-preservation and self-destruction. Biblically, the heart (*leb*) refers primarily to the inner nature of the person and is seen as the seat of human will, thoughts and emotions. Because of the feelings of euphoria that anesthetize the person's deep emotional wounds and chemical changes throughout the brain that reinforce the behavior, the human will, *chooses* the idolatry of lust above God and, in acquiescence, God gives the person over to their own lusts.

Two Types of Addiction

There are two basic types of addiction, known as arousal addiction and satiation addiction. Both of these types are alluring, crafty and powerful highs and both types find a gratification in pornography. Those affected by arousal addiction would be persons with an inflated ego, but who feel wearied by menial tasks imposed by others or discontented with where they are in their career and/or salary. This is the disenchanted that set out to change the world for Christ only to find himself or herself trapped in petty disputes about what color to paint the Sunday School room or what type of music they will use in the worship service. Invariably they are asking questions such as, "Is this what I've been reduced to? Is this what I am to give my life for?" The cause is no longer worthy of the investment. They need something — *anything* — to help them once again feel alive and they rationalize to themselves that they somehow "deserve this." Types of arousal addictions would include amphetamines, cocaine, alcohol, stealing, pornography or an affair. The drug of choice then releases hormones into the central nervous system, causing intense sensations of power and elation. The behavior causes the frustrated person to feel alive and rejuvenated.

Satiation addiction manifests itself in persons with a much lower self-esteem or people who suffer with depression, people who feel weighed down by the tremendous demands of work and perceived expectations of those they work for. They feel overworked and overwhelmed, underpaid and under appreciated. They are looking to escape from the pressures for awhile. Some forms of satiation addictions would include using marijuana, heroin, valium and alcohol or can manifest itself in such behaviors as overeating or watching too much television. Others pour themselves all the more into their work in a desperate attempt to be affirmed. They search outwardly for some sort of emotional high, through the praise of others or synthetically through drugs or alcohol. The satiated person will turn first to anti-depressants to dull the pain and then to addictive behaviors, such as sexual vices, to escape the pain. Both arousal and satiation addictions can and often do cross boundaries with one another, particularly in cases where the habit began at a very early age[66] When the emotional high for the arousal addict dissipates he or she is still trapped in their dismal circumstances; when the euphoria for the satiation addict wears off they are still empty inside. Except now, feeling intense shame and self-hatred for what they have done, they are brought to new depths of despair. So they escape to the only outlet that has offered any moment of relief from this pain and return to the addiction.

Pathology of Pornography Addiction

"When an evil spirit comes out of a man, it goes through arid places seeking rest and does not find it. It says, 'I will return to the house I left.' When it arrives, it finds the house unoccupied, swept clean and put in order. Then it goes and take with it seven other spirits more wicked than itself, and they go in and live there. And the final condition of the man is worse than the first."
Matthew 12:43-45

During those moments when the person gives into his or her addiction, depending on the particulars, they may feel excited, ashamed, anxious or a host of other emotions. But whatever they are feeling, they are feeling it with great intensity. It is this intense emotional surge that draws the person back to the addiction. In a desperate attempt to fight their addiction, the individual will employ other practices, surrogate compulsive behaviors to keep from returning to pornography. These would include behaviors, such as overeating, reckless spending, anger, resentment, or a host of others. But the emotional issues are still there and so also the proclivity to return to the former addiction. The demon is not gone – simply wandering about for a time. The sin has not been dealt with; it simply lies dormant until their resistance is down. Much of the overweight problem in our country has to do with unresolved issues and the church is a perfect reflection of this. I cannot help but look at the number of overweight pastors and/or their spouses and wonder what pain or stress has led them to that point. These unresolved issues and unguarded thought patterns will eventually cause the sleeping giant to awaken. The original addiction will not give up and you will find that these other compulsive behaviors will refuse to leave as well. As persons begin the process of recovery from their addiction they begin to uncover a host of other addictive behaviors below the surface.

As the cycle of addictive behavior begins to revolve it begins to pull the person addicted away from God and others. The mood change created by their acting out seduces their emotions into believing these behaviors can offer intimacy: their emotions lie to their conscious thinking, rationalizing that, since their emotional needs are now being fulfilled through the addiction, there's no need to struggle to maintain meaningful relationships with others. One sex addict began to realize this when he understood that his pornography and masturbation were direct results of his fear of loving his wife. "It is safer," he said, "to masturbate and look at a magazine. What you want me to do is impractical. I'd rather be with a caged lion than attempt to love her."[67] They further reason that, if people knew the horrible truth they would be repulsed and all they had worked for would slip from their fingers: their marriage would end, their family taken away, their career would be ruined, their reputation destroyed. So they pull away, isolating themselves from the very persons who could help them out of this addiction. Sin becomes a full-time preoccupation. The more they indulge, the more they pull away from others, the more they pull away, the more isolated they become. As loneliness sets in their need for another "fix" is fueled.

When the person finally returns to their senses they are gripped by fear. They pray: "Have mercy on me, O God, according to your unfailing love; according to your great compassion blot out my transgressions" (Psalm 51:1). They vow never to do it again, rededicating themselves in life and ministry. But the devil doesn't give up that easily. He has his hooks in that person and he will not let go without a fight. As the individual pulls, sin yanks the string back again until the person is reduced to the equivalent of a spiritual *Yo-Yo*. Eugene Peterson calls such persons "wind-whipped waves" (James 1:8 MSG). The cycle has begun: the pain returns and they run to their addiction; grieved, they pray for forgiveness. The addict struggles in his or her own power to overcome until the pressure gets to be too much and back again they go. Depending on the strength of their resolve the cycle may take a day, week, month, or even years before it returns.

For the sexaholic, the progression is relentless and inevitable. Within any given moment of our lives, however, we were unaware of the extent it had driven us and refused to see where it was leading. Like revelers riding a raft down the river of pleasure, we were unaware of the awesome power of the rapids of the whirlpool ahead. First addicts, then love cripples, we took from others to fill up what was lacking in ourselves. Conning ourselves time and again that the next one would save us, we were really losing our life.[68]

The addict is being given over to the baser side of themselves; their personality has been permanently altered. As they progress in the addictive behavior they can feel their true self being swallowed up. Even if they find the courage to surrender the addiction to God, bring their sin into the light, and get involved in a 12-step recovery program, their personality has been forever altered. The altered personality has caused indelible changes in the addict's psyche. While the individual can remain free and clean from their addiction for the rest of their lives, they must never forget that pornography (as with all compulsive behavior) will remain a weak spot in their armor and must be well guarded.

Effects of Pornography

Now that we've identified the insidious nature of pornography addiction, it's important to see the destructive effect pornography has on the individual and how far reaching those effects are to those around them. There are at least four particular victims of pornography addiction: the addict himself/herself, the culture in which they live, the family which they influence, and the church in which they serve.

A. Pornography and the Addict

Sex addiction is kind of a steamroller to hell. The double life, the inconsistencies, it all takes great energy... The hallmark of addiction is that sex becomes the organizing principle of daily life, with every spare moment devoted to fantasizing, planning the next experience... agonizing over the guilt and shame it leaves behind.[69]

Pornography has been called the "victimless crime." I am convinced, now more than ever, that pornography produces nothing but victims and that the first and greatest of these victims are the addicts themselves. Who else has suffered the torment so closely and for so long? Unlike any other creature, the addict lives the double-life of perpetrator and victim.

It is important to see that pornography addiction is a type of drug. The drug is seen in the way it affects one's brain chemistry; peptides such as endorphins govern the electrochemical interactions within the brain creating emotional highs of euphoria. Dr. Patrick Carnes, in his book, *Don't Call it Love*, explains: "Addictive obsession can exist in whatever generates significant mood alteration...One of the more destructive parts of sex addiction is that you literally carry your own source of supply. By focusing on external chemicals like alcohol, we have missed the significance of being able to get high on our own brain chemicals."[70]

Dr. Carnes illustrates: "Addicts report symptoms that absolutely parallel the withdrawal experience of the cocaine addict. Physical symptoms – including dizziness, body aches, headaches, sleeplessness, and extreme restlessness – are very common. Many addicts who have recovered from a chemical addiction and a sex addiction say that recovery from sex addiction was far more difficult...while the initial physical symptoms are less severe, the withdrawal experience is more prolonged and more painful."[71]

Two chemicals in the brain that are greatly affected in addiction are the Dopamine, pleasure sensors and Serotonin, which gives a sense of well being. During the height of the experience of using our "drug" the dopamine levels increase dramatically, opening the floodgates of our brains and bringing a sense of euphoria. Immediately following the release is a drain in the serotonin, causing great bouts of depression and a desperate need to reconnect with those pleasure sensors again.

The phenyl ethylamine (PEA), dubbed the "molecule of love," is structurally identical to amphetamines, creating a high-arousal state which soon tapers off. The phenyl ethylamine peaks in the presence of fear, risk, and danger, all common elements of pornography addiction. One addict described it as "a rush, almost a euphoria that would come over me...similar to the way epileptics have this sense of aura before a seizure." The biochemicals of sex stimulate the pleasure center of the brain. Dr. Candace B. Pert had conducted research on these pleasure sensors in hamsters, reporting that blood endorphin levels increased 200% from the beginning to the end of the sex act, relieving both physical and emotional pain.[72] Equate this to the sex addict and add the increased adrenaline from the fear of being caught and the scales soar off the charts.

No shackles of sin are more binding than those that hold fast the addict;

their own heart, mind and body are fighting against their recovery. Deep within the person is a whisper of renewal from God's Spirit while from the bowels of the addict's own belly screams for them to feed its lusts. The mind is so adversely affected to the point where they cannot even trust their own sense of reasoning; thoughts are governed by sin's all-pervading influence. It is no longer a matter of knowing right from wrong because the mind of the addict lies to itself and is no longer able to discern the truth. The sexual addict is dramatically altered physically, emotionally, rationally and spiritually; he or she has become their own worst enemy. They spend their waking hours, and many times their sleep time as well, striving to feed that craving lust while begging to be free. They have become the embodiment of the proverbial person dying of thirst while at the same time craving salt.

B. Pornography and Culture

"Pornography always has in it somewhere a hatred of man, both of man as a human being able to respond to ideals, and of man as an animal. Pornography is not an affirmation but a denial of life, and commercial pornography is a denial of life for the sake of money."[73]

Our first inclination is to blame humanity's plight on the promiscuous society in which we live today. While Western culture must share in the blame, we must also recognize there is a more sinister character lurking about in the shadows. Paul reminds us that "our struggle is not against flesh and blood, but against the rulers, against the authorities, against the powers of this dark world and against the spiritual forces of evil in the heavenly realms" (Ephesians 6:12). The world, in fact, is simply fulfilling its due course: "Cursed is the ground because of you… It will produce thorns and thistles for you" (Genesis 3:17b, 18a). When God created Adam, he gave charge of the earth into his hand; when Adam sinned, earth's ownership was given over to Satan. That's why, when Christ was tempted by the devil, he could offer to give Jesus the kingdoms of this earth (Matthew. 4:9). We know that after the cross Jesus proclaims that he has received all authority over heaven and earth (Matthew 28:18), but Paul makes it clear that as he was still waiting for his full deliverance from his body of death (Romans 7:24), so the earth itself eagerly awaits its full redemption (Romans 8: 18-25). The world is still sin-scarred, able to be redeemed, but infected and spreading because of sin's influence. Our culture, therefore, not only influences the person toward corruption but is, in fact, corrupt, addicted, victimized, cursed and in need of redemption too. While the pornography industry peddles the poison, Satan is the real kingpin of this drug cartel. It is apparent that in recent decades the American culture has taken a dangerous turn morally in regard to human sexuality. The following are some sobering statistics of how pornography has infected our culture:

Porn outlets outnumber McDonald's restaurants three to one (more than 27,000 to 9,000) as of 1997, according to *Adult Video News.*

The *Los Angeles Daily News* reported in January 1995 that 300 million new porn videos are distributed each year.

According to a 1997 study by Digital Detective Services Inc., 25% of office computers in the United States contain pornography of various genres, including child pornography.

According to the 1998 issue of *Counselor's Corner* there were 19.5 million visitors each month to the top five pay-for-porn sites and 98.5 million people who visited the top five free sites.

Counselor's Corner further reported in 1998 there were more than 400,000 porn outlets available on the Internet and that there are more than 200 new porn sites added daily.

In a survey by pastors.com of more than 5,000 pastors, more than 55% had visited a pornographic website within the year, and 33% had visited a sexually explicit site within the previous three months.

Nine out of ten of the 500 men attending a church retreat in California indicated that lust, porn, and fantasy was the habitual, continual, or fatal disconnecting factor in their relationship with God.[74]

What do you call a culture where Hollywood releases 400 movies a year and the pornography industry releases 700 movies each month? J. Budziszewski rightly coined the term: *Pornotopia.* He writes: "Only a generation ago, the expression 'making love' could be used for any of the endearing things that lovers do...any experience in which the lovers lost themselves for each other, because sacrifice of self is what love means. Today, unfortunately, we use the expression 'making love' only for sex. This is misleading. Of course sex can be a way of making love, but it can also be a way of destroying it."[75]

The spiritual condition of society tends to mirror the spiritual state of the persons who make up that culture. It's interesting that the first photograph was invented in America in 1839 and it took only 11 years before the word "pornographer" was added to our dictionary.[76] Within the last fifty years in our country sex has ceased to be a viable part of what it means to be human, it has been emancipated from being an expression of life and love and a part of the human race.[77] The greatest expression of love is now devoid of love, reduced to the selfish whims of sin-soaked beasts. How did we fall so far so fast?

In an article titled "Man's Search for Himself," W.W. Horton reflects: "The chief problem of people today is emptiness. While one might laugh at the meaningless boredom of people a decade or two ago, the emptiness has for many now moved from a state of boredom to a state of futility and despair which holds promise of dangers…the human being cannot live in a condition of emptiness for very long: if he is not growing toward something, he does not stagnate; the put-up potentialities turn into morbidity and despair, and eventually into destructive activities."[78] Isolation breeds emptiness and cuts us off from life-giving sources to fill that void. The very natural recourse, then, is to become filled up with something less satisfying, thus perpetuating a behavior of isolation which continues to empty the person until there is nothing left.

C. Pornography and the Family

"To love means…to subordinate oneself to the formation of a new subject, a 'we.' This depends…upon the resolution of two subjects to accept life's most difficult task, the creation of a double-subject, a 'we,' with complete disregard for egocentricity, all prejudices, training formulas and drives. He who has enough courage so to love finds in living with his partner the strongest positive experience imaginable – the appearance of super-personal purposes" (Fritz Kunkel, "Let's Be Normal").[79]

The Scriptures remind us of the purpose of marriage: "For this reason a man will leave his father and his mother and be united to his wife, and they will become one flesh" (Genesis 1:24). This is a beautiful image of God's blessed union and a stark reminder of what pornography steals away. Christian marriage is the sacred union, joining of two whole lives into one; not robbing one's identity from the other, but finding a sense of completeness of self in each other, through Christ. Pornography, as with all sexual sin, causes separation between the couple and separation from God, robbing them of unity and completeness. Instead of two becoming one, the two become disjointed and diminished in self. In more cases than not, the addiction of pornography began early in the person's childhood development. And more times than not the man or woman trapped in the addiction are hoping to leave those images behind when they are joined together. Marriage is viewed by the addict as a salvation from pornography, a "trading up," replacing the fantasy for reality, finding for the very first time wholeness for their splintered soul. As one addict described his experience: "For the first time I had sex with a woman. It was wonderful. So much better than masturbation! I wouldn't have to do that anymore! Free at last! And what a glorious feeling, being united with a woman. This was finally the answer I'd been looking for." But the disillusioned newlywed soon discovered: "Lust allowed me that honeymoon for a short time, only to demand its due again later."[80]

This is the power of addiction. God had planted inside of us this intense desire for intimate communion with God and each other in the midst of Paradise. But once we allow our heart to drink from the shallow wells of pornography, it overpowers our will, and becomes, as Jonathan Edwards said, "like a viper, hissing and spitting at God" and us also if we try to subdue it.[81] Like that poisonous serpent, sexual addiction takes hold of its victim, separating them from those who love them, striking out whenever they venture too close. They no longer belong to their spouse; they are emotionally cut-off from that life-connection. If the addiction started early in life, chances are they were never truly connected emotionally at all. Sex addicts who were exposed to pornography or abuse as a child lives in an emotionally arrested state of development, with skewed notions of what true love really is. If the addict, then, can't express love, the spouse suffers from a loveless marriage and the children learn that love is meted out in small rations. One husband described it this way: "For eighteen years my wife continually told me she didn't believe I loved her. In truth, I loved her the best I knew how, but I was too wrapped up in myself and my (pornography) addiction to know that love was so much more than I was giving her."

The Bible's condemnation of adultery is underscored throughout the Old

Testament law. While the Old Testament polygamous unions were not always considered adulterous (Genesis 16:1-4; 30:1-5; 38:15-18), Jesus removes all doubt upon the standard God demands: "I tell you, anyone who looks at a woman lustfully has already committed adultery with her in his heart" (Matthew 5:28). Adultery tears apart the "one-flesh" relationship of marriage, damaging the spiritual union God had established. It is a betrayal that is not easily overcome, and is even offered by Christ himself as the only legitimate reason for divorce (Matthew 5:32).[82] Interestingly enough, the same descriptive words used for idolatry carry the same connotation for the word adultery. As idolatry is seen as "illicit intercourse" and "wanton disloyalty,"[83] so too adultery is fraudulent, deceitful betrayal of love and loyalty. In fact, pornography is the lustful search for the *ideal* person, a word which finds its root in the term *idol*.

The emotional isolation caused by the pornography produces a selfish, secretive, and emotionally detached individual, leaving the ostracized spouse to languish from loving malnutrition. When the sin of their partner is finally found out the feelings of such betrayal cut deep within their psyche. In many cases, the shame of the addict's behavior is matched by the shame the spouse feels, internalizing his or her feelings and concluding that their must be something deficient in them to cause their spouse to look elsewhere for satisfaction. The same sense of shame that caused the addict to withdraw and hide from community will cause the spouse to withdraw as well. The result being that they are both left with no one to discuss their pain but each other; shame, anger and betrayal will make such a connection strained if not impossible.

And as much as pornography addiction causes the marriage partner to suffer, the children, because of their inability to understand such behaviors, will reap a much more devastating set of circumstances. It is important to recognize that almost all sexual addictions begin at a very early stage in childhood. Practically every adult that suffers from pornography addiction was introduced to it as a child either through discovering pornography on their own or being introduced to it by a friend, or worse, as a predator's tool of abuse. More than 80% of all known sex addicts admit to have been molested as a child. From very early ages they are learning to associate sexual abuse with intimacy. Even before their minds are developed enough to understand human sexuality, they are experiencing the emotional adrenal rush of the phenyl ethylamine (PEA), locking forever into their psyche a sexual hunger that must find satisfaction. "I was always fascinated by the prospect of seeing my friends naked and enjoyed the chance for an overnight stay with them. These sleepovers provided the ideal circumstances for a persuasive and … manipulative child like me to convince other children that getting naked together was perfectly acceptable…I was usually very careful and calculating in setting up my trap…I was much like a spider waiting for its prey…I was seven years old."[84]

While not all sex addicts are child molesters, those molested as a child are emotionally trapped at the age in which that trauma first occurred. "The developmental damage to an individual created by early life trauma creates an inability to experience (or express) love and nurture."[85] These traumatic events during childhood leave indelible marks on the individual, causing an emotional ineptitude. Very often these disemboweled children become 'lost children,' with deep feelings of abandonment and worthlessness, allergic to their own humanity, always looking for ways to keep their inadequacies from being discovered. Many of those stuck in that stage of development have learned to identify sex and love within the same emotional context. Just as some people involve themselves in sex in order to find the love denied them as a child, so too the adult victim of child molestation continues searching for that perverse sense of love to which they were exposed to. The lines between love and lust and fulfillment and shame are convoluted in the adult child of sexual abuse.

Extend this picture out further and see the extended line of generational perversity, as these abused children grow up and have children of their own. When we hypothesize what may happen to children raised in such homes, several painful scenarios come into play, some of which include: 1) the child is raised with an emotionally detached parent and grows up lost and love-hungry. Unable to properly experience or express love, they become choice recruits for their own sexual addictions; 2) the addicted parent crosses sexual boundaries with the child, who grows up frightened and confused, equating love with abuse, pleasure with pain; and 3) the child finds the parent's pornography and is confronted with issues he or she is not emotionally prepared to deal with. I read of one account where a child awoke in the middle of the night to find his minister-father masturbating in front of the computer screen. The father swore it was his first time and pleaded with the child to keep his secret. But it wasn't long after that when his son started down the same slippery path. Innocence is lost when a child discovers the family's dirty little secret. The way in which the parents live have ways of visiting itself upon the children, "punishing the children for the sin of the fathers to the third and fourth generation" (Exodus 20:5).

D. Pornography and the Church

The church is, in all practical purposes, an extension of the family and as new families are being brought into and raised up in the church, their sexual baggage comes along with them. Molestation, pornography, and every other known type of sexual abuse found outside the church walls can also be found within. A 1995 survey of 350 male Christian church leaders revealed that 64% struggle with sexual addiction and 25% of married Christian men have had an affair since becoming a Christian.[86] In the past decade and a half we have watched televised Evangelical ministers admit to adultery and followed headlines reporting child molestation inside the Catholic clergy. These are not isolated cases any more. One local pastor confided that his church was forced to close their Christian school after it was learned that three children were molested by one of the workers. In fact, one of the pedophile's choice opportunities has been as children's workers in the small church as most of these churches do not conduct background screenings and are desperate for someone to work with the children during the worship service. According to Ralph Earle, every congregation, no matter how small, has someone in it that is sexually addicted.[87] Church conflict fuels the need to act out and acting out isolates and exacerbates church conflicts which further fuel the need to act out.

Sexual indiscretions are inevitably found out in the church and cause massive damage to the church and its reputation. This is all the more true when the sexual offender is the pastor. Because the focus of this book is on ministers we must also look at the affect that clergy's sexual sin has on the church. Many of the feelings of emotional stagnation and betrayal that are seen in the pastor's actual family are mirrored in the church family as well. All churches to some extent or another have an elevated view of their minister; in many cases the clergy often embody the divine for the congregation. When problems arise in the family the first inclination is to call the minister; no one else is given the trust and respect afforded the family minister. When a pastoral trust is betrayed, then, every experience of honor and blessing experienced through this person turns to ashes.[88]

Undoubtedly there are spiritual implications for a church when their leader is caught in sin. Jesus tells us that if a blind man leads another blind man they both fall into a pit (Matthew 15:14). In Leviticus 20 God speaks through Moses to the people on how they are not to live. He warns the people against sacrificing their children to Molech and those who do must die. In verses 4 and 5 he says, "If the people of the community close their eyes...I will set my face against that man and his family...and all who follow him." The leader of this church family is sacrificing to the god of immorality and the church is reaping the results. How can the God of light and truth bless a church where its leadership is lost in such a dark lie? "The integrity of the upright guides them, but the unfaithful are destroyed by their duplicity" (Proverbs 11:3). This truth also applies for the church in regard to laypersons involved in such sinful practices. In Deuteronomy 22:23 Moses sets down the punishment for those found in adultery and in the next verse explains: "You must purge the evil from among you" (v. 24). Paul grieves over an incident of incest within the Corinthian church, insisting the perpetrator be removed (1 Corinthians 5:1-5) and then teaches that a "little yeast works through the whole batch of dough" (v. 6), or, a little sin can infect the whole church.

As we have seen, pornography addiction is an epidemic of sin that has left in its wake victims strewn about the streets. It is an insidious illusion, offering intimacy but delivering isolation, expressed as freedom but causing enslavement. Sin has struck its death-blow and every member of the human race feels the effects of it. Marriage vows are betrayed, children are victimized, churches are cursed, and the name of Christ is dragged through the mud as the man or woman trapped in the addiction despair of life. In the next chapter we will observe the role of the minister more closely and see what it is inside the clergyperson that leaves him or her vulnerable to such deadly poison.

CHAPTER 3
PASTORS AND PORNOGRAPHY

In the previous chapters we laid the groundwork on what God's original plan for human sexuality was and how sin has stained that design. We looked at the addictive nature of sexual sin, particularly the sin of pornography and the damaging effects that pornography has on the individual; we saw how pornography infects the people and culture surrounding the sexual addict.

In this chapter we will begin to focus in on pornography addiction as it relates to the clergyperson and why it seems to be that pornography is the "addiction of choice" among ministers. We will look at the unique typology of persons who sense God's call upon their lives and the types of influences that shape such individuals. We'll examine the particular personal issues of the pastor and the social structures, including the church itself, which may lend them to reinforce such behaviors. Finally, we'll distinguish whether pornography addiction among clergy crosses gender lines and what particular sexual drives act as triggers for each of the sexes.

Pastor as a Person

Christian ministry is a unique vocation. Very ordinary men and women, who sense, what they can best describe as a divine prompting, lay aside their own personal ambitions in order to serve others. Clergypersons are no different than the rest of the human race. They have the same passions, hopes, and dreams as every one else, yet, for the sake of that call, they lay aside their own dreams for the sake of others. Moreover, these men and women also have the same stirrings as the rest of humanity: they are sexual animals, moved by the same passions of life and influenced by the same negative forces. Not all clergy have sensed God's call and not all clergy enter ministry with clear ambitions. But right motives or not, pastoral ministry is a demanding life of self-sacrifice. Other types of ministers, such as missionaries and evangelists, make similar sacrifices, but pastoral ministry is unique, in that practically everyone in their sphere of influence feels a right to dictate what and when and where these sacrifices will be made. "Most ministers have too many bosses and wear too many hats…a pastor is expected to do whatever chore anyone dreams up for him because no one knows exactly what his job is[89]."

"Pastors live in a world that never stops, where the light never goes out, and where the average work week is between fifty-five and seventy-five hours. One in eight ministers are bi-vocational or multi-vocational, and sixty percent of their spouses work outside the home."[90]

Not content to simply pastor the church (or not *allowed* to be content), the minister begins to take on other duties in the church: teaching a Sunday school class, sweeping the walkways, cleaning the church, painting the parsonage and mowing the lawn. A very close pastor friend of mine once lamented:

"I would arrive at the church three hours early on Sunday morning. I would turn up the heat, unlock the doors, turn on the lights, shovel the snow, print and fold the bulletins and pick up any trash I found. Then if there was time I would go over my sermon and pray. One testy matron of the church pointed her finger at me and yelled, "You're an *employee* of this church!" There have been many a Sunday afternoons I spent reading the classified section of the newspaper."

What happened? Was this God's intent for the pastoral call? Are laypersons taking advantage of the kindness of these under-shepherds? Or could there, perhaps, be something within the ministers themselves that allow and maybe even seek their own demise? There is something self-destructive in the character and position of the minister, as described above. Look with me at some of the personal issues that lend themselves to the pastor's susceptibility to pornography addiction.

Even before we center in on the personal development of the called individual, there is a dimension of the personality that is formed even before we take our first breath. Is there something in the genetic makeup of the person that causes susceptibility to addictive behavior?

In the Beginning...

I praise you because I am fearfully and wonderfully made; your works are wonderful, I know that full well. My frame was not hidden from you when I was made in the secret place. When I was woven together in the depths of the earth, your eyes saw my unformed body.
Psalm 139:14-16

For centuries now, "nature vs. nurture" has been the great debate in the realm of human behavior. Is our behavior destined by the genetic makeup of the chromosomes past on by our parents or is destiny determined by the environment in which we are raised and the choices that we make. In recent years new research has brought to light astounding evidence of a possible genetic vulnerability for addiction. Dr. David Goldman, chief or neurogenetics at the U.S. National Institute on Alcohol Abuse and Alcoholism reported: "It appears that the genetic vulnerability for substance and alcohol abuse is fairly general in our society."[91]

In the same way certain genes make persons more prone to heart disease, cancer or Alzheimer's, scientists now believe that other genes may make persons more susceptible to addictive compounds that affect the brain's natural reward system. Drugs forever alter the brain's natural chemicals, such as serotonin and dopamine, which are involved in controlling the person's impulses. Scientists are finding evidence that these forever-altered neurotransmitters are being passed on generationally, creating restructured genes in a person's DNA strand. For example, researchers recently found a gene that is linked to antisocial alcoholism. It is a mutant form of a gene known as HTR1B, which lowers the levels of serotonin and increases the risk of impulsive aggression. The genetic mutation had been found among a certain group of Native Americans where there are high levels of alcohol consumption.[92] This is not to say that Native American are a weaker species when it comes to alcohol, but rather individuals who suffer from alcoholism are very likely going to pass that vulnerability to drink on to their children, and they, in turn will pass it on to theirs.

A recent study was conducted at Harvard Medical School involving 352 pairs of identical male twins and 255 pairs of fraternal twins, all of whom smoked marijuana more than five times in their lives. Both groups were given a set of questions about how good or bad they felt after using the drug. Dr. Ming Tsuang, Dr. Michael Lyons and their colleagues compared the answers submitted by the two sets of twins and discovered that the identical twins' experiences were significantly more alike than the fraternal twins. Since identical twins carry the exact same genes, while the fraternal twins carry half the amount of matching genes, researchers concluded that genetic factors played a significant impact on the drug experience. Dr. Roy Pickens and his colleagues at Johns Hopkins University conducted similar studies resulting in similar results. There are approximately 100,000 genes in the human body and, of those more than 40,000 are expressed in the brain, the seat of addiction.[93]

But the human being is more than just body and mind; there is the spiritual dimension joined together to create the soul of a person. What role does human genetics play in the whole of a person, body, mind and spirit? Science has made great social and biological strides, but, as of yet, have been unable to provide us with an adequate explanation of what an emotion is or where the seat of our feelings are found. Is it in the brain, the genes, the heart or someplace else?[94] Where does the human soul reside? At what point of existence is the spirit of God implanted into our nature, or, for that matter, the sinful nature? As we discussed in chapter one, traducianism is the theological understanding that both the body and soul of the human are passed on mediately through the process of conception. The name "Eve" means "life-giver" and all human life is passed on through the woman. Likewise, death was passed through all humanity from the sin of Adam: "sin entered the world through one man, and death through sin, and in this way death came to all men…" (Romans 5:12). I do not mean to say that the ovum is the center of life and the sperm the encroachment of death, because neither the spirit of life nor the spirit of death has material substance. Rather, could it be that God's Spirit is breathed into mankind at the point of conception and at the point in time that it becomes an inhabitant of this earth it is thereby corrupted by the spirit of sin and death?

Fruits of Death

The acts of the sinful nature are obvious: sexual immorality, impurity and debauchery; idolatry and witchcraft; hatred, discord, jealousy, fits of rage, self ambition, dissensions, factions and envy; drunkenness, orgies, and the like…But the fruit of the Spirit is love, joy, peace, patience, kindness, goodness, faithfulness, gentleness and self-control."
Galatians 5:19-21a, 22-23a

Scripture tells us that both God's Spirit and the spirit of death each carry distinguishing fruits with them. These are the fruits, but the seeds of each of these pieces of fruit are housed in their respective spirits. Further, we know that God has imparted special gifts to his children in order to live and serve the Spirit of Christ. Could it not also be concluded then that Satan has imparted some of his particular "gifts" to mankind as well? Verse 24 describes them generically as "passions and desires." Could particular passions and desires be seen as distinct mutations within the individuals' DNA strands causing predisposition to particular sinful behaviors? "I, the LORD your God, am a jealous God, punishing the children for the sin of the fathers to the third and fourth generation..." (Exodus 20:5) What do we do with the overwhelming evidence of persons becoming third and forth generation alcoholics? Do we attribute *all* of this to family environment? What about the growing homosexual community that protests that they were *born* with their distinct sexual orientation? Again, while much of this can be attributed to childhood environment, especially childhood sexual trauma, could we not concede that a portion of homosexuals may have been genetically altered this way? Not overlooking the practice, but understanding, as David did, that sin infects, even through the embryonic pouch: "Surely I was sinful at birth, *sinful from the time my mother conceived me*" (Psalm 51:5, italicized mine).

But, just as those who have been born with genetic links to high cholesterol should not simply throw their hands up in the air and prepare to die early, genetic vulnerability to sinful behaviors does not conclude a predestined life of debauchery. Environment plays a huge part in the shaping of a person's character and reshaping of their nature.

Childhood Environment: "Shaking the Family Tree"

Undoubtedly, one of the most essential environmental factors in establishing the human character is the stages of childhood development. The family molds the child's self-image and sets the stage for their understanding of proper human sexuality.[95] A person's sexual development begins as early as the first hours of birth with the parents holding, touching and kissing the child, with the care and respect and affection lavished on or withheld from the child. These experiences imprint on the child's psyche how he or she will feel about themselves, the world around them and the God who created them both.

As children grow, they observe whether or not their parents are comfortable displaying physical intimacy toward one another and them. They are quick to pick up on the level of care and affection parents display. "By the time children start school and must deal with outside information and peer pressure, they are already well on their way to becoming the sexual adults they are going to be. That is, most of their values and attitudes about themselves and how they relate to others sexually are formed."[96] Throughout the stages of childhood development these thoughts and feelings will be impressed upon the child's heart and mind. Each experience carries with it the possibility for great good or the potential for catastrophe.

As we begin a discussion of family influences it is important to recognize that no family is perfect. Most families try hard to do the right thing by one another, but human beings are prone to fail now and then. Other families are a breeding ground for abuse and dysfunction. 81% or sexual addicts are sexual abuse survivors, 74% have been physically abused, and 97% have been emotionally abused.[97] It's not enough to know whether the minister grew up in a Christian home because child abuse crosses all walks of life and denominational borders. Superficial knowledge of a pastor's family background is a poor indicator of whether they had been abused. Many of the overwhelming stories of clergy fallout are simply the parent's hidden sin coming to light through the child's.

While child abuse is undoubtedly the most offensive example of boundary confusion, others would include physical and emotional withdrawal or neglect, over-protectiveness or being too strict, including strict religiosity. There are homes where the parents verbally tear at the child's sense of self-worth: "Why are you so stupid?" "You were a mistake!" This form of verbal degradation is also known as "emotional abuse." Another form of subtle manipulation occurs when a parent demonstrates an emotional dependency upon the child. "What would I do without you?" or "You're the man of the house now." In this situation the child is given far too much emotional responsibility in the home; the behavior has become commonly referred to as "emotional incest." Children are simply not prepared emotionally to handle that type of inferred responsibility. Strict religiosity affects the child negatively when biblical standards are held to the letter of the law and children are not allowed to be children. Parents become almost Pharisaical in raising their children and children are afraid to talk with parents about personal issues, including their sexuality. Any time harmful things are allowed to happen to the children the boundaries are too loose and any time that healthy things are not allowed to happen the boundaries are too tight.

One more form of neglect that we hardly ever consider would be what some experts call, "sexual abandonment." This is when the parent(s) fails to adequately teach or model healthy sexuality to their children. Children are being taught their sex education through television, friends at school, and "finding dad's Playboys," but rarely are they taught nor do they see modeled before them an honest picture of human sexuality. A clear understanding of sexual identity lies at the core of human identity and gives a proper perspective for human relationships.[98]

Other family issues that cause vulnerability toward sexual addiction would include such things as failing to teach children how to honestly communicate their feelings. Deep emotions, such as anger, fear and sadness are never discussed or allowed to be displayed. Another issue would include confused roles in the family. Some children become the heroes who get the work done, the scapegoat who bears the brunt of the responsibility, the lost child who seems independent and is left to do things on their own, the saint who always does what's right, and the handful who always bucks the system. The typical list for future clergy would include the hero, the saint, and the lost child. It is as if their childhood was grooming them for the pastorate. A final issue has to do with coping strategies. How do the family members cope with life and especially with stressful situations? Do they drink/use drugs, work, fight, withdraw, eat, go shopping, use pornography? Substance and behavioral issues are coping mechanisms to mentally escape for a while and/or anesthetize the feelings.[99]

Probably a higher percentage of clergypersons come from dysfunctional families than not and these figures seem unaffected by whether the individual was raised in a Christian home or not. Some enter, freed of their own personal hell, wishing to help others get free as well. But once ordained they discover that more healing was necessary and hell has caught up with them. Others enter ministry as a desperate attempt to overcome their own personal dysfunctions, hoping such a commitment will deliver them from the sin that has held them. A 1988 study[100] of unusually high-functioning clergy members further demonstrates the painful situations from which ministers emerge:

91% reported chronic physical dysfunction and problems with weight in their own or their spouse's family of origin.

83% reported chronic emotional disorder and suicide attempts
75% reported diminished sexual interest and sexual acting out as children.
66% reported substance abuse.
58% reported affairs and problems with the law.
50% reported chronic or episodic physical violence.
25% reported incest.
8% reported compulsive gambling.

The people who emerge from these family influences are disoriented men and women, damaged disciples who mask their low self worth by appearing strong and brash, persons desperate to earn love and respect but never able to accept it, codependent martyrs who find their worth in the praise of others, lonely, isolated individuals who crave connectedness but are unable to connect. These are people who carry deep wounds, and, bearing the mark of those sins upon their own psyche, they run inside the church in a desperate attempt to be fixed and free. Sadly, what they find inside the church is other damaged men and women, examples of the same family dysfunctions they've sought to be delivered from. "Church members bring their own family-of-origin issues into congregations. Most pastors realize that church systems are frequently as 'crazy' (or dysfunctional) as the families from which they themselves came. So pastors constantly face interactions that can create enormous stress, reminding them of what they have experienced all their lives...The stress of these family issues create a loneliness that creates vulnerability."[101]

Pornography, thus, becomes an escape, where the pain of childhood trauma and current stresses can be momentarily eluded. Confused roles during childhood have caused confused identities in adulthood; childhood traumas leave adult children emotionally arrested at that stage of development, causing them to be unable to distinguish proper relational roles and incapable of dealing with the normal stresses of adulthood. Pornography becomes a form of self-medication, a coping strategy for feelings of low self-worth or self-pity. Poor education and modeling of human sexuality during childhood leave children vulnerable to a variety of improper sexual experiences, including pornography and masturbation. Further, as discussed earlier, in practically every known case of pornography addiction, the individual discovered pornography and masturbation at a very young and vulnerable age. The mental changes in brain chemistry have left deep-seated imprints upon the child's personality that follow them into adulthood. When similar stresses affect the individual the mind is quick to recall the emotional release it had experienced in the past through pornography and they are immediately drawn to pornography again.

Personality and Its Shadow Side

Childhood development and experiences forever alter and establish the personality of an individual, shaping them into the person they will become, how they view the world around them, and how they relate to others. Over time our genetics and personal history consolidate into fairly stable personality traits. An excellent indicator for discovering these personality traits is the Myers-Briggs Type Indicator. Developed by the mother-daughter team of Katherine Cook Briggs and Isabel Briggs Myers, the Myers-Briggs test was developed using the personality typology developed by Carl Jung, the first psychologist to study adult development. In his study, Jung categorized the adult development along four continuums:

EXTRAVERSION ——————————————— INTROVERSION
SENSING—————————————————————INTUITION
THINKING————————————————————FEELING
JUDGING—————————————————————PERCEIVING

While not discounting the notion of God's call on a person's life, childhood experiences seem to establish certain personality traits that tend to pull the individual toward a certain life's work. More importantly, the particular traits of an individual will indicate the type of person they will be in life and work and, interestingly enough, the strong side of a person's personality is naturally reinforced, most times to the neglect of the shadow-*side* of the personality. The shadow-side of the personality is the less-dominant personality types found in the person. These subordinate traits of the personality can be compared to a person's peripheral view, where they see coming images from either side of their direct sight. Neglect of the periphery and a person is left vulnerable to what comes against them from the side. The same is also true for the shadow traits of the personality. For example, if a pastor's strong personality traits are extrovert, intuition, feeling and judging, which is the most common personality type for clergy,[102] he or she will quite naturally nurture those strong areas in their spiritual and emotional development to the neglect of the introvert, sensing, thinking and perception personality traits.

Strong extroverts prove to be fiery preachers and great evangelists, while their neglected introvert side lacks the depth and perspective that comes through quiet times of study and reflection. The strong intuitive person develops a more contemplative spirituality, but lacks the ability to carry it into the everydayness of life. The one who is service-oriented proves to be a wonderful chaplain but lacks true leadership abilities. Feeling types rely heavily on "gut feelings" but rarely stop long enough to reason out such situations. This in particular is significant when you consider that 70% of all clergy, male or female, are feeling types[103]. The thinker remains objective in all situations but fails to show compassion and build rapport. The judger is a strong systematic leader but lacks the gentleness of a perceiving pastor. The spontaneous or perceiving person needs discipline while the judger needs more spontaneity.

While all ministers display areas of ministry they are strongly suited for, these shadow areas of the personality leave the pastor ill-prepared with the large variety of persons and wide spectrum of needs in the local church, adding to his or her anxiety. Further, since all dimensions of the personality are necessary to make a person whole, underdeveloped dimensions leave the pastor spiritually fragmented and vulnerable for attack. Left unnourished and to their own devices the shadow areas will find other places to feed that natural hunger.[104] For example, the extrovert who is outgoing and charismatic becomes a target for love-starved church members. If he or she neglects the quiet time of introspection with God they leave themselves open for spiritual attack. On the other hand, the introverted pastor who withdraws within tends to cut themselves off from life-giving relationships, thus becoming isolated and very lonely, a prime target for inappropriate sexual behavior. The intuitive person must find a way of feeding the sensing side of the personality or its sensual cravings will satisfy themselves through primitive sensuality; the sensing person usually requires more intuition to keep from going down dangerous paths. Feelers allow emotional wounds to go deep and may run to pornography for emotional relief; the thinker tends to let his or her need for emotional release to go unsatisfied for too long, finding immediate gratification through pornography. The strong leader doesn't see the potential danger signs of sexual sin; the perceiving leader is too quick to give into their sensual feelings.

The Alban Institute conducted an extensive survey of 1319 ordained clergy (1247 ordained males and 72 ordained females) to study personality types in ministers. According to their findings, clergypersons with the NF, iNtuitive-Feeling, personality types are most at risk for sexual impropriety. The intuitive type is sensual and needing to connect emotionally with another. They are spontaneous, usually acting before they think. Feeling types are warm and caring; they have the tendency to become lost in caring for the needs of someone and are unaware of the long-term consequences. Feeling types are much more likely to become enmeshed in other people's lives emotionally and sexually. Of those surveyed, a large majority of clergypersons tested as being intuitive, and more than 70% of the pastors as feeling types.[105] Interestingly enough, because spirituality and sexuality interface with each other, those personality types that lend them to being the most spiritual are also at the highest risk for being sexually seduced.[106] In fact, the more devout the individual the more vulnerable they are to inappropriate sexual involvement. When you consider that pornography, as with all inappropriate sexual behavior begins with seduction, we begin to see why pornography seems to be the "drug of choice" for clergy.

Church Context and Expectations

"The Greatest Job You'll Ever...Love?

The loneliest place to be is in the pulpit...
The minister is a target, used by the people in the church.
Steven Arterburn

Consider this scenario: A man enters a convenience store at the very moment it is being robbed and is shot in the chest by the burglar. He staggers out into the street where he is immediately hit by a car and has both of his legs broken. The ambulance driver, speeding toward the hospital looses control and the ambulance rolls four times down a steep embankment. The man sustains a concussion. Finally the man reaches the hospital, survives surgery, has the bullet removed and both legs set and is then wheeled to a private room for recuperation. The nurse brings in his dinner tray and moments later he chokes on a chicken bone and dies. Some may conclude that it sounds as if this individual was destined to die, others would say that circumstances had stacked the deck against him. His intestinal fortitude sustained him during those tough bouts, but it was the place of perceived safety and healing where he was done in.

In a very similar fashion we wonder about the one called into pastoral ministry. While for many the church is a place of strength and refuge, many times, for the pastor, it is a very lonely, very painful place. Patterns of personal dysfunction mark the would-be pastor, from the very beginning.[107] Family dysfunction and arrested maturation tears their soul and distorts their perception, personality traits starve their spiritual and emotional immune system. Wounded, shaken and disoriented, they enter the ministry where they expect to find healing but are instead choked to death by the unreasonable demands and expectations of other wounded individuals. Past wounds reopen, infection sets in, and sin is allowed to finish its deadly business.

Unrealistic Expectations

Dr. James Dobson describes church ministry as a "bottomless pit"; his cousin, H.B. London refers to it as "the terrible tyranny of the unfinished."[108] The pastor is expected to deliver a couple of heart-searching, soul-winning sermons on Sunday and then another for the mid-week service. Many of them teach a Sunday school class, lead a Saturday Bible study and hold services at the local nursing home or prison. They balance the church budget, chair the committees, conduct the weddings and funerals and a host of other respective jobs. And if the pastor is part of a denomination or ministerial association, the list of responsibilities only increases. The pastor is chiefly responsible for growing the church, increasing the income, leading various ministries, promoting worth-while causes, visiting the sick and lonely and, in his or her spare time, mow the lawn and sweep up. Sunday night, after he or she has preached their last message, turned off the lights and locked the church doors, they still cannot relax because they know in a few short hours they will have to do it all again. A dear clergy friend of mine was interviewing with a pastoral search committee in which they pulled out a several-page, single-spaced list of expectations for their new minister. After perusing the list she was asked if she felt she could meet the requirements of the position. Without batting and eye she said, "Jesus himself couldn't do all that!"

Clergy families live their lives in a fishbowl. Pastors have shared horror stories of parishioners walking into the parsonage without bothering to knock, reasoning, "the church owns it" and forgetting that it is also someone's home. Church members impose expectations upon pastors and their families that they themselves have no intentions of keeping. In fact, a recent Barna Research survey found that four out of five adults expect ministers to live up to a higher standard of behavior than they expect from others.[109] Both the character and work of a pastor is lived out under a microscope. Is there any wonder why they are insecure, why they display a false persona, and why they fall? Insecurity is hammered hard on the crucible of negative events in ministry. Whether real or imagined, the clergy mind tells them that they are not allowed to be human.

Is it really as serious as all of that? Consider the following survey results of the personal and professional lives of pastors:

(1991 survey of pastors by the Fuller Institute of Church Growth)

90% of pastors work more than 46 hours a week.
80% of pastors believed that pastoral ministry negatively affected their families
33% said ministry was an outright hazard to their family
50% felt unable to meet the needs of the job
45% report significant stress-related crisis at least once in ministry
90% felt inadequately trained to cope with ministry demands
70% say they have a lower self-esteem now compared to when they started out in ministry.
40% reported a serious conflict with a parishioner at least once a month
70% do not have someone that they consider a close friend.[110]

Focus on the Family surveyed 5000 ministers and found that 40% of them have considered leaving their churches in the last three months.[111] What are the implications for clergy and addiction to pornography? It's easy for ministers to give help – it's hard for ministers to get help. Pastors feel overwhelmed with the tremendous amount of work and idealistic expectations. The pastor is vested with the responsibility of bringing growth and vitality to the church, dismissing Jesus' words that he will grow the church and the scriptural evidence that it is his Spirit that breathes new life. This daunting task is laid on the shoulders of the minister, yet he/she must accomplish this task and do so with little authority, unclear goals and uncommitted members. They are to work twelve hours a day, six days a week and do so under the scrutiny of every person who walks through the church door (and a few who don't). They desperately seek out some form of relief, some escape from their reality. Completely vulnerable, they remember that one escape from their past that has always been there and always proved faithful in providing temporary relief: pornography.

Along with the unrealistic expectations of ministry, there are other factors that play a role in clergy breakdowns and pornographic susceptibility, such as dysfunctional church families, isolation in ministry, church conflict, and lack of self-care:

Church Dysfunction and Insecure Leadership

Church ministry has rightly been described as a family, and as such, there are usually varying levels of dysfunction to be found inside each church. The man or woman of God many times is coming out of their own family dysfunction only to step into another. And just as the minister brings his or her baggage inside the church, so does everyone else, except now the church's baggage becomes the pastor's responsibility. Many times ministers who come from broken environments enter into adulthood in an emotionally arrested state. They look like a grown up, but inside they are still very much a child.

Immature leaders will mask their insecurity in a number of ways. One way is to appear strong, almost overbearing. But it is, in most cases, a façade, a phony image to hide their lack of self-confidence. One common phenomenon is that many times people are attracted to ministry because they crave the attention and affirmation of the adoring congregation. Mental Health professionals call this a narcissistic personality disorder. This disorder is common among clergy and causes them to become tenacious in their duties, afraid of disappointing anyone. Their diminished self-worth causes them to overcompensate in ministry. Perhaps this is where the unrealistic expectations of ministry originate, not in parishioners mandating such efforts but ministers self-imposing extra duties on themselves. Often the narcissist's behavior is self-destructive.[112] "Frequently these pastors have chronic feelings of envy and unsatisfied ambition. They are usually charming and proficient manipulators who run from criticism."[113] Another way that pastors mask their insecurities is to appear to always have their spiritual act together. Afraid of letting the church know that they are upset or angry or scared or hurting, they must always appear as the model of righteousness. They follow the example of Benjamin Franklin who once admitted to a Quaker friend: "I never really learned to acquire humility, but I've become quite good at faking it."

Isolation and Unaccountability in Ministry

Ministry is undoubtedly one of the loneliest professions in the world. You would think the opposite were true. The minister socializes all week: from his breakfast and lunch meetings to dinner invitations in parishioner's homes; shaking hands on Sunday and afternoon visitation. But in truth, practically every clergy-lay relationship is superficial, and they are expected to be so. Ministers are cautioned by their colleagues and denominational leaders *not* to get too involved with the members of their church. Instead, the pastor invests himself or herself in half-hearted relationships at the cost of spending time with their family, the only relationships where he or she is encouraged to draw closer.

Not only do they isolate themselves from the people they serve, but pastors will isolate themselves emotionally from one another because of jealousy and competition, fearing to trust each other.[114] This is especially true for the male clergy who tend to find their identity in the success or failure of their church. I think back over my first church. We were small but growing. I was involved with a cluster of pastors from my denomination and we took part in joint-services at different times in the year. The problem was, with such a large gathering of people, there were only a few churches large enough to incorporate the crowd. My fear and the fear of many of the other pastors was that when our parishioners saw the professional job and excitement generated at the large churches, they may feel a desire to leave for greener pastures. I wish I could say these fears were irrational, but, in truth, that very thing happened time and again. George Barna Research has documented that more than eighty percent church growth in the U.S, is either biological growth or transfer growth, children born into the church or people leaving one church to join another.[115] Consumerism in the church has played a large part in contributing to pastoral paranoia and clergy mistrust.

For similar reasons pastors are hesitant to open themselves up to their bishops/superintendents for fear they may jeopardize future opportunities for advancement. The struggling pastor reasons to himself/herself: "Jesus himself told the parable of the servant who was faithful in the little things being put in charge of greater things (Matthew 25:21). What's going to happen to me if I tell my district superintendent that I can't handle the little things?" The forlorn shepherd of the small flock regretfully concludes that he or she must suffer alone, working all the harder to make their church flourish, so as to get noticed by the powers-that-be and be lifted from their disparaging set of circumstances.

To further exacerbate the intense loneliness of the ministry family, consider the fact that in almost all cases they have left home and their own extended family in order to serve the spiritual needs of other families in other communities. When the extended families of congregants come together for weekend gatherings and holiday meals, the ministry family is usually by themselves, missing those connections with parents, siblings, grandparents, and others. If finances allow they will make a yearly pilgrimage home, but more times than not meager salaries do not make such excursions possible, and even if it does, one week a year with family can hardly compare to the fifty-two weeks of the other members. Sometimes young clergy couples cannot find time to go out together because there is no one to care for the children as extended families tend to provide. A very large portion of emotional support is given up when the pastor accepts a call from a church.

Tied closely to this issue of isolation is the matter of unaccountability. The minister's schedule is enigmatic. Ministry requires that he or she lock themselves in their office for hours at a time or to make middle of the night hospital visits. Because the minister is considered above reproach and no one really knows what a clergyperson's day entails, no one tends to question the minister. With the emergence of the Internet, not only do pastors have a ready supply of resources for sermon preparation, but they are only a few clicks of the mouse away from literally thousands of illicit pornographic web sites. Who is to say which is going on behind that closed door? When the pastor is out in the middle of the night making a hospital visit, they may be only a few blocks from the neighborhood strip club or massage parlor. X-rated videos are as close as the family video store and magazines, such as *Playboy* and *Penthouse* are sold where they buy their gas.

Church Conflict and Boundaries Issues

Undoubtedly, the majority of civil adult conflict takes place inside the church. Lay persons argue over practically everything and in most every case the target of their disfavor is the pastor. Pastors spend enormous amounts of energy dealing with eruptive disputes. They are continually being confronted and continually needing to confront. The problem is, as discussed earlier, the clergyperson who is emotionally arrested in their development will avoid conflict, especially direct confrontation. The conflict is not isolated to the church either. There is a large amount of conflict that comes from the home as well, especially as it has to deal with time and money management. The minister will hardly ever complain about the meager compensation for fear of being seen as too worldly, while, more times than not, it is the spouse that has to make ends meet. As one minister's daughter put it, "Our family is the only one in the congregation that lives below the poverty line."[116] A survey by *Leadership* magazine indicated that 70% of pastors' marital conflict has been over their compensation.[117]

Time management is another source of conflict in the pastor's marriage. As the pastor seeks more and more to be available for his or her church members, he or she becomes more and more unavailable to those at home. When the pastor is home, he or she thinks of things that need to be done at the church, and at church they pine to be home with the family. The conflicted minister is pulled to and fro as a tug-of-war rope. Lamenting, the pastor blames the demanding church, the nagging spouse and/or the sadistic God who put them in this situation to begin with. Unable to stand the pressures one day more, the pastor looks for an escape and there, in the privacy of his or her own office are an array of explicit web sites and chat rooms to connect with "old friends" who never complain or judge, never make demands...and never satisfy.

Underlying Issues

Looking beneath the surface

"So, if you think you are standing firm, be careful that you don't fall."

I Corinthians 10:12

"You can't judge a book by its covers" - or so the saying goes. And you cannot tell a spiritually and emotionally strong minister by what you see in the pulpit or beside the hospital bed. In the same way you cannot tell which minister will take a moral tumble by the smile on his/her face or the size of their congregation. A minister is similar to the polar ice burgs on the icy waters. It is not the small visible portion of the ice burg that proves treacherous for the ships, but the massive portion submerged from sight. Likewise, it isn't the visible behaviors of the clergyperson that will sink the pastor and the church, but those dark and painful issues that are beneath the abyss.

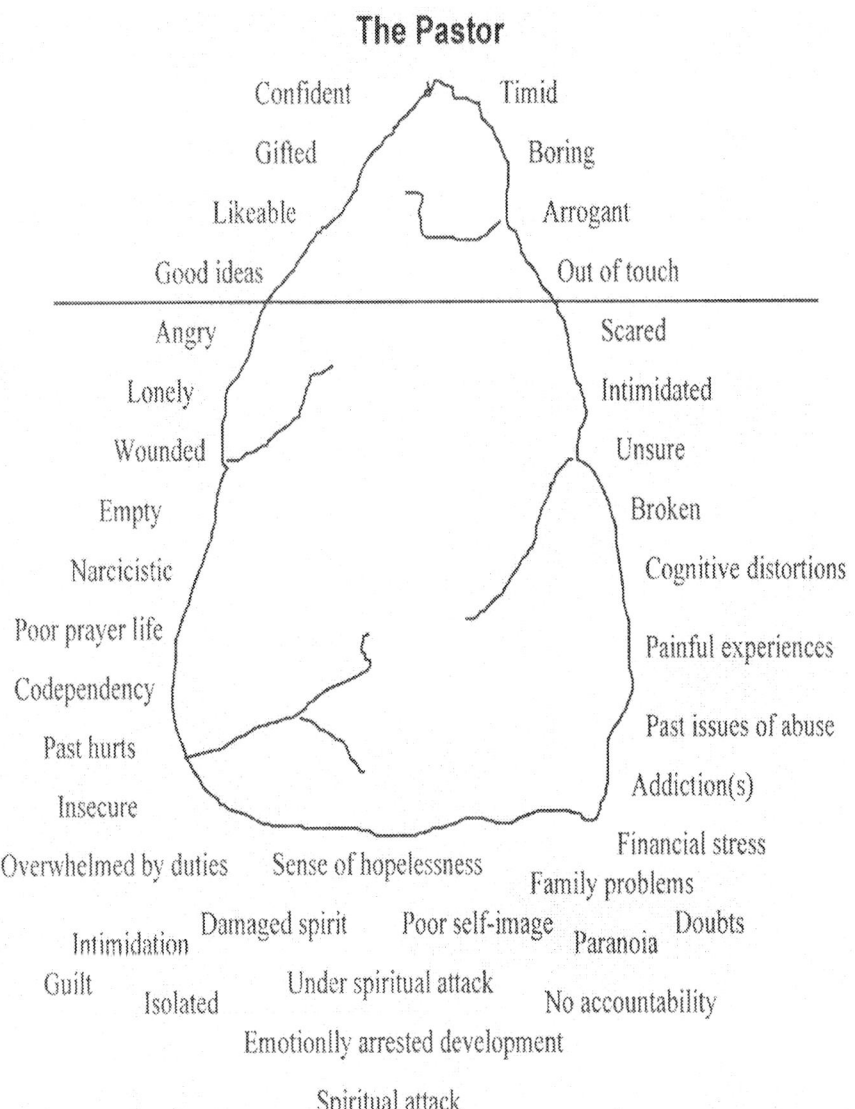

Spiritual attack

As discussed earlier, ministry is a very demanding job and the pastor has more than his or her share of the load to carry. Because of this many clergypersons give of themselves to the neglect of their own health and welfare. Believing they are following Christ's mandate, they, "deny themselves, take up their cross and follow" (Matthew 16:24b). But many times the pastor confuses his or her cross with the crosses of other people. We are called to "carry each other's burdens" (Galatians 6:2) by doing for others *what they are unable to do alone*.[118] "Each person should carry *his* own load" (Galatians 6:5). Christ alone bears the entire weight because he alone is able to handle the immensity of the load. Pastors have a tendency to develop a Messiah-Complex when it comes to the church. If we're going to take Jesus' responsibilities we shouldn't be surprised when we find ourselves nailed to a cross. Some see themselves as the good shepherd who "lays down his life for his sheep," forgetting that Christ is the Good Shepherd (John 10:11) and the only one qualified for the job.

In truth, it is, in most cases, a co-dependent disorder among clergypersons, a need to be needed by those around you, finding a sense of worth in outside approval because they can't find it within themselves. Codependency is all-too-common in persons who enter ministry, not necessarily hoping to save the lost but to find themselves, to heal their own damaged soul. The codependent pastor lives in constant fear of losing the approval and presence of those he or she cares for."[119] Because of this emotional deficiency clergy begin working later hours at the church, give up their days off, and stop taking time for physical fitness or personal hobbies. Lack of self-care on the part of the pastor leaves him or her vulnerable for spiritual attack.

Vulnerabilities Unique to Gender

The Male Pastor

There are areas of vulnerability in ministry that are unique to the specific gender of the clergyperson.[120] For example, a very large portion of the clergy in America are male, yet, in almost all Christian churches in the West, the highest percentage of congregants are women and the majority of lay-ministry is performed by women. The male pastor is the person they look to for moral support, spiritual guidance, and emotional strength. Because ministry is intimately spiritual and our experiences are profoundly emotional, boundaries have a tendency to lower between the minister and persons in the church. The personality of the male pastor makes him vulnerable. The typical male pastor is sensitive, caring, and giving, at least that is the persona he displays at church, which become attractive qualities to distraught, emotionally-starved women in the church. Inside, the male pastor is unsure of himself and in desperate need of validation from other sources. Emulation by one or more of these women in the church can be a hard magnet to resist.

Because the pastor has invested the lion's share of his time and energy at church, relationships at home generally become strained. The male pastor who counsels and comforts lonely vulnerable women receive affirming words and warm embraces in return: defenses are down and sexual temptation is glaringly strong. The male pastor has only a few options at this point: he can run home and reestablish a right intimate relationship with his wife (an up-hill battle, indeed!), or he can give into his temptation and begin a clandestine affair with one of the women in his church. A third option, however, may avail itself to the male pastor: he may struggle with his emotions for a time, isolating himself from both church and family, and then reason to himself that pornography is the lesser of two evils. After all, pornography has filled that emotional vacuum before and the chances of being caught are significantly less.

The Female Pastor

On the other hand, female clergy also have a unique set of temptations because of the "mystique of the holy woman," which can prove to be intriguing and powerfully alluring to some men. Also, female clergy are, in most cases, very warm, loving, and relational, perhaps even more than the wife waiting at home. Because of the position, the clergywoman is intimately involved in the lives of the church people at some of their lowest, most vulnerable times, and because women are primarily relationally stimulated, sexual temptation among female clergy is very much a reality.[121] Following the formal definition of pornography from chapter one and Jesus' definition of adultery in Matthew 5:28, emotional and relational fantasy on the part of female clergy is pornographic in nature and is a very real precursor for further sexual infidelity. Ann Bartram, a female pastor, points out that women pastors can have strong emotional feelings toward their parishioners. Experience has shown her that clergywomen become relationally enticed and are most vulnerable to sexually acting out with needy, vulnerable and lonely men in the church. She adds to the factor the codependent tendencies of the pastoral role as a set stage for a very possible boundary crossing.[122]

Again, just as the male pastor may run to the computer to surf explicit web sites rather than get involved with actual adulterous relationships in the church, the female pastor, at her lowest points of loneliness and highest points of temptation is more likely to turn to Internet chat rooms and search on-line personals, fantasizing about relationships she knows she cannot have. Dr. Glen Robitaille, a pastor-counselor friend of mine coined the term "fem-porn" to mean any form of media that acts as a stimulus for women sexually or relationally. For instance, Clint Eastwood's movie, *The Bridges of Madison County*, is, a very familiar movie and favorite among women, where Eastwood plays a worldly photographer who whisks into a small town and tenderly sweeps a middle-aged married woman off her feet and into his bed. Enchanted by his stories, his glamorous lifestyle, and his sensitive emotional qualities, this woman soon becomes enchanted by this stranger and, subsequently, disenchanted by her own husband. For every woman who watched this movie, fantasies began to erupt of a tender, understanding, sensitive man who is both charming and romantic. All of the sudden the lump asleep in the easy chair at home no longer stirs the fires. For others it's the faceless thousands of chat rooms on the Yahoo personals, each of them handsome, enchanting, and fun to chat with. Most of us are familiar with at least one person who ran off and married someone they met on-line. I have personally met a number of recovering sex addicts who used local chat rooms as a means for establishing contact with women, making arrangements for an anonymous sexual rendezvous.

The pastor lives on the razor's edge of anxiety and vulnerability. Overwhelmed by the work of ministry, isolated from life-giving relationships, and haunted by the ghosts of their past, the pastor finds himself or herself weak and defenseless, susceptible to whatever flaming arrows the devil may shoot in their direction. As they obsess about their current state of crisis, their anxiety increases. Distorted thoughts perpetuate, and intensify the anxiety to where the individual in unable to reason clearly. They can no longer find the strength of faith to hold to God, in fact, their mind rationalizes a need to mentally block God off in order to allow sin to present another alternative. Unable to fight these intense feelings any longer, the clergyperson must find a way of escape. At this point in Satan's game of rationalization, pornography actually begins to make sense. If Pornography has proved itself somewhere in the person's past, chances of escape are slim at best. As they use their drug the symptoms of anxiety decrease, negatively reinforcing the behavior and greatly diminishing their power to overcome. "What a wretched man I am! Who will rescue me from this body of death?" (Romans 7:24).

The question we are left with, then, is where is the line drawn in the sand? When walking sin's path, where is that border from which we step from being a sinner saved by grace to a backslidden saint fallen from grace? Is there a point of no return and have these ministers crossed that point? These are questions we will seek to answer in chapter four.

CHAPTER 4
IDENTIFYING THE DARK SIDE OF THE PASTOR

The Path to Perdition

"The way through the world is more difficult to find than the way beyond it."

Wallace Stevens,   *Reply to Papini*

If we deliberately keep on sinning after we have received the knowledge of truth, no sacrifice for sins is left, but only a fearful expectation of judgment and of raging fire that will consume the enemies of God.
Hebrews 10:26-27

Human Will Overrides Divine Grace

Trying to identify the point at which a person loses his or her salvation is not only difficult, it is next to impossible. How can anyone possibly look at someone else and determine whether God's mercy and grace has been removed? In Galatians 5:19-21, Paul gives us a good idea of the types of sin that will disqualify a person; he calls them the "deeds of the flesh." But while he lists immorality, impurity, sensuality and others that find their source in sexual lust, he also lists such things as enmity, strife, jealousy, anger, dissentions, factions, and more. If these "deeds of the flesh" are our guidelines for disqualification, we can be assured that these fallen clergypersons will not languish in Hell alone. In fact, I would venture to say our churches will be able to continue right along in Hell after this life is through, and I doubt that very many of those churches will see a drop in attendance, clergy or laity alike.

When trying to discern whether or not a person has done everything possible to assure their passage to Heaven, I am quick to remember that there really is nothing *we can do* to make Heaven a reality; it all must lie with Jesus who *already did* everything that was necessary. If we must do something or not do something, then it is no longer grace at work. I remember working as a youth pastor a number of years past when my father was killed in a car accident. To my best knowledge Dad was not a Christian. He had stopped drinking and even began attending church, but salvation is not found in sobriety nor is it acquired through church membership. Distraught over my father's spiritual condition, my pastor at the time offered me one brief sentence that has become my lifeline: "No one knows the extent of God's grace."

Grace for us is something we discover over time, receive in allotments, and disperse in small portions. But for God, grace is a part of who He is, its fullness is found in Him and offered to us in abundance. We hold out our thimble-sized cups, asking to be filled, but having no idea how much grace is available. Does this mean we should sin more to acquire more grace? As Paul retorted, "God forbid!" But when sin does bound in us, grace does much more abound. It seems that those who write on this subject from their own personal experience rarely mention that point of eternal forfeiture, while those who write from the perspective of an outsider peering in are quite quick to draw a line in the sand for others. Personally, I am not convinced that we can "lose" our salvation at all. God's comforting words to us are, "Never will I leave you, never will I forsake you" (Deuteronomy 31:6; Hebrews 13:5). But at the same time I believe that we can *choose* to leave him. After all, freedom to choose Christ must include the freedom to change our minds. Further, while our acts of sin are indeed breaches in our covenantal agreement with God, I do not believe that every sin committed enacts our withdrawal from God's saving grace. Rejecting Christ is a volition of the heart. Instead, I think a person will be able to sense when they have stepped beyond God's grace and mercy, in the same way they sense in their spirit when salvation becomes theirs. In the meantime, let me share with you my perspective of what that path of sin and death looks like.

Everything I Know of Theology I Learned from Pornography[123]

Here is a statement that will get a minister's credentials pulled in a hurry! As the recovering clergyperson begins looking back on the deep crags where their sin had taken them and begin to peer over the horizon of where God is bringing them, essential theological truths are being formed in their mind, and imprinted on their heart. For example, they begin to understand the dimensions of human spirituality and the insidious ways that sin separates from God. They begin to grasp the inward workings of the sin nature, the damaging effects of environmental influences, and how the human will rises above them all to choose their own path, thus holding them personally responsible. The recovering pastor can see more fully the process of backsliding and even begin to recognize the very point at which they begin to forfeit their salvation. Addiction offers the person enslaved a distinct sobering vantage point where they are better able to see through the gates of Hell and understand the exact nature of Hell's torment. And most importantly, recovery teaches the man or woman of God *experientially* how great and vast and deep and wide is God's love for them. They know it deep within them, this truth that is far beyond human comprehension.

The recovery process of sexual addiction not only teaches valuable theological truths, the convalescing minister becomes a student of anthropology, learning first hand the intricacies and fallacies of this animal created in God's image. In this chapter, we will look at some of the more common developmental deficits found in God's called, shadow sides of God's marvelous gifts. We will see the underlying unmet needs and the damage they cause in the human psyche. Finally, we will look at some suggested ways to find healing for these shadow areas as a precursor for personal recovery and ministry restoration.

As we look at the spiritual spiral of the one addicted to pornography, see the menacing clouds that seem to engulf the child of God:

An Attitude Change:

"Or take ships as an example. Although they are so large and are driven by strong winds, they are steered by a very small rudder wherever the pilot wants to go."
James 3:4

And just as a tiny rudder sets the path for a sea journey, so also something as small as a change of heart can change the course for a sin-journey into addiction. Just as the winds push the sails of the ship, the pastor has many people and circumstances pushing him or her forward. But it is something within the vessel itself that chooses the direction it will move. We cannot control other's actions, but we are responsible for our reactions. "Guard the good deposit that was entrusted to you — guard it with the help of the Holy Spirit who lives in you" (2 Timothy 1:14). Former Nazarene General Superintendent, D.I. Vanderpool used to share a story of when he and his family took a trip to the see the giant Sequoia redwoods in California. He told of standing beside a towering tree called General Sherman, and as he peered up at the giant, in his mind he held a conversation with the General. Dr. Vanderpool asked the General: "How old are you?" and the winds stirred to the tops of the General, as if to reply, "Before Moses was born, I was here." Dr. Vanderpool continued with his interview: "I suppose you have seen a number of fires through the years."

"Yes," the General admitted, "I have stood through many fires."

"How is it," Dr. Vanderpool inquired, "that you were able to survive?" And General Sherman answered, "It's because the fire was not able to reach my heart. The center of who I am was protected and so I was able to survive."

And so it is with all of God's creation. Several places throughout the Scriptures we are admonished to guard our hearts, or minds, our tongues and our souls (Psalm 141:3; Proverbs 4:13, 23; 21:23; 22:5; Mark 13:33; Luke 12:1, 15; Acts 20:31; 1 Corinthians 16:13; Philippians 4:7; 1 Timothy 6:20, 2 Timothy 1:14). It is the change in attitude that sets the course for addiction, a change in heart, mind, soul and tongue. The addiction had little to do with the pornography; pornography was the means of escape. Likewise, it had very little to do with the stressful events of the pastorate; the events were the strong winds, or driving forces, that brought us to our escape, but they did not set the course. The rudder which steers the ship is the heart, mind, and soul left unguarded and vulnerable to attack.

What were the attitudinal changes that led the man or woman of God to escape? We now better understand the events that lay waste to ministers: mounting pressures, petty battles, sour dispositions…these are the events. But events don't *make* a person sin; it is *what we do with those events that lead a person to sin.* We thought we had let those painful events roll off our backs; we thought we had given them over to God. In reality they were there all along, pushed down inside the person of God, a cauldron of resentment and contempt, bitterness and hostility, anger and envy, rebellion and rage. In 12-step recovery programs, step three is: "We made a decision to turn our will and our lives over to the care of God as we understood him." Probably a more accurate way to phrase that would be that we "made a decision to turn our will and our lives over to the care of God *as we understood turning our will and lives over.*"

The problem lies not in how we view God but in recognizing what it means to fully surrender. In our minds we erroneously came to understand the role of the under-shepherd as being responsible to do the lion's share of the work and receiving an equally large portion of the headaches. We allowed ourselves to become the martyr, one "being crucified with Christ." But there was unsettledness within the minister as he or she recognized the unfairness of this arrangement. While the minister's work is distinctly different from that of the lay person it is not to be proportionally different. Deep inside the center of the psyche was planted a seed of discontent that bloomed into deep roots of resentment; resentment toward the people who make unrealistic demands on the pastor, resentment toward themselves for allowing others to run rough-shod over them, and resentment toward God as they perceived Him calling them to such a life. Pornography was simply the vehicle of rebellion and way of escape; the pornography was simply a manifestation of inward thoughts and attitudes, the nails that the ministers themselves had forged.

"In your anger do not sin. Do not let the sun go down while you are still angry, and do not give the devil a foothold" (Ephesians 4:26). Paul doesn't say don't get angry because anger is a natural emotion. But the sin comes into play when we *decide* what we will do with that anger. The minister chooses self-pity and resentment begins to take root.

Thus we create our own predisposition toward addiction.

A Decision to Persist in Wrong:

"It is true there is difficulty in entering into godliness. But this difficulty does not arise from the religion which begins in us, but only from the irreligion which is still there. If our senses were not opposed to penitence, and if our corruption were not opposed to the purity of God, there would be nothing painful in us. We suffer only in proportion as the vice which is natural to us resists supernatural grace."

Blaise Pascal,
Pensees

Not only does the minister allow events to change his or her attitude, but they decide to keep hold of those attitudes. The clergyperson begins to think thoughts like, "I don't need to put up with this! This church will fall apart without me!" Before long they are matching faces from the congregation to go with each of their specific hurts, choosing to allow resentment to stay and grow, choosing to hold on to those attitudes while pushing those persons away. Polarization begins to happen and the pastor learns to develop a double life. They put up a good front and paste on a happy smile, while inside they are hurt and angry and bitter. They become masters of passive-aggression, withholding praise and attention as a form of punishment, "forgetting" to follow through with commitments, conversations hold a bite of sarcasm, speaking with a caustic tone;[124] points in sermons began to mirror real events, as if to say, "You know who you are!" Chances are they don't have a clue. Many of those "real events" turn out to be the pastor's own distorted thoughts and wounded emotions. Other times the events are real, but the offending persons are impervious to receiving coded messages. The clergyperson is now empowering these negative attitudes, which develop into compulsive behaviors; these negative attitudes become the first of their addictions and a precursor for many more, including sexual addiction.

One person described his addiction to resentment like this: "I know I get a 'hit' off that resentment every time I play back the scene with that person in my mind. It's like taking a drink from something deep inside me. Why? What's it doing for me? At times I swear I'm hooked on resentment more than I ever was on lust and alcohol."[125]

I remember situations from my own pastoral experience. There was one woman in particular that became my personal thorn in the flesh. I can still hear her in my mind, calling out, "Pastor", dripping with a caustic sardonicism that would make your skin crawl. Unwilling to bring her complaints to me, she would let her displeasure be known in other church circles until it would make its way back to Several times I needed to confront this woman, but I was too much of a coward. Instead, I would play out these wild scenarios in my mind, putting herself in her place with the same grace as Dirty Harry with an abscessed tooth.

Resentment empowers the addiction and disembowels the pastor, eating away at him or her. In their mind they replay the scenario, and each time he or she comes out on top. The pastor is not the submissive servant in his or her thought world. In their minds they put sister so-and-so in her place or they really give it to brother what's-his-name, as they wish they could in real life.

Here is where the fantasy life begins to gain power and shape the duplicity of the pastor's life. Outside the pastor is meek and mild, inside a raging fire. **Addiction is a spiritual matter, and it needs to be dealt with from the inside out.** "O Jerusalem, wash your heart from wickedness, that you may be saved. How long shall your evil thoughts lodge within you?" (Jeremiah 4:14)

Thus, our wrongs hold us in bondage; we sin against ourselves.

Guilt and Punishment:

"For every wrong there is a reaction that negates life, adding to the pool of our emotional and spiritual distress."
Author unknown

"But if you do not do what is right, sin is crouching at the door" (Genesis 4:7b). The pastor is beginning to reap the penalty of all those negative things they think and do. The word "crouching" in this verse is the same word as an ancient Babylonian word, referring to a demon waiting to pounce. Every bitter thought, every act of aggression becomes a syringe of poison shot into the bloodstream, every unhealed emotional scar festers and infects. The person of God knows it's wrong, but they won't let go, they *can't* let go. This is why cognitive therapy and accountability are so important; their way of thinking is too distorted to be trusted. The child of God feels guilty about these attitudes and somehow they know it's killing them. Ashamed, they begin to pull away from others, those to whom they are bitter for escape, and also loved ones out of shame. The isolation can be a time of self-introspection, but more times than not it becomes a time of replaying the perceived wrongs done, fostering those bitter feelings, and allowing those attitudes to become even more entrenched.

After a time of swimming (or, rather, sinking) in these distorted thoughts and festering wounds, feelings begin to take on a life all their own. The pastor asks God to deliver him or her from their negative thoughts, all the while convinced that these thoughts and feelings are valid. The pastoral petition is half-hearted, needing to be free from them, yet still feeling justified in them. As they pray they also think and as they think they also remember and as they remember those fantastic scenarios play out in their head once again. They hate the bitterness that is taking root...but they also like it because the feelings awaken those carnal dimensions of the sin nature that they thought were dead. Apparently not. Somewhere along these lines Satan begins to awaken (or reawaken) the pastor's sensual senses. Just as our senses convince us that we are justified in our resentments, so too they begin to justify other sins of the flesh. Those doors of temptation are beginning to open and the pastor is starting to investigate. For Eve it was seeing how fresh and delicious that piece of fruit looked on the tree. In my case, it was that mysterious e-mail that opened into a naked picture. I was amazed at how fast I gave into my sin nature, how quickly my addiction was able to grab hold of my throat. What I didn't perceive at the time was how much time and effort the devil had put into setting the stage.

"You ran well. Who hindered you from obeying the truth? This persecution does not come from him who calls you. A little leaven leavens the whole lump" (Galatians 5: 7-9) – or, a few sinful thoughts, allowed to rise, will corrupt the whole spirit of a person.

Thus, we defile ourselves.

Self-Obsession:

"As we make the conscious spiritual choices setting into motion the addictive process, we become increasingly more selfish and self-centered. A rebellious attitude sets in."[126] In order to keep from looking at their faults the man or woman of God begins to focus in on the faults of others. In fact, the most blatant sinful behaviors that they see in others are usually the ones taking root in themselves; these behaviors seen in others are simply mirrors to their own soul and become the focus of their scorn. Like the man with the log in his eye who is focused on the splinter in his brother's eye, both objects are made from the same substance, yet it is the speck of the other rather than the plank in themselves that they see. Many times it is the minister who vehemently condemns sexual sin that is found out to be struggling with it, as if their angry words stem from a heart of self-loathing. The clergyperson seeks to hide his or her sin by preaching against it. The pastor who strongly denounces sexual sin has experienced first-hand, or, at least seen, the devastation such sin causes.

That "plank" becomes a type of protective blinders. It makes it almost impossible to see others or themselves for whom they really are, and what they can see they refuse to see. Defensive walls are built, closing them off emotionally from others. They become unteachable, hardening their heart to

God and others, becoming gods unto themselves. "The problem is that we are the problem. The good things on earth — food, drink, sex, recognition, power, wealth — are not spoiled; we are."[127] They play the part of the "humble servant," but, in truth, they are now the center of their own universe, and they are actually becoming addicted to themselves. "No wonder so many of us found masturbation to be infinitely more than childhood experimentation. It got us high on ourselves, short-circuiting any meaningful connection with others and God. In our great and lofty pursuit of 'finding' our lives we shut out the possibility of ever receiving life."[128] As one person wrote, "It got awful lonely sitting on that throne of God."[129]

"For men will be lovers of themselves...unholy, unloving, unforgiving, slanderers, without self-control...traitors, headstrong, haughty, *lovers of pleasure rather than lovers of God*, having a form of godliness but denying it's power (this power of self that they revel in now, that they will later find themselves enslaved to). From such people turn away! For of this sort are those who creep into households and make captives of gullible women (using the opposite sex to satisfy their own insatiable appetite) loaded down with sins, led away by various lusts" (2 Timothy 2:2-6a, italicized mine).

Thus, we make ourselves god.

Blind and Delusional:

From the moment the person begins making excuses for their attitudes and covering up their sinful obsessions, they begin to lose sight of the truth about others and themselves. In A.A. they call this *pride-blindness.* For example, even though they have been unable to stop the sexual compulsions, they are hesitant to admit that they are addicted; they delude themselves into believing they are still in control. They lie to themselves, rationalizing their behavior, but aware that there are too many holes in their story. In order to cope spiritually, they begin compartmentalizing their behaviors, separating different dimensions of their life: "This area is family, over here is my spiritual life and ministry, back in the corner is that secret place that is just for me." Some ministers even begin to keep a mental score between the good things they do and the bad. One minister, in particular, while driving home from a hospital visit reasoned to himself: "I have visited my sick parishioner and even prayed with her roommate. It's my time now and I think I've earned this," as he pulled off at the local massage parlor.

94

"The way of the fool is right in his own eyes...deceit is in the heart of those who do evil" (Proverbs 15:1a; 20a).

Thus, we delude ourselves.

Separation:

I don't think anyone is free. One creates one's own prison.

Graham Sutherland

Just as the opposite of love is apathy so too the opposite of the human will is being emotionally uninvolved or detached. Love and will describe a person reaching out to connect to God, to significant others, to life itself. It is a search for intimacy. The opposite would be to pull back, retreat within oneself, to keep intimacy shallow and at arm's length.[130] The minister, at this point, has begun to isolate themselves from others, including emotionally isolating from loved ones, and at the same time they are separating themselves from God. It may not appear so to them but it becomes quite apparent to those around them. The minister becomes the model of what Timothy writes, having "a *form* of godliness," but one that's hollow. The longer the pastor lives this double life, the more coats of varnish he or she puts on the façade and the more of their true selves they give away until soon there is nothing left, a hollow shell. Theirs has become a life of hypocrisy, playing the part of light and truth, being swallowed up by the dark shadows of falsehood.

The process of separation is taking the person of God to a place of even more boding evil, as they begin to separate from God and *themselves*. There is an inward duplicity, where they refuse to let go of resentments and all the sinful fruits they have bore within them, yet, the light of Christ is still there, however faint; no longer able to dispel the darkness, it simply struggles to stay lighted. "For he who doubts is like a wave of the sea driven and tossed by the wind. For let not

that man suppose that he will receive anything from the Lord; he is a double-minded man, unstable in all his ways" (James 1:7b-8). At this place on the path we begin picking up patterns of mental, emotional and even spiritual schizophrenia. Genuine mental health issues arise in the person, actual demonic oppression is at work. The damaged disciple is left isolated, alienated and depressed, with nothing to fill his or her scattered thoughts but excuses of why they are justified in what they do and anguish over where they are. With each lie, with each sinful act they are drawing farther away from their true selves and the light of Christ diminishes more and more, until finally the darkness descends and the flame is snuffed out. If not already gone, they are dangerously close to losing their salvation – and they know it.

Thus, we lose ourselves.

The Negative Connection:

The Christian cannot survive disconnected from God. St. Augustine wrote: "Our hearts are restless until they find their rest in Thee." The addict has created within themselves an emotional vacuum. They try to fill that gaping hole with themselves, but they are too small to fill a God-size crater. There is another chasm created when the saint pursues self – the basic need to connect with another human being. Without these two connections our existence is intolerable. "Without this essential core of our being plugged in somewhere, life is unbearable. We can't just leave the plug of our soul dangling."[131]

They are desperate to connect with someone, but they have cut off their emotional ties long ago. To reconnect would take investing large measures of self into relationships – not exactly something the self-centered addict is accustomed to giving. Ironically, the demand to give oneself for the sake of God and others - the key element that sent them spiraling out of control, is now the key element of saving them from themselves. Self-absorbed, one's entire way of thinking about sex has been distorted: satisfaction is now being seen exclusively in the physical dimensions of a relationship – the *sexual* dimensions of a relationship. Sex void of its legitimate spiritual context; the addiction — sex addiction or love/relationship addiction, become the source from which they feed their spiritual hunger; pornography, lust and self become the addict's unhealthy trinity, the source of their lives. But the negative connection doesn't satisfy. Hunger intensifies and so does the need to seek more sex, harder pornography, riskier exploits. Lust becomes the negative force connecting us with the worst in us and others, connecting us with what someone has called our "negative gods" — perhaps reconnecting us with Satan himself.

"Professing themselves wise, they became fools, and changed the glory of the incorruptible God into an image like corruptible man...*Therefore God also gave them up to uncleanness, in the lusts of their hearts, to dishonor their bodies among themselves"* (Romans 1:22a; 24, italicized, mine).

Thus, we pervert ourselves.

Spiritual Death:

Radio Personality, Paul Harvey tells a disturbing story of how an Eskimo goes about the task of killing a wolf. Early in the morning the Eskimo dips the blade of his knife into a bowl of animal blood, being sure to coat the entire blade and then he allows it to freeze. After awhile he applies a second coat, then another and another, until the blade is indistinguishable, completely covered over by the frozen blood.

Next, the hunter cuts a hole in the ice. He sticks the handle of the knife in the ice, blade side pointing up, and then leaves it there overnight. Sometime throughout the night the wolf follows the scent to the knife and there begins to lick the frozen blood. Very soon the wolf develops a taste for the blood and begins to focus all his attention on that blood, licking faster and more furiously, until the blade is completely exposed. At this point the wolf's craving for the blood reaches a feverish pitch; he is unaware of the lacerations the sharp knife is making in his mouth and tongue, unaware that the blood he is now lapping up is his own. "His insatiable thirst is now being satisfied by his own warm blood. Hs carnivorous appetite just craves more — until the dawn finds him dead in the snow!"[132]

In a very similar fashion, the minister consumed by their own lusts and resentments soon find themselves being consumed instead. The person of God has entertained thoughts and attitudes contrary to God's nature and design and embraced them as their own. They set up house and began to live comfortably in this negative state of being, ignoring that inner voice, allowing those toxic thoughts and behaviors to poison who they are. Thoughts turned inward and anger outward; walls were built, blocking the life-breath of God and others, and soon they find that they are being blocked off from their very selves. They become blinded and delusional, lying to others and to themselves, rationalizing this sin that is swallowing them whole. The void created by their self-obsession becomes so painfully real that they sink deeper into their sinful lifestyle and with that they sink deeper into despair.

Can there be any doubt that this person has been enveloped into the darkness? "The insanity of our delusion damns us to a condition where truth about ourselves cannot penetrate. We must finally ask, then, doesn't all of this add up to spiritual death?" Grievously, it does. "There is a sin that leads to death" (1John 5:16b). (You will have to decide for yourself whether it includes eternal death). Diseased attitudes became the irresistible driving force, perpetuating them from all that is good and right, propelling them downward, toward their final demise. Can there be any doubt that this is that "way that seems right to a man, but in the end leads to death?" (Proverbs 16:25). Our compass has been damaged and the rudder has misguidedly taken us to a place where we do not wish to be. Here is a clearer understanding of Hell as the "final death." The place from the hell experienced in the life of an addict is not a far step from the Hell they may experience in the next. "The stakes are higher than we figured. Had we ever glimpsed the truth for a moment, the torment would have been greater than we could bear. Thus the illness *must* perpetuate itself, both within and without. To stop means the very threat of death. But unless we do stop and face the truth about ourselves, we remain in death."[133] The individual is in such dire straights, such deep spiritual and emotional anguish that the only relief they can find from their torment is to act out again…Their distorted mind tells them that it's the only thing they have left.

Thus, we destroy ourselves.

Depending on your religious conviction you must decide whether this hell I speak about is our own personal hell in which we find ourselves here on earth or whether we have actually forfeited our inheritance as God's children and are destined for eternity in Hell (*hades*). I can't make that distinction for you. All I can say is that I personally felt as if I was being swallowed whole and completely cut off from God. I fully believe that where sin abounds, grace does much more abound and that no one can snatch us from God's hand, but I also believe that we may choose to leave of *our own volition* and no matter have devastatingly hard sexual addiction is, it is a sin of *choice*.

Making Our Own Hell

"These are wells without water, clouds carried by a tempest, for whom is reserved the blackness of darkness forever…they allure through the lusts of the flesh, through lewdness, the ones who have actually escaped from those who live in error. While they promise them liberty, they themselves are slaves of corruption; for by whom a person is overcome, by him also he is brought into bondage. For if, after they have escaped the pollutions of the world through the knowledge of the Lord and Savior Jesus Christ, they are again entangled in them and overcome, the latter end is worse for them than the beginning. For it would have been better for them not to have known the way of righteousness, than having known it, to turn from the holy commandment delivered to them."

2 Peter 2:17-21

Hell is not a place of intolerable heat and little demons with pitch forks. Hell is this progression into the inner torment we have been living in already, yet now with a full awareness of where this collision course takes us and all we have forfeited. The insufferable heat of Hell is seeing each of those wrong choices we made; we supply our own demons as we recognize the missed opportunities of grace afforded us by God through those around us. "Brothers, if someone is caught (overtaken) in a sin, you who are spiritual should restore him gently" (Galatians 6:1a). When we consider the issue of restoration for ministry, we must first recognize that we are seeking to restore men and women to the Kingdom. Since, as we see, sexual addiction is a spiritual process, it follows that the program of recovery that will be most effective must also be essentially spiritual.

The Dark Side of the Pastor:

Inside of each human being is the potential for greater good and baser bad. Both nature and nurture influence our direction toward vice or virtue; there is within each of us a measure of light and shadows of darkness. No one enters a sin soaked world unblemished. Throughout childhood and into adulthood we seek to cope with these conflicting urges. We repress and deny or confess and cast away; many grieve over those dark tendencies, some embrace and indulge in them. Ignore the feelings, explain them away, blame others for making those feelings come. The truth is there is in each of us a measure of light and shadows of darkness. The irony is seen in the fact many of the dark shadows are simply distorted images of light. Many of the impulses to do wrong stem from a misinformed call to do right. The key to maintaining control is to recognize those dark dimensions, surrender them to God and so find the correct behavior and response. In this section we will explore some of the more common distorted dark areas of the clergyperson and offer suggested ways to correctly view and implement these thoughts and behaviors.

The anxious/depressed pastor:

"Pain is the price we pay for being alive"

Rabbi Kushner,

When Bad Things Happen to Good People

A very common personality disorder in ministers is deep-seeded feelings of intense anxiety, followed by extreme depression. There are literally thousands of ministers today that are unsure of themselves and find pastoral ministry a scary place to be. A 1992 study conducted by the Alban Institute discovered that more than 20% of the nation's 30,000 clergy suffer from long-term emotional stress. "One recent year when the Southern Baptist Convention paid out $64 million in medical claims benefits for pastors, stress-related illnesses were second in dollar amount only to maternity benefits."[134] Anxiety involves feelings of both fear and inability; persons feel exposed and vulnerable. Clergy who are depressed often focus on their short-comings, exaggerate them, and minimize any positive qualities they may have; the anxious pastor typically overestimates the situation and underestimates their ability to control it. I remember one pastoral couple who interviewed with a church that had a reputation for chewing up and spitting out clergy. Following the stress-filled meeting the pastor's spouse was so overwhelmed that she literally became physically sick, vomiting uncontrollably for days.

Intense anxiety and depression is crippling. It causes deficits in a pastor's thinking and ability to reason. These distorted thoughts monopolize their concentration, causing chronic feelings of distress. The more anxious the pastor feels, the more they obsess over the situation and the worse the obsession becomes. The typical response to anxiety and depression is escape. For the minister this may mean dropping a stressful ministry project, leaving the church where they serve, or leaving ministry altogether. For others it may mean mental or emotional escape. This type of escape generally comes in two forms: either they will emotionally resign from pastoral leadership, in much the same way an older employee, nearing retirement may simply go through the motions, or they will involve themselves with some mood-altering, addictive behavior. The greatest problem with escapism is that it works. The anxious or depressed person retreats from the source of their consternation only to find the intense feelings dissipate, thus reinforcing their behavior of choice and setting indelible patterns into place; when anxious situations reoccur the pastor returns to his or her escape of choice.

Generally, the profession of the clergy will limit the types of addictive behaviors they may engage in; more times than not clergypersons will choose an addictive behavior that is generally accepted in the church. For example, in Alcoholics Anonymous it is not uncommon to find a number of Catholic or Episcopal priests in alcohol recovery, the reason being that alcohol consumption is an acceptable practice in the Catholic and Episcopal Church. By the same token, in the more Fundamental and Evangelical denominations, excessive eating is not only acceptable but many times encouraged. The old saying being, "Where two or more are gathered in My name, there will be a covered dish." The same can be said of the pastor who compulsively overworks himself or herself. It is common practice for clergy to spend ten to twelve hours a day, six or even seven days a week at the church. But often these obsessive behaviors will only fuel the anxiety: overeating leads to obesity, which leads to more stress and depression. This is true also with overworking, which exacerbates frustrations and leaves the individual too tired to fight those negative emotions. When the more acceptable obsessive practices fail to alleviate the pressure, Satan will weaken the pastor's resolve and he or she will begin to be drawn in other directions. Pornography, at this point, becomes the favored drug of choice because it provides the minister with a high level of secrecy, especially Internet pornography.

Now that we have identified the disorder, there are steps that we can take to correct our thinking and quiet the intensity of anxiety and depression:

1. Spiritual:

The first and greatest step is to identify and confess these feelings to God and another person. "I will lead the blind by ways they have not known, along unfamiliar paths I will guide them; I will turn the darkness into light before them and make the rough places smooth" (Isaiah 42:16). Neither medicine nor therapy makes the kind of astonishing promises as God does. He will lead us to see the fallacies in our blurred thinking. As his light pierces the darkness of our thinking the rough circumstances we now dread will become smooth paths for us. Our need for another is found in the definition of the word *confess*. Confession in the Greek means to "say again." There is power in hearing hope and encouragement resounds in our ears; many times the power of our distortions is broken when brought out into the light of reason and reassurance.

2. Physical/Emotional:

Anxiety and depression wreak havoc on our minds and bodies. Sometimes, in order to be able to deal with our deep issues, it is necessary to first care for the physiological and emotional components of anxiety and depression. Simple solutions as exercise or relaxation techniques can release endorphins into the bloodstream, allowing the body to better cope. Prescription medications, such as antidepressants or anti-anxiety meds may be needed to help regulate the chemicals in the brain related to stress and depression.

Sometimes just getting away from the problem for awhile can take the wind out of its sails. A night's retreat for reflection or a weekend away with the family can help a pastor regain perspective. A number of denominations have campgrounds available for the burned-out pastor and there are a number of Christian retreat areas available on-line at either no cost or a nominal fee. Ask a church member to borrow their cabin or just splurge for a hotel room with a pool. Soak in the hot tub with your spouse and play in the pool with the kids. For the past couple of years Christi and I would break up the winter months by taking the boys on an overnight trip to Great Wolf Lodge in Sandusky, OH. Great Wolf Lodge is a beautiful hotel with an indoor water park, complete with water slides and lazy river. I'm not sure who looks forward to it more, my boys or me. One thing is for sure, there's nothing better for making large problems small than spending a couple days making a memory with your family. A note of advice though, let the focus of the weekend be on the family and not on you or the church — *it has to be about them* — leave the laptop and cell phone at home!

3. Cognitive:

A simple but particularly effective way to control anxiety and depression is to modify distorted thinking. This is hard work because many of our blurred thought patterns have been with us since childhood. Some mental distortions may include unrealistic expectations, such as our planning to grow the church twenty percent each year. Others would include automatic thoughts, like, "I don't deserve love" or "I fail at everything." I know for myself, it wasn't enough to be the best pastor I could be; I had to be better than all my predecessors in that church. It wasn't enough to set goals, I had to break records. See Paul's words again in light of our understanding of cognitive thinking: "We demolish arguments and every pretension that sets itself up against the knowledge of God (or, every distorted thought), and we take captive every thought to make it obedient to Christ" (2 Corinthians 10:5). Through the help of a trained Christian therapist, ministers can modify these all-or-nothing thought patterns, creating a profound effect on one's anxiety and depression. As one person described this type of therapy, "We are changing our stinking-thinking so we can experience that healing-feeling." The following exercise can help you identify the automatic thoughts that you have, recognize the distortions in those thoughts, and prompt you to find a more rational way to view the situation:

THE DAILY MOOD LOG[135]

STEP ONE: DESCRIBE THE UPSETTING EVENT

STEP TWO: RECORD YOUR NEGATIVE FEELING — and rate each one from 0 (the least) to 100 (the most). Use words like sad, anxious, angry, guilty, lonely, hopeless, frustrated, etc.
Emotion Rating Emotion Rating Emotion Rating

1._____ 3._____ 5._____

2._____ 4._____ 6._____

STEP THREE: THE TRIPLE-COLUMN TECHNQUE —

Automatic Thoughts Distortions Rational Responses

Write down your negative thoughts, identify the distortions, and substitute more realistic thoughts. Estimate your belief in each automatic thought and estimate your belief in each one (0-100).

1.

2.

3.

"Stand fast therefore in the liberty by which Christ has made us free, and do not be entangled again with a yoke of bondage."
Galatians 5:1

Common Disorders in Clergy

It's hard to believe that in this day and age, there are still Christians who deny the validity of Christian counseling services. As we discussed earlier, in chapter three, there are a number of common personality disorders found in ministers. A clearer understanding of ourselves as individuals can go a long way in helping us understand who we are as Christians and clergy, in relation to church ministry. Listed are some of the more common personality disorders found among the ordained clergy:

The Obsessive-Compulsive Pastor:

Simply put, people with obsessive-compulsive disorder (OCD) are persons who have obsessions and/or compulsions. Obsessions are recurring negative or upsetting thoughts, mental pictures, or impulses. For the pastor, these can best be seen after a heated confrontation with a congregant, where the words and events replay again and again in the pastor's mind. Compulsions are actions that someone feels they have to do to keep from feeling anxious or to prevent something bad from happening. Examples of this may include such things as tapping one's fingers on the table or the ritual of washing one's hands several times a day. It can also be seen as an irrational need to maintain order and structure in every dimension of one's life. Again, an example of compulsive behavior for the pastor would be one who has their hands in many, if not all, areas of church ministry, unable to relinquish control to anyone else. Most people with OCD suffer from both obsessions and compulsions.

The OCD pastor is consumed with perfectionism in both personal and professional life. Further, the obsessive-compulsive pastor tends to be very status conscious. Unable to find security within themselves, they are persistent in their quest to receive reassurance and approval from others, such as church members, colleagues and denominational leaders; consequently, they feel anxious when they are unsure of other's perception of their performance and standing.[136] Their year is focused on attendance numbers, church statistics and accomplishing something grand at the church. The church is viewed by the pastor as an extension of himself or herself; successful ministry equals validity for their existence. While the obsessive-compulsive clergyperson is outwardly seen as a strong, highly moral leader, in most cases they are an emotional powder keg of repressed anger and resentment. While the undue pressure to perform is, in most cases, self-imposed, the church leader will likely deflect those feelings onto the church people as tyrannical requirements.

Again, as with the anxious, pastor, the compulsive tendencies of a leader are not in and of itself negative if viewed properly. A desire for excellence is a noble *and biblical* calling. Such aspirations, though, lose their luster when they are allowed to go unchecked; excellence gets lost in the shadows of fixated, irrational thinking. Over four million people in the United States suffer from OCD; one person in forty will have it at some point during their life. When anxieties reach beyond what the pastor feels he or she is able to bear OCD can become debilitating.

There is no exact cause for OCD. Genes play a role; learning and life stresses also contribute to the disorder. Perhaps past childhood trauma or other family dysfunctions caused these innate needs inside the leader. 90% of the thoughts of the obsessive-compulsive are common in all people, yet for them these thoughts are more distressing and they cannot let them go. "When they find they are unable to control these upsetting thoughts they look for other ways to relieve their anxiety…Soon they must do the action again and again in order to feel better. Before long, the action becomes a compulsion."[137] The obsessive-compulsive searches out some compulsive behavior in order to feel a sense of emotional control. These may include prayer or reciting Scripture — for others the fuse to the emotional "powder keg" of resentment is already lighted and they rebelliously grab for control through negative, destructive behaviors, such as viewing pornography. The gun powder soon explodes and all that's left to do is assess the damages.

Again, the best treatment for overcoming these obsessive-compulsive thoughts and behaviors is spiritual, physiological, and pharmacological. Admitting our shortcomings to God and another human being is always the right first step in overcoming any disability. "God opposes the proud but gives grace to the humble...Come near to God and he will come near to you...Humble yourselves before the Lord, and he will lift you up" (James 4:6b, 8a,10). Sometimes, when you have a problem with a defective product, the best thing to do is call the Manufacturer.

Further, cognitive therapy has proven essential in helping to correct inaccurate thinking. Studies have shown that cognitive-behavioral therapy is about 80% effective in relieving OCD, equipping the person with the tools necessary to reevaluate situations and think correctly about them, helping the person regain control of their life. Medications have also proven about 50-60% effective in relieving the symptoms by increasing the level of serotonin in the brain. It stands to reason then that medication taken in conjunction with the therapy allows the individual to relax and focus on the sessions.

The Narcissistic Pastor:

"Ministry attracts persons who crave affirmation through the attention of an audience and/or have a desire for power. As a result, a percentage of persons with severe character and personality disorders are finding themselves among the ordained."[138]

The ancient Roman writer, Ovid, had written a play titled: *Metamorphoses*, a story of a mythological young boy named Narcissus. Narcissus was the son of the river-god and a nymph. Because of this Narcissus is pictured as unstable in his identity, somewhere between fluid and fantasy. Although, outwardly, he is described as having a strong face like marble and his neck is likened to polished ivory, inside he is weak and unsure. Narcissus was extremely handsome; many found themselves physically attracted to him. But something caused Narcissus to scorn all romantic advances. One of those disparaged lovers, vexed, placed a curse on the head of Narcissus: "May he fall in love and not have what he loves." When Narcissus was sixteen he was walking near the fabled river Styx when he approached upon a calm pool of water. Kneeling down to take a drink, Narcissus catches a glimpse of his likeness and is instantly transfixed on his own beauty. Overcome by the reflection, Narcissus is unable to bring himself to turn away. Ovid shifts the imagery of the story from water to elements of fire in which Narcissus "takes on a delicate glow" and is suddenly transformed into a flower — the Narcissus, which today continues to grow on the river banks, reflecting their own rare beauty at the water's edge.[139]

Mental health professionals call it "narcissistic personality disorder" and a prime profession for finding such individuals is in pastoral ministry. The typical narcissistic minister needs the admiration of a congregation to enhance their own image and shore up their feelings of personal inadequacy and self-hatred. He or she will promote magnificent church/ministry projects and seek to caste a grand vision for the work of their church, yet underneath these ambitious efforts and grandiose visions are feelings of inferiority; their efforts are a signal of an over dependence on external admiration and acclaim. Narcissistic clergy frequently have chronic feelings of envy and restless ambition; they are unable to sit back and enjoy the fruits of their work because outward recognition never fully satisfies feelings of personal inadequacy. "Though narcissism seems to be diametrically opposes to the concept of spiritual, servant leadership, it is all too common in the church and among spiritual leadership."[140]

For years theologians have seen the story of Narcissus as one of vanity. Narcissistic behavior is seen as self-absorption and self-obsession — ego run amuck. If this is the true picture of Ovid's main character then what does that say of the narcissistic pastors in God's play? Are pastors vain, self-aggrandizing individuals, focused on their own pursuits at the expense of caring for the masses and bringing glory to Christ? If this is the true narcissist, the term "minister" ("servant") has become an oxymoron. He or she is no better than the celebrities who are paid to attend some charity fund raiser, pose for the camera and walk away pleased with themselves. But before we abandon all hope and respect for our clergy leaders, let's examine the character of Narcissus closer.

Narcissus Reexamined:

Metamorphoses is not the story of ego loving ego; this is a story of ego finding and loving psyche; narcissism is a shadow quality of the soul's deep need to be loved. "Narcissism is a condition in which a person does *not* love himself. This failure in love comes through as its opposite because the person tries so hard for self-acceptance."[141] The character, Narcissus, is the product of fluidity (the river-god), ever-changing and uncertain, and fantasy (the nymph), unable to grasp reality. Yet, his head is compared to the solid marble — the narcissist appears strong-headed; his neck is like ivory — he is stiff-necked, focused and undeterred. The narcissistic leader, then, is one who appears strong-willed, a solid, perhaps overbearing leader. But inside the person is unsure of themselves, driven by extravagant ideas in order to validate who they are. For example, the narcissistic minister will be the one who promotes grand visions for the church: far-reaching ministries and exhausting building plans, and such. He or she is thinking to themselves, "If I can pull this off I will have succeeded beyond what my predecessors have done and have proven to myself and everyone else that I am a great godly man/woman." Many churches have felt the strain of over-ambitious projects in an attempt to make the pastor feel good about themselves. "Because ministry provides the ready justification that grandiose visions and risky ventures are necessary to accomplish God's kingdom work, the church and Christian congregations provide fertile soil for budding narcissists."[142] Narcissistic leaders overestimate their own achievements to others while jealously refusing to acknowledge the same qualities in another, their distorted thinking concluding that to promote another somehow diminishes them.

Again, in the story, Narcissus is seen as handsome beyond compare but uninterested in his many suitors. Some theologians have concluded that Narcissus' looks caused him to be vain. In truth, I'm not at all convinced that Narcissus ever saw his own reflection, nor did he completely believe what others had told him concerning his appearance. It isn't until he sees his reflection in the river Styx that he fully sees himself and then is unable to turn away. Had he known of his beauty the story would have been quite shorter, opening and closing on the same page with Narcissus continually looking at himself. Again, an irony of the narcissistic leader is that these people usually *seem to* have an over inflated ego, seeing themselves as special with a sense of entitlement. Narcissistic leaders have grand fantasies (a very nymph-ish quality) of accomplishing tremendous success in life, again, in order to validate who they are. Such individuals are usually charming and proficient manipulators, taking advantage of others to indulge their own desires.

The narcissistic clergyperson lives for the praise of their congregants and peers, but deep inside they are unable to process this praise and allow it to feed their soul. The pastor, thus, is reduced to the equivalent of a lap dog, always hungry for the approval of others. For this reason ministers continually work long hours at church and rarely will ask for a raise, even when the family is desperate. The church's perception of the pastor is more important than the reality of circumstances. This is also why confrontation and church conflict is so devastating to the pastor; even constructive criticism given gently is often perceived as punishment, reinforcing their own notions that they are not good enough. Instead they wander from project to project, praise to praise, hoping the next kind word will be the one to nourish their love-starved soul. Instead, it lands like a drop of water on a parched tongue, whetting it just enough to make them cry out for more.

The final picture from Ovid's story that I want to look at is the closing scene: Narcissus passes through the forest area and stops beside a quiet pool of water. Dehydrated from his journey, he bends down to drink from the fresh water and catches a glimpse of himself there. He is transfixed by the image and soon transformed. Narcissus glows with the fire of self-discovery and is transformed into a beautiful flower, planted by the riverbed. Confused and cursed to wander the earth looking for a true perception of himself, Narcissus comes to a clearing in the forest and there among the trees is a quiet pocket of the ever-flowing river; a place of rest from the continual motion inside this son of the river. Thirsty from his never-ending journey, Narcissus prostrates himself before the quiet reflection pool and catches a clear picture of who he is — not just the watery image of a man, but the deeper, truer self. Narcissus was at a point of introspection and there he discovered who he really was. The cold embers of an extinguished soul are set ablaze as he faces truth for the very first time - a sort-of "baptism by fire!" Instantly he is absorbed into the solid ground and up springs the flower.

In like manner the narcissistic minister goes about through the ceaseless motion of ministry, hoping that it will lead to wholeness. After years of wandering he or she comes upon a forest glade. The towering trees cast long shadows; the area is dark and foreboding. But they dare venture in and there, in the clearing, find a quiet oasis that beckons, come. In desperate need of respite, the minister collapses beside the water's edge and begins to lap up the sea. There, quite by surprise, our forlorn friend looks deep within and discovers his/her own soul. An intense examination of the self ensues, burning up all the dross and miraculously they are transformed into their true self, beauty that far surpasses their former self, firmly established in the solid earth, connected to it's past (the water), and facing the sunshine of God's light.

As with the previous disorders, there is a positive dimension of narcissism. For one thing the church needs grand visions and ambitious efforts. God himself gives us his Spirit in order to accomplish great things for him: "I will pour out my Spirit on all people. Your sons and daughters will prophesy, your old men will dream dreams, your young men will see visions" (Joel 2:28). The dark shadows fall when these are attempted in order to make a fragmented leader feel whole. Narcissism is a deep-seeded thirst that prompts the man or woman of God to pilgrimage. Notice what it took for Narcissus to find emotional and spiritual healing: 1) He had to come away to a quiet secluded place (a place more introverted than most narcissistic people like to spend their time); 2) He was willing to fearlessly search and eventually embrace his past (Narcissus was conceived from the river); 3) He had to devote the time to squarely examine himself; 4) He had to endure the pain that God's fire brings before transformation. "Care of the soul requires us to see the myth in the symptom, to know that there is a flower waiting to break through the hard surface of narcissism."[143] Narcissism is neither evil nor righteous — it is a path of the personality that can take us to further paths of evil or righteousness. To walk through these steps into such a life transformation requires the honest work of the pastor, their God and a trained Christian therapist — and time.

The following self-test for Christian leaders is from Gary McIntosh's and Samuel Rima's book, *Overcoming the Dark Side of Leadership: The Paradox of Personal Dysfunction*. If answered honestly, it can be a wonderful tool of self-discovery that can lead to a pastor's own journey of the soul:

5 = strongly agree
4 = agree
3 = uncertain
2 = disagree
1 = strongly disagree

1. Fellow leaders in my church or organization frequently question whether my proposed goals and projects are feasible and realistic.
1 2 3 4 5

2. I am obsessed with knowing how others feel about my sermons, lessons, and performance.
1 2 3 4 5

3. I find it difficult to receive criticism of any kind, reacting with anger, anxiety, or even depression when it does come.
1 2 3 4 5

4. At times I find myself thinking: *I'll show them; they could never make it without me*, when I experience conflict situations or opposition to my proposed plans.
1 2 3 4 5

5. In spite of achieving what others would consider significant success, I still find myself dissatisfied and driven to achieve greater things in an effort to feel good about myself.
1 2 3 4 5

6. I am willing to bend the rules and press the envelope of acceptable behavior to accomplish my goals.
1 2 3 4 5

7. I find myself feeling jealous of the success and achievements of associates, other churches, or organizations in my area.
1 2 3 4 5

8. I am often unaware of or unconcerned about the financial pressures my goals and projects place on those I lead or the church or organization I serve.
1 2 3 4 5

9. Success or failure in a project has a direct bearing on my self-image and sense of worth.
1 2 3 4 5

10. I am highly conscious of how my colleagues and those whom I am accountable regard my accomplishments.
1 2 3 4 5

11. I need to be recognized or "on top" when meeting with a group of fellow pastors, denominational officials, or associates.
1 2 3 4 5

12. I see myself as a nationally known figure at some time in the future or I have plans to attain such a position.
1 2 3 4 5

Add up the circled numbers and place the total here: _____

If your total comes to less than 20, you probably are not narcissistic. If your total is between 21 and 40, you probably have *some* narcissistic tendencies. If your total is 41 or more, you probably are a narcissistic pastor.[144]

Codependent Clergy:

"It is not easy to find happiness in ourselves, and it is not possible to find it elsewhere."
Agnes Repplier,
"The Treasure Chest"

It's no longer simply a matter of a person finding a sense of worth through outside approval, but an innate need to be needed by others. Like cancerous cells that cling to one another and grow, the codependent dysfunction attaches itself to another's need or dysfunction and begins to feed off of it. Just as some men and women enter the field of psychology out of some pathological need to have others dependent upon them, so too some men and women enter the pastorate with a savior-complex, seeking to save the lost in a desperate attempt to find themselves, to heal their own damaged soul.

Codependency is a conscious or unconscious fear of losing the approval and presence of others. Much of the codependent personality can be traced back to unsuccessful enmeshment in early childhood.[145] As we discussed earlier, in chapter three, misplaced boundaries in the family can be emotionally damaging to children and can (and most likely will) follow them into adulthood. One such boundary breakdown would include misplaced roles in the home. Because of the absence of one of the parents, whether physical or emotional, oft times the remaining parent struggles with bouts of loneliness and will turn to the child (usually the eldest) for the emotional support needed. The child becomes, in all practical purposes, a surrogate parent to their siblings and a surrogate spouse to the parent. As the child grows their role is crafted and reinforced. Ironically, the child who is forced to act like an adult often develops into an adult with the emotional needs and behaviors of a child.

Codependency can also be a learned behavior while growing up. If a person in the family, particularly a parent, has an addiction, the child observes the behavior of the family codependent (often the other spouse). They are taught through word and example how to clean up the messes of the addicted member and cover up their shameful behavior from the rest of the world. The confused child has empathy for the codependent, assisting in similar behavior patterns and adopting that behavior as their own. A key word to describe the codependent is balance. The codependent adapts to the situation in order to counterbalance the unacceptable behavior of the dependent family member. They react to the pain and needs of those around them and they balance the inconsistencies of their family life in order to portray a positive image to the outside world. Everything inside that child is telling them their life is out of control and every nerve is sensing the need to set things straight. Codependent adults become masters in the art of balancing several crisis situations at one time. Like the circus performer who spins several plates simultaneously, eventually the exhausted performer collapses under the strain and the plates come crashing in around them.

Codependents in the Church

"What is a codependent? That's easy. They're some of the most loving, caring people I know."[146]
Mark Laaser

The Christian church is a breeding ground for codependent personalities and the pastor one of its strongest advocates. "It has been my experience that when you learn the methods of codependence, even the most casual glance at most churches will reveal the presence of codependent behavior."[147] Is this not the central call of the Church?: To care for the needs of others above our own? We're even taught to list the priorities of love as: "God, others, and self." Scripture tells us repeatedly to care for others (Philippians 2:4; Mark 12:31; Luke 6:31), and even promotes a healthy form of self-hatred (Luke 14:26). But there is a marked difference between Christian love and codependent behavior. Codependency is not putting other's needs above our own, it is a pathological need to have *and to keep* others dependent upon us — we need to be needed! Codependency takes our best intentions to produce good fruit for Christ and distorts it into something that is dark, disturbing and perhaps even demonic. "Codependency constantly takes the good and uses it for evil ends."[148] Disturbing dependency, packaged as love, but, in truth, an addiction all its own.

113

The Codependent Clergy

"In some way or another we often sell our souls to the raters and grade givers of the world, hoping that by winning their acceptance or by minimizing the possibility of their rejection, we will ease the pain of the initial insult(s) given to our psyches."[149]

The minister is the poster child for codependent personality disorder. The codependent pastor takes on far more than his or her fair share, both physically and emotionally. They hold themselves responsible for the actions and attitudes of others, often blaming themselves for another person's inappropriate behavior. They go to great lengths to keep from disappointing someone, avoiding conflict and confrontation. On the surface, the codependent seems "dependable." They will overextend themselves in order to please those around them, but then they resent the people for making them work so hard. Unable to recognize themselves as too weak to say no, they blame others for taking advantage of "their graciousness."[150]

The following are some of the indicators of a codependent pastor.[151] Codependent pastors tend to:

Think and feel responsible for other people's feelings, thoughts, actions, choices, wants, needs, well-being, and ultimate destiny.

Feel anxiety, pity, and guilt when other people have a problem.

Feel compelled — almost forced — to help that person solve the problem.

Anticipate other people's needs and wonder why others don't do the same for them.

Say yes when they mean no, doing things they don't really want to do, doing more than their share, and doing things other people are capable of doing for themselves.

Not know what they want or need or, if they do, diminish them as unimportant.

Try to please others instead of themselves.

Find it easier to outwardly express anger about injustices done to others, rather than injustices done to them.

Feel depressed because they spend their whole lives giving to other people and nobody gives to them.

Find themselves attracted to needy people/find needy people attracted to them.

Abandon their routine to respond to or do something for somebody else.

Over-commit themselves.

Feel harried and pressured and believe deep inside that other people are somehow responsible for those pressures.

Blame others for the spot that codependents find themselves in.

Feel angry, victimized, under appreciated, and used.

Find other people become impatient or angry with them for all the preceding characteristics.

This list of indicators looks remarkably similar to the perceived job description of most pastors. While codependency is more a response to another's personality disorder, it develops into a disorder in and of itself and begins to take on a life all their own. Dr. William L. Playfair, in his book, *The Useful Lie* describes the codependent as being "too concerned about others. They love others too much. They do not love themselves enough, or even at all."[152] While I would agree with the latter, I am not at all convinced about the former. When Jesus said "love our neighbor as you love yourself," he spoke as much truth in the words he didn't say as those he did. Those who love themselves understand the concept of love and can transfer that same love to those around them. By the same token, those who do not love themselves have false conceptions about love and they transfer that false idea of love to their neighbors. How can an empty vessel fill another empty vessel; how can a malnourished heart nourish another's? The effort of the codependent on behalf of another is not to offer love, but a desperate attempt to receive love.

"Compliant people have fuzzy and indistinct boundaries; they 'melt' into the demands and needs of other people...Compliant people take on too many responsibilities and set too few boundaries, not by choice, but because they are afraid."[153] It's not love; it is fear of never being loved.

A Common Denominator:

While every minister does not have all of these personality issues, it would be safe to say that the majority of ministers have at least one, more likely several of these issues and more inside of them. As we look for the crimson thread that passes through each of these character defects it is abundantly clear that such clergypersons face the deep-seeded pain of disconnectedness. And here is the crux of the situation: The minister embarks on a pilgrimage; they speak of it as "a calling." Perhaps they were called — perhaps it just seemed the natural path to take. Regardless, they are not yet prepared for ministry because they are not yet made whole and free: childhood traumas, latent addictions, emotional emptiness — all these need to be cared for, even before classes in Bible, theology, and homiletics begin. Instead, the novice enters this most sacred rite, fragmented and frightened, hoping to hide their scars but not at all convinced that he or she can.

They enter into a "dyslexia of reality."[154] Desperate to connect to Reality, lust denies the human soul true connection, offering, instead, fantasy, an illusion that will never satisfy. "I did not plan to veer from the path," one pastor laments, "Nothing could have been further from my mind. I loved God with every ounce of my handicapped heart."[155] Henri Nouwen refers to such persons as "wounded healers," broken people seeking to bring healing to others. But how can someone who is broken bring wholeness to someone else? Can someone who is empty fill up another? Is it possible to love God and love your neighbor as yourself (Matthew 22:37-39) when, in fact, you *don't* love yourself? Such people are not "wounded healers;" they are just wounded. The people chatter, "Physician, heal yourself" (Luke 4:23), as if such were possible. Men and women of God have sought that remedy their entire lives. The only answer available to us is to allow God to first heal the men and women called out for ministry so they can then be instruments of healing for the rest. The task is too great for damaged disciples. What would such healing look like?

CHAPTER 5
RECOVERING THE SHEPHERD

"I have strayed like a lost sheep. Seek your servant, for I have not forgotten your commands"
Psalm 119:176

Sometimes it's the shepherd who needs to be restored, and not the sheep.

In C.S. Lewis' *The Great Divorce*, he tells the story of a ghost who desires to enter heaven but he has a small red lizard perched upon his shoulder who prompts the ghost to return to hell where they can pursue their passions; the ghost is torn between his own desire for heaven and the lizard's influence to go back. Suddenly, before them stands the "flaming Spirit" who offers to kill the lizard. The ghost desires relief but wishes something a little less drastic than death for his crimson companion. He has grown accustomed, even attached to the small lizard. The Spirit is insistent that only a quick and complete death could bring relief to the tormented apparition.

An inner struggle ensues until finally the ghost realizes he must be rid of this scarlet reptile, even if by killing the lizard he might be killed as well: "It would be better to be dead than to live with this creature." He submits to God's will and asks for his help. As the Spirit strikes death's blow, "the ghost gave a scream of agony such as I have never heard on the earth. The Burning One closed his crimson grip on the reptile: twisted it, while it bit and writhed, and then flung it, broken backed on the turf." But then a miracle occurred: the slain serpent was transformed into a great stallion. The ghost, finally free of this pestilence, mounted the horse and rode off toward heaven.

For those trapped in past afflictions and sinful addictions this analogy is strikingly clear: we are the ghost, a vapor of our God-imaged spiritual self. We desire to be connected with the Father, but our destructive demons entice us to continue in our hellish life of debauchery. The flaming Spirit is the Holy Spirit who is a consuming fire. He tells us we can be healed of our past and freed of our sin. The Spirit promises to completely destroy it, but, incredibly, we aren't willing to be completely done with those things. After all, they have been with us for so long, and, although they are slowly killing us, they have become sort of a companion and friend; when all else failed us, these things stayed faithful. But the Spirit of God speaks the truth that we already know in our hearts: "Half measures avail us nothing."

Repentance and Reconnection

"Dyslexia of Reality"

In her book, *When Godly People do Ungodly Things*, Beth Moore coined the term, "dyslexia of reality," which simply means we got things turned around. Ingrained in each human being is this deep-seeded need to connect with Reality, or, God. But because of our distorted sin nature and traumatic past issues, we are unable to make this life-giving connection. Instead, we are enticed to connect with the negative spiritual forces which promise life but only lead to death, trading our birthright for a mess of pottage. People who get involved with sexual sin are often starved for love, chasing after the things in their past when the true connection is right there in front of them. Or, as G.K. Chesterson put it, "A man who knocks on the door of a brothel is knocking for God."[156]

If the problem is that pastors have made the wrong connection, the natural process of recovery must involve changing the plugs, if "dyslexia of Reality means we have gotten things backwards, the solution must involve turning things around. In fact, the word *repentance* (Gr. *metanoia*) means to turn things around, a change of purpose,[157] or a change in who we follow after. So if the problem came from being disconnected from God and a misconnection with sin, then the solution to our problem is to disconnect ourselves from sin and to do what we must to reconnect with God. That's not as simple as it sounds. Every Christian who has tried to fight pornography addiction has attempted this, but to no avail. I know in my own case, I would pour out my heart in desperation to God, pleading for forgiveness and begging to be delivered from this curse. But, inevitably, I would be back to feeding my addiction a day or two later. I now see that what I was doing was asking God to deliver me of my pornography addiction *because I wasn't willing to let it go*. I was like that ghost in C.S. Lewis' tale, wanting to connect with God, but unwilling to fully and finally surrender my crimson lizard. Deliverance from sin means to be done with that sin. When pressures begin to mount, we no longer run to our addiction, but run to God. *And even if relief doesn't come, we station ourselves at the cross, willing to die connected to Life rather than live connected to Death.*

Reconnecting with Life

"Lord, Lord, Lord,
Please come to help me;
I turn to you alone
For my refuge."
Agathonice of Pergamos

If addiction is a matter of substituting the Truth for a lie, exchanging the True God for gods of our own making, forfeiting Life as we spiral toward death — then how do we reverse the process? In essence, how do we reconnect with Life? Look with me at the first three steps of

The Twelve Steps of Sexaholics Anonymous:

1. We admitted that we were powerless over lust — that our lives had become unmanageable.
2. Came to believe that a Power greater than ourselves could restore us to sanity.
3. Made a decision to turn our will and our lives over to the care of God as we understood him.[158]

Very simply put, we turned away from lust, plugged into God, and surrendered ourselves to his care. Or, as they say in SA: "I can't — God can — I think I'll let him." The problem is our efforts have been half-hearted at best. We knew we were powerless over lust, the unmanageability of our lives made that starkly clear. Yet, we continued to fight for release in our own strength. We believed in our hearts that God could restore us to sanity and often asked him to do it. But deep down, our own experiences at failure made us doubt that he would. We made the decision countless times to surrender our will and our lives to God, but, in truth, we didn't fully give our mind and will over to the task. The essence of step three is absolute lordship to Christ. It's no longer a matter of surrendering our freedom of choice and asking God to revoke free will. It is submitting to his absolute Lordship, even in the center of our free will. This means that we say no to lust, regardless of whether God removes lust's hold on us or not. It's like a diabetic saying no to sweets while standing in the middle of the candy store.

"Cheap Grace — Costly Grace"[159]

"By the grace God has given me, I laid a foundation as an expert builder, and someone else is building on it. But each one should be careful how he builds. For no one can lay any foundation other than the one already laid, which is Jesus Christ. If any man builds on this foundation using gold, silver, costly stones, wood, hay or straw, his work will be shown for what it is, because the Day will bring it to light. It will be revealed with fire, and the fire will test the quality of each man's work. If what he has built survives, he will receive his reward. If it is burned up, he will suffer loss; he himself will be saved, but only as one escaping through the flames."
1 Co 3:10-15

Paul is speaking in a whole different context here, but there are lessons that can be learned here about lordship as well. It is by God's grace that we are able to be established and by which we build. But we should take serious consideration how we build, first and foremost, being careful that we build our faith upon Christ, but also giving consideration to the substance to which we build with. Are we building our life of faith with costly metals and stones or are we using cheap materials and slapping on a fresh coat of paint? In other words, are we building with, what Dietrich Bonhoeffer called, "cheap grace" or "costly grace?" Look at the way Bonhoeffer described cheap grace:

Cheap grace is the deadly enemy of our Church…Cheap grace means grace sold on the market like cheapjacks' wares…thrown away at cut prices…Grace without price; grace without cost!…In such a Church the world finds a cheap covering for sins; no contrition is required, still less any real desire to be delivered from sin….Cheap grace is the preaching of forgiveness without requiring repentance…absolution without personal confession. Cheap grace is grace without discipleship, grace without the cross, grace without Jesus Christ, living and incarnate.[160]

Yet, now see how he defined costly grace:

Costly grace is the treasure hidden in the field; for the sake of it a man will gladly go and sell all that he has. It is the pearl of great price to buy which the merchant will sell all his goods. It is the kingly rule of Christ, for whose sake a man will pluck out the eye which causes him to stumble, it is the call of Jesus Christ at which the disciple leaves his nets and follows him…It is costly because it cost a man his life, and it is grace because it gives a man the only true life…Costly grace is the sanctuary of God; it has to be protected from the world, and not thrown to the dogs.[161]

Paul says it is fire that will test the quality of our work; it is also fire that will test the strength of a man or woman's faith and character. Some have built well, recognizing the cost as death to self (literal or actual), others have committed themselves to Christ up until the point that life struggles become more than they are *willing* to bear. I have preached costly grace, but I have lived cheap grace. I had determined in my heart that, if the time had ever come, I would stand strong before a hangman's noose, like Bonhoeffer, rather than deny my Christ. Yet, I had never determined to stand up under the strain of my sin's shame and find the help that only comes by bringing my addiction into the light. My thought was if God did not rescue me from myself then I would take this hidden sin to the grave with me. "Recovery's ultimate goal is integration…It's about bringing your spiritual values into your sexual behavior; it's about honesty; it's about accepting who we are, including our past."[162]

In the next chapter we will take a closer look at spiritual restoration, but for now, let's focus in on the specifics of recovery, what it's going to take to trade in our cheap grace in order to purchase a grace more rich and lasting.

Walking in the Light

"This is the verdict: Light has come into the world, but men loved darkness instead of light because their deeds were evil. Everyone who does evil hates the light, and will not come into the light for fear that their evil deeds will be exposed. But whoever lives by the truth comes into the light."

John 3:19-21a

"This is the message we have heard from him and declare to you: God is light; in him there is no darkness at all. If we claim to have fellowship with him yet walk in the darkness, we lie and do not live by the truth. But if we walk in the light, as he is in the light, we have fellowship with one another, and the blood of Jesus, his Son, purifies us from all sin."
John: 1:5-7

"What fellowship can light have with darkness?"
2 Corinthians 6:14c

As we have discussed in the previous chapters, the greatest pull toward pornography addiction is isolation and its strength is drawn from remaining hidden in the shadows. So too, the only way to find true freedom from pornography addiction is to step out of the shadows, into the light, and there in the light we reconnect in fellowship with God the Father and with each other. We want to walk in the light of Christ, yet we cling to the shadows of our past, our sin, and our shame. John says that if we claim to live by the light of God and yet continue walking in the darkness of our sin, we are deceiving ourselves, we are living a lie. Living in undisclosed sin means that we are living in darkness; we are not practicing what we preach. Again, I don't believe we have necessarily (as of yet!) crossed the point of losing our salvation. Remember Paul's words in 1 Corinthians 3:15, "he himself will be saved, but only as one escaping through the flames." In other words, we may make it but it will be by the skin of our teeth! But the question then is what about those we serve? What about the life's work we have dedicated ourselves to? Can we be guardians of Truth and yet perpetuate a lie?

"Therefore confess your sins to each other so that you may be healed."
James 5:16a

The key to our being healed of our painful past and sinful addiction is confession — not only to God who already knows our struggles, but to one another, to members of our community of faith, those we have been deceiving. We need to confess to our brothers and sisters so they may provide us with the strength and help necessary for such a battle as this. "The prayer of a righteous man is powerful and effective" (James 5:16b). If sin continues in strength through dark isolation, its power over a person is broken more and more with each word of confession. If Paul is right that Light has no fellowship with darkness, then it is also true that as we walk in the Light the darkness must flee.

But clear discernment must be made when considering which persons we are to confess our sins to. Remember, Paul says that the prayers of a *righteous* person are powerful and effective. Here is a clear indication that the persons to whom we confess must be men and women who demonstrate true godly faith. Galatians 6:1-2 gives us a clearer understanding of such individuals: "Brothers, if someone is caught in a sin, you who are spiritual should restore him gently. But watch yourself, or you also may be tempted. Carry each other's burdens, and in this way you will fulfill the law of Christ." By this passage we can discern a list of criteria for those to whom we confide: A truly spiritual individual will (1) seek to restore you, rather than add to your ruin. They will (2) deal gently with you, acting in love and mercy. They will (3) be humble and discerning, someone who understands the treacherous path of pornography addiction. Finally, they will (4) help you bear up under the load as you walk through the slow painful path of recovery.

In other words, the people to whom we trust our darkest issues with are to be advocates, people who will come along side of us and help defend us as we battle our demons. The Greek word for advocate is *paraclete*, and refers primarily in Scripture for the work of the Holy Spirit, strengthening, encouraging, defending, holding accountable and keeping our confidence. (Not to be confused with the word, *parakeet*, which is a strange bird that repeats everything said to them!) "Two are better than one, because they have a good return for their work: If one falls down, his friend can help him up. But pity the man who falls and has no one to help him up!... Though one may be overpowered, two can defend themselves. A cord of three strands is not quickly broken" (Ecclesiastes 4:9-10, 12).

We will discuss further in the next chapter who we should let into our confidence as we discuss the process of reconciliation. Let me just emphasize four armies of support that you will need in your camp: (1) your spouse, (2) your district leaders, (3) an experienced Christian counselor, and (4) a sexual addictions twelve-step program. In these four sources you have people with a vested interest in your welfare, resources for support and accountability, wisdom and insight into why we do the things we do, and a group of individuals who understand. I will later emphasize the importance of the first three groups, but if I can make a quick plug for the twelve-step program for a moment, consider the importance of a band of brothers and/or sisters who *experientially* understand what you are going through. In fact, these men and women have either been or are right now where you are. I remember many times, sharing a deeply troublesome part of my past, and looking over to see several wry smiles, as if to say "Been there — done that!" They accept you the way you are, but they care too much to leave you there. They're similar to a platoon of soldiers, fighting side by side, binding your wounds and watching your back.

A Plan of Recovery

Pornography addiction is a calculating downward spiral. Just as there are set patterns into this addiction, there are certain steps a person must take to find recovery. The following twelve steps can be instrumental in helping a person overcome their addiction to pornography:

Twelve Steps to Overcoming Pornography Addiction[163]

1. Stop lying to others and yourself: People trapped in addiction refuse to admit there is a problem, even to themselves. *He who conceals his transgressions will not prosper, but he who confesses and forsakes them will find compassion* (Proverbs 28:13).

2. Accept responsibility for your behavior: Blaming others accomplishes nothing. Our sin is not the result of a neglectful spouse, demanding work or a depraved society. Only when we own our sin can God do something about it. *They have become filled with every kind of wickedness...they who do such things deserve death* (Romans 1:29a-32a).

3. Surrender: You will never overcome this addiction on your own, because, deep down you *want* that addiction. Your body and mind crave it. It is only through surrender to God's will that we can hope to have victory. *Submit yourselves to God. Resist the devil and he will flee from you* (James 4:7).

4. Confess your sin to God and to another person: Sin thrives in the shadows; its power is broken only through the light of disclosure. *Therefore, confess your sins to each other and pray for each other so that you may be healed* (James 5:16).

5. Get rid of your stash: You can't wean yourself from sin: sin is death, pornography is a cancer that must be completely cut out or it will grow and spread. *Flee from sexual immorality* (1 Colossians 6:18a).

6. Study God's Word concerning sexual purity: The best way to save your soul from death is to fill it with high doses of Life. *Therefore putting aside all filthiness and all that remains of wickedness, in humility receive the Word implanted, which is able to save your souls* (James 1:21).

7. Set up strong boundaries: The enemy doesn't give up his prize without a fight. Temptation will come and your own mind will let him in the door; be cautious: *Do not enter the path of the wicked, and do not proceed in the way of evil men. Avoid it, do not pass by it. Turn away from it and pass on* (Proverbs 4:14-15).

8. Establish means of accountability: set up trusted persons who know of your issues and will hold your feet to the flames; give them permission to ask anything and determine to be completely honest. Here is your daily strength. *Two are better than one…If one falls down, his friend can help him up. But pity the man who falls and has no one to help him get up!* (Ecclesiastes 4:9-10).

9. Give yourself time to work through the process of recovery: More times than not, God chooses a slow painful process of deliverance. *Be joyful in hope, patient in affliction, faithful in prayer* (Romans 12:12).

10. Find a good Christian counselor: People addicted to sex often carry significant emotional baggage that needs to be unpacked. A good psychotherapist can help you discover the deficits in you that make you susceptible to sexual addictions. A Psychiatric examination may be necessary as well in order to prescribe psychiatric medicines that may prove useful in treatment, such as antidepressants. *Plans fail for lack of counsel* (Proverbs 15:22a).

11. Find a twelve-step program: There are many twelve-step recovery programs for sex addicts. These are people who completely understand because they too have been where you are now. *A cord of three strands is not quickly broken* (Ecclesiastes 4:12b).

12. Pray: While there is a progressive order to these steps, prayer should be a part of them all. In every step God is our Refuge, our Strength, our Deliverer, our Revealer of Truth and our Comfort. He has not forsaken you.

*Be strong and courageous. Do not be afraid or terrified ... for the Lord
your God goes with you; he will never leave you nor forsake you*
(Deuteronomy 31:6).

Don't get discouraged: Make no mistake about it the journey is
painful and fraught with danger. But you will make it. If you fail, be
quick to get back up. *Where sin increased, grace increased all the more*
(Romans 5:20). Hold on to the cross of Christ with white knuckles and
work these steps. Each morning, before you even get out of bed,
surrender that day to God in prayer. Not surrendering your entire life,
that's too broad a time frame and much larger order than you can fill
right now. Get specific: surrender lust, surrender anger and
resentment, surrender impatience and unkindness. Surrender your
right to such things. Because God has given us free will to govern our
own lives, surrender involves giving up that right. "Everything is
permissible for me — but not everything is beneficial. Everything is
permissible for me — but I will not be mastered by anything" (1
Colossians 6:12). Lordship of Christ means laying down our *rights* (not
abilities) to do things our own way. This means that when a sexual
image passes before our eyes, we don't have to decide whether we
will drink in that image or not. We have surrendered that to the
Lordship of Christ, the option has been taken off the table, it's no
longer available to us.

Every day ask to be emptied of self and filled with Christ, put on the
full armor of God and ask God to direct your path. Throughout the day,
when God reveals a time of selfishness or some other character defect,
immediately repent and make things right. Remember, God is doing
more than delivering you; he is remaking you, whole and complete.
Each evening when you lie down, review your day in prayer, asking
God to reveal any blunders or moments of weakness. Repent of those,
and ask for a refill of his Spirit. Also, ask God to guard your dreams,
those moments of unconscious thought; he can even redeem these.
Make this a regular practice until it becomes a habit; after awhile these
can become your new compulsive behaviors.

The following is a general idea of what the nature of recovery
will look like:

The Nature of Recovery:[164]

1. Detoxing:

Stopping the habit by abstaining from the panacea, also known as "sobriety." Making peace with the pain, anxiety, boredom and emptiness that follows. Finding a home in the suffering is where you will experience some of your greatest spiritual and personal awakenings.

2. Detraumatizing:

Addressing major past events that have caused high levels of depression and anxiety. Repairing relationships with others. Cultivating cognitive thoughts and skills associated with genuine intimacy (friendships, family members, relationship with spouse...).

3. Centering:

Learning to function without the chemical highs of our addiction. Serenity: learning to live on a more even emotional level without being given over to anxiety, obsessive thoughts or compulsive behaviors.

Spiritual Deliverance

"Forasmuch then as the children are partakers of flesh and blood, He [Christ] also himself likewise took part of the same; that through death he might destroy him that had the power of death, that is, the devil; and deliver them who through fear of death were all their lifetime subject to bondage" (Hebrews 2:14-15, KJV).

As we discussed earlier, pornography addiction is a violation of God's plan and purpose for humankind. It is a form of idolatry that robs the individual of God's influence and blessing and casts them into a spiritual state of bondage not easily broken. For this reason, it seems that talk of spiritual restoration would be incomplete without spending at least a few minutes focusing on spiritual deliverance. After all, we are reminded that "our struggle is not against flesh and blood, but against the rulers, against the authorities, against the powers of this dark world and against the spiritual forces of evil in the heavenly realms" (Ephesians 6:12). Immediately our minds reflect on television preachers laying hands on individuals and watching those persons fall down writhing on the floor. I must admit, that I've never witnessed such things first hand. I'm hesitant to comment on such practices, but I will say that if Jesus considered it necessary to commission his disciples to "drive out demons" (Matthew 10:8), then I suppose there's a need for such ministry and perhaps we should be among the first ministered to.

Playing in the Devil's Back Yard

"Whoso means to rescue and preserve the subjective element shall lose it: but whoso gives it up for the sake of the objective shall save it."[165]
Walter Lowe

Carbon monoxide is a subtle killer. Invisible and odorless, it creeps in upon its victim completely undetected. As the gases sneak up on the individual, it replaces the oxygen in the person's blood. The person becomes disoriented, their judgment is impaired, and soon they lose consciousness until death finally exacts its due. And as the carbon monoxide damages, disorients, disables and destroys the physical life, so too Satan and his army move upon the person of God who wanders into his back yard through pornography.

Certainly, Scripture gives us many examples of devil-possession, satanic agents incorporating the bodies of human beings, temples made to be the dwelling place of God, had become the habitation of demons. The senses, the nerves, the passions, the organs of men and women, supernaturally induced to the vilest of lusts. Here is a clear example of what happens within the sexually addicted person. The question that immediately comes to our minds is, is it possible for Christians to be possessed by the devil or are all such cases involving Christians a form of demonic oppression. In truth, there are three common ways that satanic forces attack human beings: oppression, possession, and demonization.

1. Demon Oppression: Demon oppression, also known as "demon infestation" (sounds too much like when the kids are sent home from school with lice) involves the strength in which Satan tempts us to do wrong. The entities surround the individual but do not enter him or her. Demon oppression happens to unbelievers and believers alike, although their power of influence is diminished greatly in direct proportion to the believer's crucified nature and will. In demonic oppression/infestation, these dark forces gain temporary influence in certain areas of the individual's life, dimensions of the person's character that are not surrendered and, therefore, unredeemed. Such would be the case of the pastor who gives into lust or lying, jealousy, gluttony, or a host of other sinful habits.

In most cases, demonic oppression does not require deliverance, but true repentance and inner healing to remove demonic access. Yet, if those practices have long been indulged or is deeply-rooted in past childhood experiences, deliverance may be required. "Here the unclean one has managed to install itself securely in some area of the person's character structure (or, "members")...the...person is obsessed and unable to maintain righteous intentions. A man may set himself to be virtuous, but when triggered in that area, he has little or no ability to control himself. The demon is in charge." These deeply entrenched practices become a home to these demonic forces.[166]

2. Demon Possession: By possession we refer to the in-dwelling presence of one or more demons, who take full control affecting the person both neurologically and physiologically. The demon(s) thinks, feels, speaks, and acts through the person. There is much debate in Christian circles over whether a Christian can be possessed or not. The late Dr. V. Raymond Edman, former president of Wheaton College, in seeking to answer whether Christians can be possessed, wrote, "Theory says no, but the facts say yes."[167] How can a Christian be possessed by a demon when he or she already belongs to God through Christ? How can we be possessed by Satan when Ephesians 1:14 tells us we are "God's own possession"? "What fellowship can light have with darkness?" (2 Corinthians 6:14b). A Christian is always God's possession, purchased by Christ's blood, God's Spirit abiding within them. The Spirit himself testifies with our spirit that we are God's children" (Romans 8:16). The fault is not in differing opinions, but in our definition of demon possession. The truth is the word "possessed" paints a false picture. The word most commonly referred to in Scripture is actually better translated "demonized" or "to have a demon." While there is true and complete demon possession in our world, it is not something that happens often in the United States and it never happens to Christians.

3. Demonization: "Do not give the devil a foothold" (Ephesians 4:27). Here's a riddle: what happens to a Christian who refuses to live as a Christian? He or she opens doors they have no business opening and Satan is

more than obliged to walk through. What happens if a Christian continually harbors hatred, unforgiveness, pride or unclean thoughts? "These are areas of disobedience and Satan is the prince of the power of the air, the spirit that works in the children of disobedience."[168] Our bodies are temples of the Holy Spirit, but, just as the ancient Israelites became disobedient, worshipping idols in God's temple, so the disobedient Christian allows false deities into God's new temple. By playing around in the devil's back yard, we have allowed him a foothold in our lives. Merrill Unger wrote:

Christians can and ought to enjoy complete deliverance from the power of Satan and demons as a result of Christ's perfect work of redemption. But what believers can and ought to enjoy and what they actually do enjoy are two different things. When Christians fail to recognize what they have in Christ and refuse to appropriate the resulting privileges, they invite defeat, and can be held captive by demonic forces to a pitiable degree. Believers can be hindered, bound and oppressed by Satan, and even indwelt by one or more demons, who derange the mind and afflict the body.[169]

The best way I can distinguish between possession and demonization is, the demonized person has a demon or several demons inside them, while in possession the demon(s) have the person — it's a matter of ownership. Let me try and explain this a little better. The Bible alludes to the fact that Satan can gain a foothold in the Christian. The Greek word for "foothold" is *topos*, from which we derive the geographical term *topography*. While the Christian had, at some point in their life, given ownership of their life over to God, somewhere along the line they took some of that property back for themselves and have, in a sense, rented out a section to Satan and his crew. "Such does not describe a momentary demonic action. It is, rather, a place Satan has secured, a semi-permanent station on some corner of the map of a Christian's life."[170] Demonization takes place when sin is allowed to go unrepented, thus, allowing Satan a foot in the door to come and do his dirtiest in us. Someone once said, "the enemy can't enter the person of God, but a *friend* can." Just as Jesus stands knocking on the heart's door, patiently hoping that we would allow him entrance, so too the devil and his band pound at the soul of the child of God, accusing him or her with lies and demanding to be let in. If we waver in our faith and open the door he is more than happy to come in. This is why Jesus warns us not to let the devil have a foothold. Would he warn us if it were not possible? Before a person enters into deliverance, he or she must deal with the sin issues and character flaws that gave those unclean spirits access in the first place.[171]

But, in truth, the question of oppression vs. possession is the wrong debate to be involved in. These are distractions, rabbit trails the devil is glad to lead you down in order to take your mind off recovery. When the devil has a death-grip on your heart and life, the question stops being about his exact coordinates and more about how to get rid of him.

"Submit yourselves therefore to God. Resist the devil, and he will flee from you. Draw nigh to God, and he will draw nigh to you. Cleanse your hands, ye sinners; and purify your hearts, ye double minded…. Humble yourselves in the sight of the Lord, and he shall lift you up."
James 4:7-10 (KJV)

Now that we have identified how Satan works his devilment (couldn't resist!), we need to take direct action against him in order to cast he and his crew away and reclaim that territory for God.

Casting Out Demons

There are certain qualifications that must be in effect before attempting to take on the demons in your life, the first being a firm assurance of your own salvation through Christ (John 10:27-30). Secondly, Jesus tells us that we must have a certain measure of faith (Mark 11:22-24; 16:17) and a good knowledge of the Word of God (Hebrews 4:12). We need to recognize and be sure within ourselves that Satan is already defeated by Christ (Colossians 2:15; Hebrews 2:14) and have a humble dependence on and trust in God. Self-pride only brings defeat (Proverbs 3:5-7). Further, there are two conditions to obtaining a person's deliverance: first, they must fully and completely surrender to God. Romans 12:1-2 is Paul imploring Christians to give themselves fully to God so that he may fully transform them. Second, they must deal with *all* issues of sin in their lives. Ephesians 4:26-27 is a warning for all believers that Satan will be waiting for the next available opportunity to return. Galatians 5:19-21 provides a list of sins that are contrary to God's Spirit, including sexual immorality. The person seeking deliverance must be willing to thoroughly deal will these sins if they hope to recover.

After these things have been settled, the person seeking deliverance is ready to do battle. The following is a pattern of prayer that covers all the bases. It is not necessarily to be prayed verbatim, although that's certainly alright. The key is that you think of each declaration made and mean it from the depths of your soul. After praying for deliverance, believe it in faith and accept God's promise of deliverance as truth: "But when he asks, he must believe and not doubt, because he who doubts is like a wave of the sea, blown and tossed by the wind. That man should not think he will receive anything from the Lord" (James 1:6-7a). Believe as if your life depends on it, because it does. Don't be anxious, worried that you missed something in your prayer and forfeited deliverance — after all, who brings the soul's freedom? Instead, be assured that he who began a good work in you will be faithful to complete it until the day of Christ Jesus (Philippians 1:6).

Father God, in the name of Jesus Christ my Savior, I come to you.
You know my heart, my desire to love you and serve you,
You also know my weaknesses and my failures.
Father, I have strongholds in my life, areas of disobedience.
I have not loved you with my whole heart,
I have not given you complete Lordship over all my life.
I know now that by holding areas of my life back from you
I have allowed Satan a portion of my self.
I have given to him what rightfully belongs to you.

My desire Lord is to overcome these areas,
including my past wounds and especially my sexual addictions.
But, also, Lord, I need help in overcoming many character failures in me,
including pride, jealousy, resentfulness, and _____.
I ask you to take these areas of my life,
for if they continue, I will surely act upon them again,
enforcing the bonds that hold me and bringing dishonor to my Lord.

My desire is to love you better and to honor you with my life.
May my life be fully consecrated to you, holy and clean
that I may show forth your love and your light to others,
and that you may be glorified.

I ask you to forgive me and cleanse me of my sins.
I thank you that, through the blood of Jesus,
You can forgive and now have forgiven me.

I thank you for the price paid for my redemption,
I thank you for my adoption,
And I thank you for Your promise of recovery.

I am powerless over these things, Lord,
and I ask you to take Lordship in these areas of my life.
They have held me fast for so many years,
but they are shameful in your sight and I want to stand before you clean.

Purge these sins from my heart and life,
purify me by your Holy Fire,
Burn up the dross and make me pure and holy.
Empty me of myself so that I may more fully be filled with you.

Father, I know that these things won't leave without a fight,
but I know that I am more than able to overcome
through your power that strengthens me.
In my darkest moments, Lord, I know that you will be there.
Assure me of your Presence and help me to walk in your Light.
Thank you for your grace that restores me and your mercy that sustains me.

Jesus, you are the Rock upon which I stand, you are the Light for which I seek, you are the rest for which I long for. By the Power and Authority given to me through your blood and assured me through your Word, I command any tormenting spirits that are oppressing me and my home and my family to leave, in the name of the Lord Jesus Christ. You are no longer welcome here; your lease on my life has been revoked. I am a child of the Living God, co-heir of his Kingdom and all rights and privileges are now fully and forever surrendered to him. I surrender any generational sins that have held me and my family captive. Your work order has been canceled and, in Jesus' name, you too must leave.

I take every thought and every deed captive,
submitting them to you, Lord Jesus.
I ask, Holy Spirit, that you make a thorough search of my heart and soul,
cleansing me of any form of unrighteousness, anything displeasing to you.
Fill every nook and cranny of me with you.

By Your Power and Authority,
Help me to withstand every temptation that comes my way,
And repair the damage to my walls,
those weak areas that have been entry points for Satan.

Thank you, that even when sin abounded in me,
your grace did much more abound!
May I never again be bound by the yoke of slavery.
Thank you for your love which endures forever
And your grace that helps me to overcome.

I am yours — fully, finally, and resolutely yours.
The dye is caste,
it is sealed with the blood of the cross!

I pray these things in the precious name of Jesus Christ.

Amen

.

"... Resist the devil, and he will flee from you.
James 4:7, KJV

Behold, I give unto you power to tread on serpents and
scorpions, and over all the power of the enemy: and
nothing shall by any means hurt you.
Luke 10:1, KJV

CHAPTER 6
RESTORING THE ADDICTED PASTOR

All this is from God, who reconciled us to himself through Christ and gave us the ministry of reconciliation.
2 Corinthians 5:12

Restoration is a complex word to define. What does Paul mean when he says that God reconciled us through Christ? What does it mean that he calls us to such work? How can the church help in restoring ministers and their families to spiritual wholeness? What would such a ministry look like? Is it possible for persons who have been involved in pornography to be restored to ministry? In this chapter we will look at the issue of biblical restoration, particularly addressing the question: "Can persons who have been involved with pornography addiction be restored to ministry?" Further, we will establish a grace-filled process of restoration ministry for the Church. Finally, we will discuss preventative measures to strengthen and protect clergy from such moral failure and establish possible steps to voluntarily disclose their pornography addiction, so they may deal openly with spiritual recovery and the Church can regain a sense of moral integrity.

Defining Biblical Restoration

"Since then, we know what it is to fear the Lord, we try to persuade men... For Christ's love compels us, because we are convinced that one died for all, and therefore all died and he died for all, that those who live should no longer live for themselves but for him who died for them and was raised again. So from now on we regard no one from a worldly point of view. Though we once regarded Christ in this way, we do so no longer. Therefore, if anyone is in Christ, he is a new creation; the old has gone, the new has come! All this is from God, who reconciled us to himself through Christ and gave us the ministry of reconciliation: that God was reconciling the world to himself in Christ, not counting men's sins against them. And he has committed to us the message of reconciliation. We are therefore Christ's ambassadors, as though God were making his appeal through us. We implore you on Christ's behalf: Be reconciled to God."

2 Corinthians 5:11b, 13b-20

Reconciliation, *katallasso*, is a term used to describe what God does for humanity through the grace of atonement. Human sin has brought about an objective guilt and separation that must be covered or removed if fellowship between God and his creation is to be restored; reconciliation is the act of covering over the guilt and the removal of the separating gulf. Because it is humanity's sin that caused the separation, it is humanity that stands in need of reconciliation; because God is the innocent party that's been affronted, it is his persistent grace alone that can offer reconciliation, and he does so through the atonement of Christ's blood. God's grace sets aside the cause of the person's alienation, offers provision for forgiveness, and welcomes back the one who has caused the estrangement.[172]

In the same way, God calls Christians to the ministry of reconciling those who are away from God and bringing them back into right relationship with him. The conflict comes in our understanding of what it means to minister reconciliation. According to this passage in 2 Corinthians 14, we are reminded that *all* died because of sin, so none but Christ stands worthy to judge another. We further see that we are not to judge others according to what we observe in the flesh, and that, since God does not count an individual's sins against them, neither should we. The Christian is not to stand in judgment over their brothers or sisters, but to exercise love and grace in all areas of reconciliation ministry. On the other hand, we are reminded that God reconciles the prodigal to himself, not by changing the nature or standard of his righteousness, but by enabling the wayward one the grace to lay down his or her own nature and acts of unrighteousness. God makes the repentant sinner new: "the old has gone" and must be gone.

Finally, we see that reconciliation is not a passive act. Christ's love, expressed through the cross, not only "compels," but is compelling. The verb *reconciling* is used of God in the active tense. As God commits the message of reconciliation to his followers, he refers to them as "ambassadors," those who *travel out* as his representatives. Phrases like "making his *appeal*" and "we *implore* you" demonstrate the imperative nature of reconciliation ministry. We can draw from these terms the understanding that the Church is not to wait for sin and spiritual separation to come to her attention, but must use due diligence in finding the lost sheep *or shepherds* and bringing them back into the fold. The need is too great to leave the work as incidental; it must be intentional.

Through this understanding of 2 Corinthians 5, we can see that the ministry of reconciliation has a three-fold approach: First, reconciliation is to be performed in love and true humility, not standing in judgment of another, for "all have sinned" (Romans 3:23) and no one is justified to "cast the first stone" (John 8:7). We must remember that, while clergy sin causes many victims, sin is a spiritual affront against God alone: "Against you, you only have I sinned..." (Psalm 51:4a), and God alone is warranted to stand in judgment. Second, we are, however, not to lower the standard of God's righteousness. There is a vast difference between gentleness and passivity. C.S. Lewis wrote: "The demand that God should forgive such a man while he remains as he is, is based on confusion between condoning and forgiving. To condone an evil is simply to ignore it, to treat it as if it were good. But forgiveness needs to be accepted as well as offered if it is to be complete: and a man who admits no guilt can not accept any forgiveness.[173] The Church needs to make sure their standards are not higher than God's, which is many times the case, but also, that they do not fall below God's standard (which happens far more frequently). Third, the Church cannot afford to hide her head in the sand regarding those secret sins infecting the church. National statistics average the number of pastors living in undisclosed sexual sin between 50-64%. A national survey conducted recently among one denomination's district leaders found that only 4% of these cases have been found out.

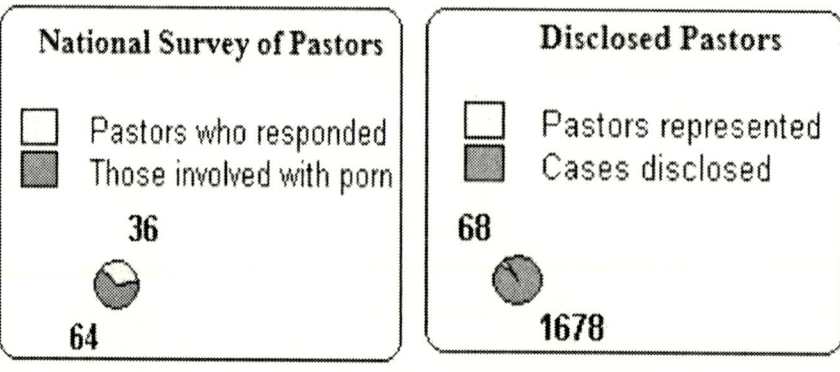

Compare these numbers to one another and it becomes starkly clear that ministers do not feel free to disclose their sin to their bishops for fear of serious ramifications, and, likewise, the bishops are afraid to know the truth for fear of the possible fallout that may take place within the church. The proverbial closet door is stuck shut and churches and denominational leaders are pressed up against the door to try and keep it that way. "Rescue those being led away to death; hold back those staggering toward slaughter. If you say, 'But we knew nothing about this,' does not He who weighs the heart perceive it? Does not He who guards your life know it?" (Proverbs 24:11-12). Burying their heads in the sand will not restore the Church, nor will it absolve its leaders. The Church must find a way to open that door so that those clergypersons may find the personal freedom and restore the moral integrity that comes only through reconciliation with God on his terms. "The Body has to be taught how to guard her virginity. Oh, that the church would start dealing openly and honestly with crimes against the Body."[174] Not a witch-hunt to punish the guilty, but a diligent search to seek and save those who are lost.

A Hidden Time Bomb

As the Christian Church seeks to institute a biblical plan of reconciliation for clergy caught in the sin of pornography addiction, it is important that they soberly grasp what is at stake: marriages, families, churches, the integrity of God and his Bride...not to mention the very souls of those lost in their sin.[175] "Of the resources for recovery, people are the most precious,"[176] or, as someone once said, "A minister is a terrible thing to waste."[177] The Church cannot close its eyes to this epidemic of sin that threatens its destruction.

God's call is emphatic: "Rescue those being led away to death; hold back those staggering toward slaughter" (Proverbs 24:11). God's call to the Church is to minister reconciliation and it may be the only hope we have. Phineas Bresee, founder of the Nazarene Church, once wrote, "God speaks in no other way as he does through human lips. The most divine power manifested in this universe is the love of God out of a pure heart, spoken through pure lips, melting the heart of a sinner and lifting a lost soul from the very brink of hell. God manifested in the flesh, speaking through lips of clay, is the password to victory."[178]

It is essential for us to recognize that the Church's primary function in such matters is to reconcile the fallen pastor with his or her God through Christ, but we have not, as of yet, discussed whether or not it is possible to restore the minister to pastoral office. To this matter we now turn our attention.

"Who may ascend into the hill of the Lord? And who may stand in His holy place? He who has clean hands and a pure heart, who has not lifted up his soul to falsehood, and has not sworn deceitfully. He shall receive a blessing from the Lord and righteousness from the God of his salvation."
Psalm 24:3-5

According to Barna Research, between 1991-2002 church attendance has dropped 6% in our country[179] and more than 80% of current church growth in Protestant churches is biological and transfer growth, rather than evangelism.[180] Considering the outrageous number of undisclosed sexually addicted pastors in our pulpits, could the dramatic stagnation of the Christian Church in the West be, in part, because the mantle of God's blessing has been removed from these pastors? Perhaps we should stop looking at secular media as the blame for the church's ineffectiveness and begin asking if it can be the result of spiritual hypocrisy.[181] If this is the case, we have another reason for why the Church needs to actively seek out those pastors trapped in pornography addiction: not just for the sake of those who are lost, but for the Church's preservation as well. How long will God permit such blatant sin from among his called?

Here the question begs to be asked — should the Church take a stronger stand, demanding the permanent removal of ministers caught in sexual sin, establishing, once and for all, a standard of righteousness among God's ordained clergy? Or should the Church, instead, take a more relaxed stand, allowing these ministers to openly confess their sin with little or no repercussions, in order to deal with this spiritual epidemic in the light of truth? Is there a Scriptural basis for restoring fallen ministers to Christian service at all? How does God view the fallen clergyperson? How does Christ view the damage inflicted upon his Bride, the Church?[182] Where is the standard that balances mercy and justice?

A Plan of Restoration

The word "restore" comes from the Greek word, *apokathistemi* - "reestablish," or "renew." The biblical understanding of restoration primarily deals with regaining one's spiritual well-being (Psalms 23:3; 51:12; Lamentations 5:21), or a spiritual renewal of the individual (Galatians 6:1; 1 Peter 5:10).[183] It does not, however, speak directly to restoring a person to a position of spiritual leadership. In fact, some would argue that Hebrews 6:4-6 gives the description of one who has personally accepted Christ and later rejects him, concluding that it is "impossible" for them "to be brought back to repentance." This passage, taken in proper context, however, illustrates the point that there is no other salvation available to them, because there is no other salvation available to anyone. The assumed clause, therefore, is that they must (and therefore are able) once again to return to Christ, the only path of salvation and restoration.[184]

If we look to Scripture, it's not hard to find examples of personal spiritual renewal and restoration to Christian leadership. Peter himself denied Christ three times (Matthew 26:69-75; Mark 14:66-72; Luke 22:54-62; John 18:16-18, 2-27), but is exonerated and restored by Jesus himself (John 21:15-19), becoming a stronger, more stable minister for having had the experience. Another example is found in the book of Acts, involving Barnabas' cousin, John Mark. On Paul's first missionary journey, Barnabas and Mark were his companions, though John Mark eventually abandons them and the work at Perga, in Pamphylia. When Paul and Barnabas were preparing for their second missionary journey, Barnabas wanted John Mark to accompany them, but Paul refused (Acts 15:36-39). In time, Paul's heart softened toward John Mark and he encouraged the Colossian church to accept him (Colossians 4:10; Philemon 24), and, by the end of Paul's life Mark is in full favor with Paul again (2 Titus 4:11).

The Old Testament offers examples of men of God who had fallen, yet had been restored to God's position and work. After David's sin with Bathsheba (2 Samuel 11:1-5, 14-18) we see God's favor returning to David;

Acts 13:22 assures us that he was "a man after God's own heart." God restored David to the point that his very own Son, Jesus, would be descended from David and Bathsheba (Matthew 1:6). Moses was still used of God after killing the Egyptian (Exodus 2:11-12) and explosive striking of the rock at the desert of Zin (Numbers 20:8). Abraham received God's favor again after lying to the Pharaoh (Genesis 12:13) and later to King Abimelch (Genesis 20:2) in displaying a willingness to subject Sarah to adultery; the New Testament recognizes Abraham as a model of faith and friend of God (Romans 4; Hebrews 11:8-10). His son, Isaac was restored after a similar fall (Genesis 26:7) and his grandson, Jacob also received God's favor back after numerous events of lying and cheating (Genesis 12:13; 25; 31; 27:19-29). In fact, Jacob's name, which means "supplanter" (one who follows on another's heels), was changed by God to "Israel," meaning "prince with God." Noah was found drunk and naked (Genesis 9:20-21), and Samson's indiscretions led to the breaking of his Nazarite vow (Judges 16:15-22). Manasseh stands out as one who fell and led God's people astray so that they did evil, "more so than the evil nations around them" (2 Chronicles 33:9-10). Yet, when he "humbled himself greatly" before God, he was returned to Jerusalem and reinstated as king (2 Chronicles 33:12-15). "God does not take away life; instead, he devises ways so that a banished person may not remain estranged from him" (2 Samuel 14:14b).

A Divine Mandate

Possibly the clearest verse of Scripture dealing with restoring a person to ministry is found in Galatians 6:1: "Brothers, if someone is caught in a sin, you who are spiritual should restore him gently. But watch yourself, or you also may be tempted." The word "restore" in the Greek here is *katartidzo*, which is a verb, meaning "to mend, to equip completely (the fallen one),"[185] giving inference to making something useful for service again. The tense is in the continuous present, suggesting the need for patience and perseverance as the process of restoration takes place.[186] Bagster's *Analytical Lexicon of New Testament Greek* defines its meaning as "to restore to a forfeited condition, to reinstate," further defining the notion of reinstating a person to position and service.[187]

It is plain to see from Scripture that both rehabilitation of the man or woman of God and the restoration of their ministry are not only possible, but encouraged. Yet, the question still remains whether restoration to pastoral position is to be immediate or over some prolonged period of time.

A. Approach One: Immediate Restoration to Ministry

The first approach we'll examine is that of immediate restoration to ministry, where the clergy may be removed from pastoral office for a very temporary period of time, such as six months or less or where the pastor is not removed from position at all. The argument given for immediate restoration is that because God forgives all genuinely repented sin and because ministers are not inherently different from all other believers, it is unfair to demand higher standards and impose stricter penalties. Proponents of the immediate restoration approach look to King David as a key example of complete and immediate restoration of a sexually fallen leader: "I acknowledged my sin to you and did not cover up my iniquity. I said, 'I will confess my transgressions to the Lord' - and you forgave the guilt of my sin" (Psalm 32:5). The argument is if God immediately forgives sin, then we must immediately forgive sins. The nature of sexual sin is argued to be no worse than any other sin and so must not be judged more harshly. Paul writes that the "deeds of the flesh are evident, which are: immorality, impurity, sensuality, idolatry, sorcery, enmities, strife, jealousy, outbursts of anger, disputes, dissensions, factions, envying, drunkenness, carousing, and things like these" (Galatians 5:19-21). The argument is made then that sin is sin, if jealousy or strife does not disqualify a person from pastoral ministry, neither should pornography. A final point to be made for immediate restoration is the notion that Scripture makes no distinction between pastor and laity when it says "All have sinned and fall short of the glory of God" (Romans 3:23). The pastor is a servant of Christ, as all Christians are servants of Christ, and it is Christ to whom he or she will give account: "Who are you to judge the servant of another? To his own master he stands or falls" (Romans 14:4a); "There is only one Lawgiver and Judge, the One who is able to save and to destroy; but who are you to judge your neighbor?" (James 4:12).[188]

The Christian Church has a long history of poor redemptive practices among those who have fallen from the path. Perhaps these incidents stand out in history because they are atypical to the way the Church normally acts — perhaps not. One fallen clergyman wrote: "I wish we in the church did a better job of conveying God's love for sinners. From the church, I feel mainly judgment. I cannot bring my sin to the church until it has been neatly resolved into a warm, uplifting testimony. For example, if I had come to the church in the midst of my addiction to lust, I would have been harshly judged."[189] Or, as one author put it, "the river of justice (in the Church) is still full of piranha."[190] It is imperative that judicial steps be governed by grace-filled discernment. There is a great deal on the line.

B. Approach Two: Delayed Restoration to Ministry

The second approach involves a delayed period of time before restoring a minister to office, generally one to three years. While the first approach sounds more compassionate and most denominational leaders would agree with immediate restoration in *theory*, the reasoning for delayed restoration offers a more practical display of genuine Christian love. The issue at hand, delayed restorers would argue, is not a matter of withholding forgiveness, but allowing time for the individual to fully deal with those issues that brought them to this wretched state of pornography addiction in the first place. As we discussed in the previous chapters, these men and women have issues of past childhood trauma, patterns of family addictions, ingrained personality disorders, cognitive distortions, and cerebral chemical imbalances to contend with. Moreover, the damaging effects on the marriage and family, caused by years of pornography addiction, will require a time of focused care. Churches and denominational leaders who practice delayed restoration, in most cases, are thinking of the spiritual and emotional welfare of the clergyperson and their family. "Restoration and healing is not the same thing. To be restored is to be returned to a place of obedience, blessing and usefulness before God. Healing has to do with recovering from the damage caused by sin. Restoration is related to healing, but it may not be on the same time schedule, and different concerns may need to be addressed."[191] While the first group looks to David as an example for immediate restoration, the second group would look at the tragic destructive life that befell David as reasoning for a time of spiritual and emotional recovery.

Those stationed in the delayed restoration camp look further into Galatians 6:1 for their main source of reasoning: "Brother, if someone is caught in a sin, you who are spiritual should restore him *gently*."

As discussed earlier, the word "restore" comes from the Greek verb *katartidzo*, meaning "to mend" or to "fit properly." The tense and mood of this verse is in the present imperative, dictating that the action is intended to be sustained over a period of time.[192] The word "restore" in this passage indicates bringing something back to its original state, before the damage and wear. If a person were to restore a finely carved antique chair, he or she wouldn't simply slap a coat of paint over it to cover up marks or age, nor would they strip it down using a belt sander, removing dings and unique carvings together. Instead, they would go through painstaking time and effort to carefully restore the item to its original glory. The same is true for the pastor, damaged through years of pain and wear. Such a practice takes time and a great deal of loving care.[193] If pastors have been damaged by pornography addiction, Galatians 6:1 brings out more fully the process of this restoration: Restoration is to be done "gently," not something done quickly or haphazardly, but with much love and care. The issue is not that denominational leaders need to *require* a time out of active ministry, but rather they need to *give* the pastor a time out of ministry, seeking to be actively involved in loving and supporting the pastor, extending grace and understanding, helping facilitate the process of recovery. From this perspective delayed restoration is not a punishment in which forgiveness is withheld; instead delayed restoration is a means of grace where forgiveness is coupled with love.

Nesting

Animals have this natural instinct that after a major trauma they will nest for a time, giving themselves a period to recover. In like manner, people need a time of stillness after major upsets in order to recover from their turmoil. Grievous errors, such as sexual sin, cause mortal wounds in the clergy, his or her family, and the church they pastor. Usually there is a time of anger and deep depression that sets in upon all parties involved. A period of recuperation is crucial for healing such wounds; it allows the opportunity to seek the Lord, work through the personal issues, quiet a troubled heart, and regain perspective.[194] "Something precipitates a mistake. That something can often be fixed, and the period of recovery is the time to do it…mistakes as sin cry for new patterns to head off temptation."[195]

Qualifications for Restoration

Regardless of the timetable in which a minister is restored to office, there are certain characteristic behaviors that must be evident before he or she should be considered qualified for restoration.

Responsibility: The first and perhaps greatest of these character behaviors should be a deep sense of remorse for the sin that has been done.

There, of course, must be clear discernment of whether the sorrow is genuine or not. Jimmy Swaggart's Oscar-worthy confession on national television touched many hearts (as well as turned many stomachs!), but the inauthenticity of his compunction showed in his refusal to follow the terms of his denomination's church discipline. Remarkably, the truest way to know the genuineness of a repentant pastor is if *they remove themselves* from office.[196] Fear grips the pastor for fear of what they will lose if they voluntarily disclose their pornography addiction and in a very real sense, removal from ministry is a confirmation of those fears. For this reason, self-removal is unlikely to occur, yet, humility brought on by a deep sense of shame is not an unreasonable expectation. Initially, most persons, when confronted and held accountable to their sin will fight or flee, defending their right to remain or running away from the whole mess that they have made. I myself litigated back and forth with my District Superintendent, defending my right to stay in ministry, and even involving my wife in the pleading my case. I was outraged that another sinner (saved by grace) would have the audacity to "stand in judgment" over me. I was wrong and it took a time of letting the dust settled before I could see it.

A clear mark of discipleship is meekness and submission to those placed in authority over them. Donald Njaa points to such openness at the beginning as evidence that the beginning work of forgiveness has begun and, in some cases, sees it as enough evidence to leave the person in ministry.[197] To refuse discipline is to show one's self to be no longer a disciple, and thus disqualified. The ethic of responsibility is implied here. The word "responsibility" comes from the Latin word, *spondere*, meaning "to pledge" or "to promise." Responsibility, thus, involves taking ownership of one's sinful behaviors and submitting one's self to the interactive work of being accountable to another. Here is where a full confession of one's sin is required, and the depths of which a person is willing to confess will show it equal to the depths of healing they will find.[198]

Confession: James writes, "Is any of you in trouble? He should pray… Is any one of you sick? He should call the elders of the church to pray over him and anoint him with oil…Confess your sins to each other and pray for each other so that you may be healed" (James 5:13-14, 16b).

The question quickly comes to mind: to whom should the repentant pastor confess their sin? Paul addresses areas of concern, such as sin, and shows that they are individual issues but they also affect the church as well. Disclosure of sin must be made by the offender to all who have been offended. To this we must then ask, who has been offended by the pastor's pornography use? Certainly, the first relationship violated is that between the individual and God. An outpouring of deep remorse to God is the first step of confession. Secondly, the spouse of the individual must be told. No other person on earth is as adversely affected by the lust of one's pornography use than the spouse. The question of whether children should be informed is a delicate one; some argue yes, others declare no. The issue to consider must be would disclosure of the parent's sexual sin be understood and beneficial to the healing of the relationship and training up of the child? Perhaps the best answer is not yes or no, but when. Because addiction has showed itself to be a generational sin, it is best for the clergy parent to discuss these issues with their children, but perhaps delay of such a talk until the child is mature enough to process the information is best. In Steven Arterburn's book, *Preparing Your Son for Every Man's Battle* suggests the time for such disclosure between the ages of eleven to thirteen.[199] The next person who must be told is the leadership of the denomination, most especially the pastor's immediate supervisor. The bishop or superintendent holds a vested responsibility to both the pastors and the churches under their charge, and, therefore, has a need and a right to know. Further, it will be this leader who will establish the guidelines of the person's discipline, recovery, and possible restoration to ministry.

One other group of people must be discussed in regard to whether they have a need and a right to know of the pastor's indiscretions or not: the local church to which they serve. In a very real sense the church is adversely affected by the spiritual and moral lapse of the clergy. For one thing, the blessing of God is withheld from the church when their leader is living in disobedience. Another way in which they are affected is the time spent by the pastor as he or she acts out is time neglected from serving the people of his or her congregation. Thirdly, as the pastor resigns their position, the church is left without a spiritual leader and forced to begin the pastoral search process all over again. This can be costly as well as time consuming. Finally, the sexual indiscretions of a pastor are a deep violation of the church's trust. They have invested their lives with this person, and so, perhaps, deserve to be told. For church leaders to withhold this information may, in fact, cause the persons in the church to feel demeaned or patronized.[200]

Unfortunately, not every person in the congregation may be equipped or desire to know the events that led to the pastor's removal. In fact, there are times when disclosure seems to bring more hurt than had it been kept privately among the elders.[201] In a very real sense, the local church is similar to the children in a family and perhaps the discretion used earlier in regard to the clergy offspring need be employed here as well. Is the local congregation emotionally and spiritually stable enough to deal with this very painful message? My personal opinion is that there needs to be better training of forgiveness and reconciliation in the local churches, particularly in the area of sexual indiscretions, before such disclosures can be made public. While the decision lies with the Bishop/Superintendent, the underlying reasoning is not clergy or congregational cover-up; the conscientious objective must be the welfare of the local Body of Christ. James' words of advice are to (1) call the elders and/or (2) confess to one another. Either option is open, but the decision must be governed by love and discernment. We are not looking to cover over the truth, but rather lovingly consider the feelings of all involved and not involved.

Accountability: The parameters of restoring a clergyperson to spiritual health and then back into pastoral position are circled around accountability. Because so many areas of a person's life accounts for the fall and is affected by the fall, different areas of life must be called into account. The first accountability relationship will involve the pastor and their bishop or district superintendent. They will enter together into a covenant in which the person will agree to monthly accountability reports in addition to many other procedures. In order to deal with the spiritual dimensions of the person, a pastoral mentor needs to be employed to directly watch over their spiritual care. The person seeking restoration will enter into a covenant with this pastor, agreeing to, among other things, make him or her available for regular accountability times and following whatever mandates the district leader deems necessary.

Perhaps they may wish to employ a Web accountability program, where the sponsoring pastor is notified by e-mail when the pastor logs on to an adult site. There are several Web accountability programs available free of charge at different Christian web sites, probably the most well known today would be at xxxchurch.com. A professional counselor needs to be employed in order to call into account the emotional and cognitive areas of the person and participation in a weekly twelve-step group dealing with sexual addictions should be required for mutual support and strength. As the number of disclosed incidents increases, districts may wish to begin their own twelve-step programs. No one understands the needs of the fallen pastor better than another fallen pastor. A marriage counselor could be another area of accountability in order to help establish new healthy relational habits including healthy boundaries in the marriage.

Fruits of Recovery: Before a person is restored to pastoral ministry, he or she must show signs of growth and maturity that point toward recovery. 1 Timothy 3:1-8 sets clear guidelines of what is expected of a person called to Christian leadership and can be a good example of what needs to be expected before a person can be restored to ministry. Five key areas from this passage need to be reestablished before a minister should be considered eligible to reenter the pastorate.
He or she must:

1. "Be above reproach" (2a).
2. "Be the husband of one wife...manages his own family" (2b, 4a).
3. Be "self-controlled" (2c).
4. "Must not be a recent convert" (6a).
5. "Must also have a good reputation with outsiders" (7a).

Be above reproach: The word here in the Greek is *anepilemptos*, meaning "that which cannot be laid hold of." In Titus 1:6-7, Paul uses the word "blameless," *anenkletos*, which means "that which cannot be called into account." The idea here is that the person wanting to return to ministry must be one who has no more skeletons in is or her closet, nothing to which someone may call them into account for.[202] Once a man or woman steps into the fullness of the light, they will never desire to walk in the shadows again. When the fallen pastor deals fully with his or her transgressions and all that they have wrought in their life, they will begin to hate sin as God hates sin. Compromise is no longer a part of their vocabulary.

Be the husband of one wife...manages his own family: These verses are a stark reminder to the fallen clergy that they have not been faithful to their spouse and family, that they have sown sin, mistrust, and instability in the home.[203] There is a need, therefore, to reestablish those relationships and restore trust before returning to ministry. In every case of sexual indiscretion, boundaries were crossed and priorities askew. Trust takes time, so does relearning priorities and establishing healthy boundaries. Forgiving spouses need to know that they won't be stepping back into the same set of circumstances as before, playing second fiddle to church and ministry.

Clergy need to relearn these lessons or else they will repeat these failures.

Be self-controlled: Only time can tell whether a person has regained control over their lives or not. Further, the process of recovery not only brings cleansing from the pornography, but soon begins to clarify other underlying areas of a person's life that are out of control. Perhaps this is one of the reasons Paul mentions control over finances. Needless spending, poor time management, and uncontrolled eating habits are signs of a life out of control and not yet ready for ministry. Good godly counseling and working the twelve steps are excellent tools for helping the individual unearth damaged emotions and distorted thinking.

Must not be a recent convert: In the same sense that a new Christian is not equipped for the high-calling of pastoral ministry, so too the newly-reformed clergy is not prepared to stand behind the pulpit yet. The pastor must not only be clean, the pastor must be whole. It takes some concerted time and effort to unscramble eggs. The pastor probably won't need to retake Bible classes or relearn Greek, but he or she will need to retrain their thinking on sin and righteousness and reapply those lessons the mind blocked off from the heart. Such a traumatic fall as this will, undoubtedly, leave the clergyperson fragmented, disoriented, and unsure of God, themselves, and everyone else around them.

Must have a good reputation with outsiders: The Greek word for "reputation" is *martyria*, which means "witness" or "testimony." It is important to discern that Paul's point of qualification requires *true facts*, not good persona. The question is not personal opinions and keeping a tight lid on shameful behaviors, but knowledgeable testimony, where those who know the full story can honestly report that they have seen a marked difference.[204] 1 Timothy 3:10 further asserts "Let them be tested" (proved). The Greek word for this is *dokimadzo*, which describes a trial-by-fire testing which refines the character. It is not a process that can be undertaken lightly or finished too quickly: "Do not lay hands on anyone hastily" (1 Timothy 5:22). "New Testament leaders are *grown* – matured and seasoned over time, and verified in character and conduct *before* hands are laid upon them, confirming the grace and call of God on their lives."[205] As Uncle Buddy Robinson (1860-1942) once observed: "It is impossible for a man to be any better on the outside than he is on the inside."[206] Therefore, outward signs can be good indicators of God's internal graces.

Need for Inner Healing: Not only is the structure and reputation of the clergyperson in need of repair, but their own sense of self-worth must be reestablished so that he or she has the sense of being clean and the self-confidence to stay the course. As one recovering pastor summed up his experience, "I may not always do right, but I won't do wrong."[207] We look at justice and mercy as if they were at odds with one another. The matter at hand is not how to balance mercy and justice; mercy and justice are of the same substance because they originate from the same Source. God's justice and mercy are not some outward entity that God employs; they are, instead, a part of who God is, a part of his nature. God does not administer justice to us because some cosmic law demands it so; God administers justice because God is just. God does not offer mercy as some benevolent benefactor; God offers mercy because God is merciful. His justice doesn't override his mercy nor does his mercy overwhelm justice. Persons seeking deliverance from pornography addiction tend to seek out mercy rather than justice because they are more interested in fulfilling their desires than their needs; those who seek to restore the fallen pastor are more interested in justice than mercy in an attempt to settle some disquieted emotions within themselves. Justice must flow from mercy and mercy must desire justice for either to be genuine.

Developing a Plan of Self-Disclosure:

Recognizing the vast damage caused to the Church through the undisclosed sinful behaviors of clergypersons and understanding the mandate, procedure and spirit in which restoration ministry is to take place, is it possible for churches, and especially denominational leaders, to establish a plan of self-disclosure for pastors? What would such a plan involve? What should be the biblical mandates for governing such a plan?

In many cases, denominational leaders have established counselors in their districts as places where ministers can go for help with their pornography addiction while still holding to their anonymity. This has been done in order that the individual can get help and the presbyter can remain uninformed and, thus, circumvent their responsibility to administer discipline. It is never an acceptable alternative for those who represent Light and Truth to hide their faces from a situation and pretend that there's no problem. Yet, if the Church puts into place a strict policy of discipline, clergy will remain too frightened by his or her impending consequences to openly reveal their indiscretions. Too much is at stake for the clergyperson: They will be forced to give up their church, in which is tied their income and identity in order to receive help. Because clergy are self-employed they do not qualify for unemployment and because most have their education in religion, they are considered by most companies as unemployable. They are removed from their home if they live in a parsonage or they take a financial beating if they have to quickly sell their house. Their complete emotional support base is removed as they must say goodbye to clergy peers and laity inside the church and in the community. Many times spouses must give up their jobs and children removed from their schools in order to relocate. How can a fallen pastor deal with the underlying issues of their addiction if they must now focus on the immediate needs of food, shelter, and employment? Is it fair to further victimize the spouse and children who are already dealing with the grief of betrayal? Will they not see themselves as betrayed and abandoned by their Church as well?

Redeeming Ministry Assumes the Debt

Restoration must be wrapped in redemption (Gk. *lytron*), releasing the individual from their debt so they may be restored. Redemption is the deliverance and freedom from sin's penalty, established through the substitutionary death of Christ: he took our penalty and offers us his pardon.[208] The debt was not overlooked by God but *assumed* by Christ. Therefore, since Christ has already taken upon himself the penalty of each individual's sin, church discipline must look markedly different from ecclesiastical punishment. If removal from ministry is, indeed, an act of redeeming grace, then it must carry grace in all areas of need for the fallen pastor and his or her family.

Love is displayed through redeeming grace by taking away another's penalty, even if we must assume the penalty ourselves. In light of this, the Church as a redeeming Body must look to the material needs of those being disciplined as well as their spiritual needs. Contingency funds should be set aside for helping displaced pastoral families; perhaps some financial training in establishing a budget would be helpful. If church districts have the space, they may wish to build temporary housing facilities on district campgrounds or on regional college campuses of their denomination; individual churches may feel pressed of God to build homes of respite and renewal for dislodged clergy families. Networking with the churches in the district may help to provide job placement so as to help stabilize the home. When the smoke clears a bit, it may be necessary for the diocese to help provide professional counseling. Obviously, the denomination cannot assume full responsibility for these individuals, but there is a very clear mandate for the Church to assist, and, almost always, there is a need for that assistance.

Because the burden that follows such downfalls is so great, there may be a need to differentiate whether the grievousness of the offense requires a time of removal from ministry or if a strict probationary period will suffice. Since both immediate restoration and intermediate restoration have a strong Scriptural basis, it may be wise for denominations to create a plan of recovery that is just as stringent and encompassing, but where certain individuals can work within the parameters of the local pastorate. In such cases the probationary pastor enters into a written covenant with the bishopric to adhere to these requirements, as well as other safeguards to insure spiritual and moral integrity. Some of these may include: full disclosure to the church body or its board representatives, removal of the Internet from church and home, downsizing in ministry responsibilities in order to relieve mounting stressors, and the like.

Prudence dictates spiritual discernment in each individual case. A sample guideline, however, as to whether a situation demands removal for a time or if a probationary period is warranted should include such factors as did the incident involve spiritual adultery (lust) or actual adultery. Another indicator should involve one's receptivity to discipline; have they presented themselves as repentant and humble or are they defensive and argumentative? Another strong consideration should involve whether or not the person voluntarily confessed their sin to their denominational leader or if it were a matter of coercion or another's testimony. Here is not only a good indicator of whether a person is in a redeeming state or not; it can also be a great prompting for inducing a person to come forward voluntarily for discipline and healing. Again, we must not hide the sin from the church, especially if the pastor is to remain. The church is one of the offended parties and, therefore, needs to have a say in whether they can continue to work with this individual or not. In this particular situation, the whole of the church may need to be made aware of the pastor's indiscretion, regardless of the damage it may ensue. The church in this situation is being asked to be a part of the redeeming process, and so has a right to know the particulars.

A final question must be addressed: After the disciplinary work is done and the pastor is restored to right standing, should his or her transgression follow them the rest of their career? For example, when a person leaves his or her place of employment and seeks a position elsewhere, the agency considering the applicant will contact the person's former employment for a reference. In the case of a pastor who leaves one district and seeks a calling on another district, should the bishop of the diocese they are leaving inform the bishop of the diocese where they are going of their past pornography addiction? The issue automatically becomes a matter of privacy verses "need-to-know." There has been much conflict in recent years over the secrecy among the Roman Catholic Church regarding their priests and various sexual indiscretions, especially sexual abuses against children. Rather than inform the Church and instill a time of restoring the individual, the priest would, in most cases, undergo a short treatment plan and then be moved from one parish to another. Does the new superintendent, and the new church for that matter, have a right to know about this minister's past in order to make a more informed decision, or, at the very least, to be on their guard about possible future moral failures? And if we don't, are we setting ourselves up for a legal nightmare in the future if they again fall?

Again, we must remember that we are dealing specifically with cases of pornography; issues involving clergy abuse, molestation and the like are legal issues that carry their own mandatory rules of disclosure. The question we are dealing with has to do with a person's sinful behavior, and, therefore, must be judged by biblical standards. We must also remember that, unlike the cases involving the Roman Catholic Church, these are clergy sins that have been addressed and fully brought through a process of redemption. Therefore, the question that needs to be addressed is how should the Church handle sins that have already been redeemed by Christ and his Church? This leads us to another Greek word for redemption, *apolytrosis*, which involves deliverance upon payment of a price. In such cases as these the payment has been made through the blood of Christ (Ephesians 1:7) and such redemption has been evidenced in the life lived for Christ: "You were bought with a price, therefore honor God with your body" (1 Colossians 6:20).[209] A person can no longer be considered a debtor after the debt has been paid.

The standard for the Church, set by God, is to abound in grace and be miserly in judgment; God does not simply cast away humanity's sins because humanity is unable to stand up under its weight, God casts away the sins of humanity because he cannot bear to have anything standing between him and his beloved. He proclaims forgiveness as a deliberate act of love[210] and He modeled that deliberate act of love in the giving of his Son. Therefore, if the standard of redemption is "forgive and forget," which God proclaimed and Jesus demonstrated, it must also be the model for the Church that is called by his name. We are reminded that "all have sinned and fall short of the glory of

God" (Romans 3:23), and so no one stands on their own merit, but on the "inexplicable, inexhaustible mercy of God."[211]

Therefore, sins redeemed must not follow the restored clergyperson. Such a standard might not sit well with some: both those leaders and laypersons who want to know what they are getting themselves into, nor the general public who demands to know the "dirty little secrets" of others. Such a stand will possibly bring undue pressure upon the defending Church. But if the Church is going to be the true representative of gracious God, she must follow the lead of him who was willing to personally face attack and even death for the sake of those he loved. After the pastor has confessed his or her sins, sought reconciliation with the Father, gone through a time of recovery, and demonstrated true works of repentance, they must not only be forgiven and restored, their sin is to be thrown into the sea of forgetfulness and not be allowed to follow them throughout their life and ministry career.

I am deeply afraid for those ministers that confess their sin and walk through the process of recovery, only to find that the Church's definition of redemption falls far short of God's. One pastor confided: "I walked the very tedious road of recovery, fulfilling every mandate set down for me and then some. As the time drew closer I began to count the months, then the weeks, then finally the days. On that last night of suspension I stayed up until midnight, ushering in more than just a new year, a new chance at life. Later that day I called my District Superintendent. He congratulated me on my hard work, but then he informed me that there were no churches available for me on his district. He further instructed me that when I seek out churches on other districts I will be required to inform them of my past problem and (if by chance they were willing to offer me a second chance) many of them may require I disclose my past to the interviewing church board and maybe even the entire church body. I feel like Hester Prinn[212], allowed to walk through the community of believers, but forced to wear that damnable Scarlet Letter." I'm afraid there are many ministers made to feel the leper's sting, caste out from their churches and denominations, forced to roam unattached and uncared for, made to carry the "mark of Cain" as a brand upon their souls.

The truth is if the Church is the living, breathing Body of Christ here on earth, then we must be about the same business Jesus was about when he came to earth — offering and even providing for the redemption of all mankind, even damaged pastors. Denominations and local congregations alike are more concerned about community perception than fulfilling the Biblical standards of love to one another. If the Church is not the redemptive

Body of Christ, then they are not the true Church, but a cheap imitation at best. "Woe to you, teachers of the law and Pharisees, you hypocrites! You shut the kingdom of heaven in men's faces. You yourselves do not enter, nor will you let those enter who are trying to...Woe to you, teachers of the law and Pharisees, you hypocrites! You are like whitewashed tombs, which looks beautiful on the outside but on the inside are full of dead men's bones and everything unclean. In the same way, on the outside you appear to people as righteous but on the inside you are full of hypocrisy and wickedness... O Jerusalem, Jerusalem, you who kill the prophets and stone those sent to you..." (Matthew 23: 23, 24, 27, 28, 37a).

Denominational leaders have defended their position by stating that pornography addiction may lead to other sexual sins in the Church, bringing the wrath of prosecuting attorneys down upon them. First of all, by this line of preventative reasoning, we can also conclude that since Jesus said the person who has anger in their heart is guilty of murder (Matthew 5:21-22), we should disqualify every person who has lost their temper. In fact, since "all have sinned and fall short of the glory of God" (Romans 3:23), all persons stand unworthy of redemption and disqualified for ministry. "But wait!" we balk. "Those are sins redeemed by Christ's atonement!" So are the sins we have been talking about. Have not those pastors walked the road of redemption and be made clean and right in the eyes of the Lord? As for the prosecutors, even if he or she could make a link between pornography addiction, which is not against the law, and some sexually based crime, they will have a hard time laying the blame on a church that has demonstrated (and documented) a clear process of recovery.

Can I offer one last piece of insight for you denominational leaders faced with this clear but tough question? People who have been set free from a lifetime of addiction will do everything possible not to step into that trap again. "Once burned, twice shy," they say. Further, the process of recovery is a process of self-discovery. These individuals have at least begun the work of dealing with their emotional and spiritual baggage. They know themselves, they know their weakness and they have learned how to avoid engaging in those weaknesses. These people who have walked "in darkness have seen a great light" (Isaiah 9:1); why would they ever choose to go back to the darkness again? People who strove so long, fell so far, lost so much, and have been given a second chance have learned valuable lessons of the futility of sin and self and the vastness of God's immeasurable grace. We are told in Luke 7:47 that those who have been forgiven much love much. Who better to shepherd the flocks of God? On the other hand, if all of the studies conducted in this book concerning clergy and sexual sin are accurate, there are a lot more clergy members still hiding out in their sin. Who do you see as the greater risk for your empty pulpits?

Preventative Measures

It has been said, "The best defense is a good offense." So, too, the best way to help the fallen pastor is to catch them before they fall. This requires establishing strong safeguards in ministry through preventative measures.

The first line of defense for any clergyperson should be strong boundary walls. By this I mean, establishing clear bounds between the person and the profession. These should include such things as a clear and reasonable job description for the pastor as well as clear expectations for the congregation, especially lay leaders. Lines of authority must be clear, with healthy boundaries between the church and the pastor, not cutting one's self off emotionally, but insuring that mutual respect is shown for one another. Another important area of defense has to do with self-care on the part of the minister. Wholeness for the pastor comes in the form of personal fitness for three areas of life: spiritual, emotional, and physical. The pastor needs regular quiet time with God, blocking out a portion of their day for Scripture and prayer. Many pastors who fall prey to sin admit that regular personal time with God had been languishing. Emotional fitness comes for the pastor by having regular personal time for themselves. Pastors need to take their regular days off each week for mental freshness and spiritual power; it is where God restores the pastor's soul.[213] For those who have past emotional baggage to deal with, counseling can be a wonderful preventative measure as well. Physical exercise is important to keep the blood circulating and stresses reduced. The release of endorphins creates a sense of wellness and balance in the pastor's brain. By intentionally marking time for these three areas in his or her appointment book, the pastor will almost certainly be able to handle whatever flaming darts the Enemy may throw at them.

The next line of defense is the guards stationed on the walls. These are support teams which hold the pastor accountable for different areas of his or her life. The first support team is the pastor's own family. There is a myth in ministry, that if the pastor commits himself or herself to the work of building God's church, God will, in turn, take care of the clergy family. The increasing devastation in clergy families has shown the fallacy of this notion.[214] These people who most support the pastor are usually the least supported by the pastor; no one holds a more vested interest in the welfare of the pastor than his or her own family. Given the opportunity, clergy spouses can prove themselves tenacious at guarding the time and welfare of their pastor/spouse, acting as intermediary of church and the pastor.

Another caring support system for the clergy is the denomination or association of which they are a part. This support must come primarily from two sources: clergy peers and their presbyters. In regards to mutual support among the clergy, one former minister lamented: "The ministry is the loneliest job in the world, and with rare exception I found fellow pastors too absorbed in their own affairs to be concerned with their fellows. Pastors need to assume the role of something akin to father-confessors to one another. So much could be done in this respect to give comfort, aid, and understanding to a fellow pastor."[215] Surprisingly, one of the major reasons clergy peers refuse fellowship is jealousy. As one seminary professor remarked, "There's more professional jealousy among ministers than any other profession."[216] Because of this, district superintendents can be a wonderful line of defense, as both a source and facilitator of support. A predominant complaint among former clergy has been the lack of personal care they had felt from their past denominational leaders. One such pastor, lamenting over his years in ministry wrote: "I am aware of the terrible load of administration upon them, but I would have given anything simply to have had any one of them as a friend I could turn to."[217] Others advised: "Quit worrying so much about [financial] support, quit pushing programs…Pay more attention to the small church."[218]

For the clergyperson, admission of stress and failure to their superiors is difficult because they fear the implications this could have on their ministerial careers, especially in future church placements. In providing support and accountability, questions will arise among the clergy, such as, "How much can I say?" or "Is this professional or personal support and where do I draw the line?" Pastors project father images on their bishops and fear disappointing them.[219] The bishop is the pastor to the pastor and, as such, has a responsibility to care for the emotional and spiritual needs of those clergypersons under them. Suggested forms of preventative maintenance could include establishing a pastoral care committee, responsible for the spiritual care and morale of the clergy on their district. These could initiate programs such as pastoral accountability partnerships, where each pastor is *required* to find another clergy on the district for mutual answerability.

Another program may include district-sponsored clergy marriage retreats, strengthening the bonds of family support. Finally, district care should include the opportunity and requirement of psychological testing and counseling. Such opportunities offer the pastor greater awareness of their personal susceptibilities, such as past wounds and deep-seated feelings of insecurity. The pastor who would minister with integrity must first come to grips with his or her own personal areas of susceptibility.[220] Being made aware of our dark side can help keep us from falling prey to it.

Undoubtedly, the greatest need for the pastor is the availability of support *and* the ability to make use of it. Religious bodies tend to be reluctant in recognizing this, perhaps believing that the Church is basically a caring, high principled institution.[221] But experience has shown that the Church today is missing some very fundamental dimensions of support and the loneliness and emotional drain of pastoral leadership leaves a spiritual and emotional deficit that only intimate support can fill. There are several areas of pastoral support that need to be addressed. First, the pastor needs to have certain supportive resources made available. Some of these could include a retreat area made available so he or she can escape by themselves for a day or two to quiet themselves before God. Another resource could consist of marriage seminars or weekends away to rekindle romantic love between the pastor and spouse. Certainly, accountability and emotional support systems need to be in place. Such things as weekly meetings with an accountability partner should be made mandatory for all clergypersons.

One of the greatest needs for clergy is to have someone in their lives who love them enough to tell them the truth, no matter how painful that may be, and to hold them to a level of personal integrity. Developing trusted, intimate friendships among the church members is essential in providing emotional support for ministers. The same is true for genuine friendships with fellow-clergypersons and their bishops or superintendents. There needs to be opportunities for pastors to step out of their professional roles, perhaps on their days off, and given the chance to express themselves creatively through personal hobbies or projects of their choosing. Pastors need respect; they need people around them that affirm them as a human being, not flattery for a job well done, but positive affirmation to combat the negativity they so often receive. Finally, pastors need opportunities for personal and spiritual growth, whether that comes through a spiritual formation group or life-giving Bible study.[222] Pastors spend their week studying and preparing studies and sermons to feed others. Sometimes they need a chance to sit and be fed. Not necessarily a brief devotion before getting to the business at hand, but an unrushed time of discussion, reflection, and prayer to nourish their parched souls.

CONCLUSION

Human sexuality was designed by God to draw his creation into perfect union with himself and each other; it is a human/divine experience that leads the individual toward a more complete sense of wholeness. Sexual sin disconnects the person from God, others, and inevitably, from their own sense of self. Because of this estrangement and the fragmentation of the individual, the pain becomes unbearable; further distancing themselves from the life-giving connection of God and others, and further perpetuating destructive patterns of compulsive sexual expression. Sexual addiction is not a respecter of persons, destroying clergy and laity alike; however, there are dimensions of the clergy character and the office of the pastorate that further incline the pastor toward this particular compulsion.

Pornography addiction in the church and in the pulpit is a stark reality that we must deal with openly yet with great caution; the stakes are about as high as they can get. Pornography addiction causes victimization in children, marriages, churches, communities, denominations, and within the souls of the addicts themselves. The cancer of this sin is rapidly spreading throughout the Body and it is perpetually being passed on to future generations to come. This devastation will not simply run its due course and then die away. If the Christian Church is to survive this hellish attack, it must take the initiative, not just in standing its ground on matters of doctrine, but rising up as an agent of God's grace. The Church must never lower the Scriptural bar in regards to sin, but rather, must reevaluate where that bar is and prayerfully discern the delicate balance of mercy and judgment, discipline and grace. While all members of the Body of Christ are sinners and clergy and laity alike stand equal upon grace, we know that we who teach will be judged more harshly (James 31b) by God; to Him we leave such judgments.

The primary objective of the Church is to be an agent of reconciliation, going out in order to bring the lost sheep back into the fold (Luke 15:4). Yet, sometimes it is the shepherd, and not the sheep, which need to be returned to the fold. In reconciling the lost, the Bible makes no differentiation between clergy or laity; yet, it calls "those who are spiritual" (Galatians 6:1) — literally, those who have the Spirit of Christ within them, to "restore gently." The people of Christ have a mandate from Scripture to insure gentle but sure spiritual renewal, even to the pastor. Such recovery should be over a period of time, generally one to three years, depending upon the grievousness of the sin and the spiritual condition of the fallen. It may prove worthwhile to assign complete removal from ministry for the first half of the allotted time and a probationary period for the latter half. In this scenario, pastors are given the opportunity to demonstrate a renewed spirit before being fully released back to service. In some cases it may be expedient for the pastor to continue pastoral ministry through the period of restoration, but these cases should be in rarity and after much prayer and discussion.

APPENDIX

The Twelve Steps of Christian Transformation

It's important to recognize that, in the same way our spiritual life is to progress and deepen, so also working the twelve steps of our recovery continues, and as we progress in our recovery (hopefully) we grow closer to the Father and deeper in our understanding of who he is and who he created us to be. It is a journey that leads from death to self to life in Christ. The following exercise lists the traditional twelve steps, a Christian clarification for each of the steps, and a Scripture verse or verses pertaining to each step. Take time to prayerfully reflect on each step, pausing at times to apply the words to your circumstances.

STEP ONE

We admitted we were powerless over our dependencies –
that our lives had become unmanageable.

After "hitting bottom," as the result of our addiction
and the failure of our best efforts, we came to realize that we could not
manage life alone, that left to ourselves we fall far short.

I know nothing good lives in me, that is, in my sinful nature.
For I have the desire to do what is good,
but I cannot carry it out. (Romans 7:18)

STEP TWO

Came to believe that a Power greater than ourselves could restore us to sanity.

We come to believe that only the grace of Christ can heal us of our past hurts and compulsions and help to restore us, make us new, and make us whole. God can do for us what we cannot do for ourselves.

For with God nothing is impossible. (Luke 1:36)

For it is God who works in you to will and to act according to His good purpose. (Philippians 2:13)

STEP THREE

Made a decision to turn our will and our lives over to the care of God *as we understood him.*

We surrender ourselves to the Lordship of Christ, continually giving more as He reveals more of himself and discloses our sinfulness and selfishness.

Come to Me, all you who labor and are heavy laden, and I will give you rest. "Take My yoke upon you and learn from Me, for I am gentle and lowly in heart, And you will find rest for your souls. (Matthew 11:28-30)

"Surely he will deliver you from the snare of the fowler and from the perilous pestilence. He will cover you with his feathers, and under his wings you shall take refuge. (Psalm 91:3-4)

STEP FOUR

Made a searching and fearless moral inventory of ourselves.

We determined to take an honest, fearless inventory of ourselves, including the roots of our addiction and the subsequent damage we caused to ourselves and others.

Let us examine our ways and test them, and let us return to the Lord.
(Lamentations 3:40)

The ear that hears the reproof of life will abide among the wise. He who distains instruction despises his own soul. (Proverbs 15:31-32a)

STEP FIVE

Admitted to God, to ourselves, and to another human being
The exact nature of our wrongs.

We admit to God, ourselves and other caring individuals vested in our lives and welfare the exact nature of our wrongs and took full ownership for them.

Confess your sins to each other and pray for each other so that you may be healed. (James 5:16a)

If we confess our sins, he is faithful and just to forgive us our sins and to cleanse us from all unrighteousness. (1 John 1:9)

STEP SIX

Were entirely ready to have God remove all these defects of character.

Through recovery we discovered more subtle obsessions and character defects, the dark side of our personality and self-serving inclinations. We were ready to be done with those things contrary to the character and will of God and asked God to help us overcome them.

You also, reckon yourselves to be dead to sin, but alive to God in Christ Jesus our Lord. Therefore do not let sin reign in your mortal body, that you should obey it in its lusts. (Romans 6:11-12)

STEP SEVEN

Humbly asked him to remove our shortcomings.

In humility, we submitted ourselves to his Lordship
and trusted him for the healing of our souls.

*If we confess our sins, He is faithful and just to forgive us our sins and
purify us from all unrighteousness.* (1 John 1:9)

Humble yourselves before the Lord, and he will lift you up. (James 4:10)

STEP EIGHT

Made a list of all persons we had harmed,
and became willing to make amends to them all.

Recognizing the harm we had done to others,
we sought to make amends to all persons we have offended.

*Then Zacchaeus stood and said to the Lord,
"Look, Lord, I give half of my goods to the poor; and if I have
taken anything from anyone in false accusation,
I restore fourfold."* (Luke 19:8)

Do to others as you would have them do to you. (Luke 6:31)

STEP NINE

Made direct amends to such people wherever possible,
except when to do so would injure them or others.

We try to heal broken relationships by setting things right. As God has
forgiven us and restored us to himself, so we also seek to be forgiven and
restored to others, careful that our disclosure doesn't cause harm to them.

*Therefore, if you are offering your gift at the altar and there remember
that your brother has something against you, leave your gift there in front
of the altar. First go and be reconciled with your brother; then come
and offer your gift.* (Matthew 5:23-24)

STEP TEN

Continued to take personal inventory,
and when we were wrong, promptly admitted it.

Committed ourselves to the daily task of personal inventory and surrender,
each day asking God to search our hearts and promptly letting go
of whatever he reveals.

Watch and pray, lest you enter into temptation.
The spirit is willing, but the flesh is weak. (Mark 14:38)

So, if you think you are standing firm, be careful that you don't fall.
(1 Corinthians 10:12)

STEP ELEVEN

Sought through prayer and meditation to improve our conscious contact
with God *(as we understood him),* praying only for knowledge
of his will for us and the power to carry that out.

We seek through prayer and willingness of heart to move into deeper
intimacy with God, growing in grace and knowledge,
and becoming more submissive to his Lordship in our lives.

I have been crucified with Christ; it is no longer I who live,
but Christ lives in me; and the life which I now live by faith in the Son of
God, who loved me and gave himself for me. (Galatians 2:20)

Now may he who supplies seed to the sower, and bread for food, supply
and multiply the seed you have sown and increase the fruits
of your righteousness. (2 Corinthians 9:10)

STEP TWELVE

Having had a spiritual awakening as the result of these steps, we tried to carry
this message to others, and to practice these principles in all our affairs.

Having received a profound spiritual awakening in Christ, having been transformed, healed, and renewed, we felt compelled of God to offer the hope of recovery to those still held captive.

And when he got into the boat, he who had been demon-possessed begged him that he might be with him. However, Jesus did not permit him, but said to him, "Go home to your friends, and tell them what great things the Lord has done for you, and how he has had compassion on you." And he departed and began to proclaim in Decapolis all that Jesus had done for him." (Mark 5:18-20)

Restore to me the joy of your salvation, and uphold me with your generous Spirit. Then I will teach transgressors your ways, and sinners will be converted to you. (Psalm 51:12-13a)

The Twelve Steps to Complete Insanity[223]

Sometimes the course of recovery becomes too concentrated and we need something to help break up the intensity. I ran across his page on the web and included it to provide a much needed laugh. Be careful though, a close examination may show that many of these have been true for us in the past.

1. We admitted we were powerless over nothing. We could manage our lives perfectly and we could manage those of anyone else that would allow it.

2. Came to believe that there was no power greater than ourselves, and the rest of the world was insane.

3. Made a decision to have our loved ones and friends turn their wills and their lives over to our care.

4. Made a searching and fearless moral inventory of everyone we knew.

5. Admitted to the whole world at large the exact nature of their wrongs.
6. Were entirely ready to make others straighten up and do right.

7. Demanded others to either "shape up or ship out."

9. Got direct revenge on such people whenever possible except when to do so would cost us our own lives, or at the very least, a jail sentence.

10. Continued to take inventory of others, and when they were wrong promptly and repeatedly told them about it.

11. Sought through nagging to improve our relations with others as we couldn't understand them at all, asking only that they knuckle under and do things our way.

12. Having had a complete physical, emotional, and spiritual breakdown as a result of these steps, we tried to blame others and to get sympathy and pity in all our affairs.

Recovering Peace

St. Anselm[224]
(1033-1109)

Come now, little child. Turn awhile from your daily work;
Hide yourself for a little time from your restless thoughts,
cast away your troublesome cares; put aside your wearisome distractions.
Give yourself a little leisure to talk with God, and rest awhile in Him.
Enter the secret chamber of your heart, shutting out everything but God,
and that which may help you in seeking Him.
Now, my whole heart, say to God: "I seek your face; your face, O
Lord, do I seek."

I will seek you by desiring you, and desire you in seeking you.
I will find you by loving you, and love you in finding you.
I praise and give thanks to you that you have made me in your image,
So that I can remember you, think of you, love you.
But so darkened is your image in me by the smoke of my sins,
that it is useless unless you restore it.
I do not seek, O Lord, to search your depths,
but only in some measure to understand your truth,
Which my heart believes and loves.
I do not seek to understand so that I may believe,
but believe that I may understand.
For this I know to be true:
That unless I first believe I shall not understand.

Serenity Prayer

God grant me the Serenity
to accept the things I can not change…
Courage to change the things I can
and the Wisdom to know the difference…

Living one day at a time,
Enjoying one moment at a time,
Accepting hardship as the pathway to peace.
Taking, as He did, this sinful world as it is, not as I would have it.
Trusting that He will make all things right if I surrender to His will.
That I may be reasonably happy in this life,
And supremely happy with Him forever in the next.

Amen

Pornography Addiction Self Test[225]

Am I addicted to pornography?

The following questions are excerpted and adapted from Hope and Recovery-A Twelve Step Guide for Healing From Compulsive Sexual Behavior. These questions do not constitute a standardized test designed to diagnose addiction. Those who answer yes to many of these questions will find that they have common experiences with pornography addicts. It is the hope of the authors of these questions that those who answer "Yes" to any of these questions will carefully consider the effects their sexual thoughts and behaviors have on their lives *today*. Those who do have concerns about their sexual thoughts and behaviors need to know that they can get help and support.

1. Do you sense that your sexual thoughts and/or behaviors are causing problems in your life?
2. Have sexual thoughts interfered with your ability to function at work or at school?
3. Do you worry that your sexual thoughts and/or behaviors are more powerful than you are?
4. Do you sometimes think that you are the only person who has certain sexual thoughts or engages in certain sexual behaviors?
5. Do you fail to meet commitments or fail to carry out responsibilities because of your involvement with pornography?
6. Do you struggle to control or completely stop your thinking about or viewing pornography?
7. Do you view pornography in order to escape, deny, or numb your feelings?
8. Do you think about sex more than you would like to?
9. Do you spend more money than you can afford to spend on pornography?
10. Does it seem as though there is another person or force inside of you that drives you to pornography?
11. Do you have two standards of fidelity — one for yourself and one for your spouse or partner?
12. Do you feel empty or shameful after viewing or masturbating using pornography?
13. Have you ever promised yourself that you would never again view pornography?

14. Do you use pornography to deal with, deny, or avoid problems in your life?

15. Do you risk legal problems in order to view pornography?

16. Do you anxiously anticipate or fear trips out of town because of what you think you might do sexually while you're away?

17. When you have child care responsibilities, do you put a higher priority on masturbating or being sexual than you do on the welfare of the child(ren) in your care?

18. Do your sexual thoughts and/or behaviors interfere with your spiritual or religious life? Do your sexual thoughts and/or behaviors cause you to believe that you don't deserve to have a religious or spiritual life?

19. Have you lost a job or risked losing a job because of your involvement with pornography?

20. Do you scan printed material (novels, newspapers, magazines) or change channels on the television set just to find something that will stimulate you sexually?

21. Do you regularly view pornography or engage in fantasies involving self-abuse or other kinds of physical abuse?

22. Do you dig through other people's garbage to find pornography?

23. Would you rather masturbate than be sexual with a partner?

24. Do you drive around unfamiliar neighborhoods (cruise) hoping to find places where pornography is available?

25. Do you look at pornography or masturbate while driving?

26. Have you replaced a collection of pornographic material after destroying one collection and vowing never to purchase pornography again?

27. Has an important relationship in your life ended because of your inability to stop looking at pornography?

Daily Checklist

The following is a daily checklist, intended to help keep us focused in the right direction, protecting our minds and our hearts and growing in our relationships with God and others. You may wish to reproduce these and post a copy on your dresser, desk, car, purse/planner, or even on the fridge.

"Since, then, you have been raised with Christ, set your hearts on things above, where Christ is seated at the right hand of God. Set your minds on things above, not on earthly things."
Colossians 3:1

Spiritual Care

Am I spending time in God's Word each day?

Am I making time for prayer and meditation each day?

Have I surrendered my day to God?

Have I surrendered lust, pride, jealousy, resentments, _____, _____, today?

Have I been involved in the life of my church?

Have I involved myself in a life-giving small group?

Do I end each day in prayer, asking God to reveal strengths and weaknesses throughout the day and do I surrender my dreams to Him before bed?

Family Care

Am I making time for my family each day (quality *and* quantity)?

Am I talking with my spouse about what's going on in my life?

Am I talking with him/her about what's bothering me? My fears? My dreams?

Am I honoring my marriage vows and keeping myself for no one else but them?

Have I played with my kids today? Helped them with their homework? Talked with them about things they are interested in?

Am I expressing love to my children each day, by word and deed?

Self Care

Am I eating properly and exercising regularly?

Am I taking a daily inventory of my stress levels?

Am I taking time for myself?

Have I called my accountability partner this week?

Have I been honest with him/her?

Have I moved my computer to a public area in my house?

Have I installed an Internet filter?

Have I found myself a mentor and make myself accountable?

Accountability

"As iron sharpens iron, so a man sharpens the countenance of his friend."
Proverbs 27:17 NKJV

"Again, if two lie down together, they will keep warm; but how can one be warm alone? Though one may be overpowered by another, two can withstand him. And a threefold cord is not quickly broken."
Ecclesiastes 4:11-12 NKJV

No wonder Solomon was considered the wisest person to ever live. Growing up in America, we are taught early on that to depend on another person is a sign of weakness. Men are taught to emulate John Wayne, women are at least a little grateful for Gloria Steinhem and others from the feminist movement. And if you suffer from deep-seeded insecurities, the need for self-sufficiency only increases. We do not feel secure enough in ourselves to have a hero, at least not openly. In fact, we need to try and diminish others in order to bolster our own sense of self worth. It is a rare man or woman that will go outside of themselves to find an accountability partner.
Promise Keepers has done a monumental job in bringing men to bear on

these critical issues and others, they have been instrumental in establishing accountability groups among men. To a certain degree some of those same issues have been addressed for women at the Women of Faith events. The problem is if you are one of these insecure men or women and you have been taught to "go it alone," you more than likely have never been to Promise Keepers or Women of Faith.

It is crucial that men (and women) come to the understanding that they cannot fight this battle alone. Perhaps you are one...who has fought his (or her) way up the corporate ladder - only to find that you were the only one there when you arrived. If you are a pornography addict, you should consider that by yourself, you managed to crawl all the way to where you are. In the world of pornography use and addiction, the ladder goes down, not up. It goes straight down into a pit that has the ability to totally consume any of us.[226]

No man is an island and no one can walk it alone, we weren't supposed to. Remember the old book, *Real Men Eat Quiche*? From what I remember, it poked fun at the *sensitive* man. I don't know whether real men eat quiche or not (I kinda like it), but I do know that real men and women have the wisdom to recognize their weaknesses and the strength to step out and do what needs to be done — what needs to be done is establishing accountability partners, people who you can share your darkest secrets, shameful weaknesses, and trust to be there. The following are some ideas of what to look for in an accountability partner:

Accountability Partner

What to look for

Someone you respect.

Someone who will keep your confidence.

A friend who will ask you the tough questions and not let you get away with not answering.

Someone who will not judge you.

Someone who is willing to be there for you emotionally and meet with you face-to-face (preferably) or by phone at least once a week.

Someone who will make you a regular part of their prayers.

Someone willing to look past the pain and frustration that typifies the porn addict.

What not to expect

Accountability partners are not there to fix your problems, but to offer support and direction.

Accountability partners will not keep your secret if they have a legal or moral right to report it (child/spouse abuse, suicide threats/attempts, crimes committed, etc.).

Accountability partners are friends, not to be taken advantage of. Don't cross boundaries by borrowing/lending money, etc.

Accountability partners invest a lot of time and energy in the person. Don't violate their love and support by lying to them. If you gave into lust this week, tell them.

Don't ignore their advice. Seriously consider what they say and act upon it.

Remember that this is a *partnership*; you need to be there for them too. Don't get so transfixed on your own needs that you forget the needs of others.

Weekly Accountability Questions[227]

More than 200 years ago (December 25, 1738), John Wesley founded a small group discipleship group and berthed the concept of accountability groups. Wesley had a set list of questions that would be asked of each member each week. The following questions are based on some of the questions they would ask and we need to have asked of ourselves. Many of these questions will be asked in your own daily checklist. That's okay, the more soul-searching being done, the better. It will be easier for you to answer those tough questions asked here if you have already been asking them of yourself.

1. How is your relationship with God right now? Has God been stretching you?
2. What have you read in your Bible this past week? What has God been teaching you?
3. Have you been *enjoying* prayer this week?
4. What specific things are you praying for in regard to yourself? Others?
5. Are you sensing any spiritual attacks from the enemy right now?
6. Are you sleeping well?
7. What are you fearing at this time? What are your current stresses?
8. What specific needs are you praying for in regards to others?

9. What type of recreation have you done for yourself lately?

10. Did you take your day(s) off this week?

11. What areas of lust have you been struggling with lately? How have you been tempted?

12. What negative attitudes have you been fostering/ struggling against?

13. Have you struggled with honesty this week? Lying? Stealing?

14. Did you participate in church this week? Shared your faith?

15. Have you made time for/expressed love to your kids this week?

16. When was the last time you took your spouse out on a date? Bought her/him a card/gift/flowers?

17. If I were to ask your spouse about your state of mind, state of spirit, and energy level, what would they say?

18. Where do you see yourself struggling with God this week?

20. Have you met with your mentor this week?

21. Where are you financially right now?

22. What other personal struggles have you faced this week?

23. Have you been resentful? Proud? Jealous? Complaining? Argumentative?

24. Have you been self-conscious, self-pitying, or self-justifying?

25. Are you consciously or unconsciously creating the impression that you are better than you really are (hypocritical)?

26. Is Christ real in you today?

Available Resources

Internet Accountability Software
COVENANT EYES
Covenant Eyes Program

When people of all ages are on the Internet, there is very little accountability in regards to knowing where, when and how long they have been on the Internet. While filters can provide some help, they can also block acceptable web sites, creating frustration. Filters can also be turned off or bypassed, rendering them ineffective. The Covenant Eyes Program removes the secrecy and privacy of using the Internet. Covenant Eyes promotes self-control and personal discipline, and the individual is held accountable in their Internet use.

Many find that overcoming sin and temptation is virtually impossible on their own. Developing a relationship with another person is the best way of obtaining help. When you sign up for The Covenant Eyes Program, you are asked to provide the names of two "Accountability Partners" (only one is required, but they recommend two). An "Accountability Partner" is simply a person with whom you have an accountable relationship. Ask a friend, spouse, pastor, or counselor to be your partner. Then, on a weekly, bi-weekly, or monthly basis, they will receive an accountability log which will be a record of all of the sites you visited, including the web addresses and amount of time you were on the Internet. This log is e-mailed to your Accountability Partner.

The Covenant Eyes Program is maintained on computers at the corporate headquarters in Corunna, MI. Therefore, the history of sites visited by the member can not be erased (though they can be viewed confidentially over the Internet by the user).

http://www.covenanteyes.com/

Free X3watch Accountability Software

This is a FREE accountability program helping with online integrity. It is offered at no charge by the ministry of XXXchurch.com and it's supporters. Whenever you browse the Internet and access a site which may contain questionable material, the program will save the site name on your computer. Approximately every 2 weeks your accountability partner will receive an email containing all possible questionable sites you may have visited within the month. This information is meant to encourage open and honest conversation between friends and help us all be more accountable. This report only goes to your chosen accountability partners and is not stored or used by XXXchurch or any other organization.

http://www.xxxchurch.com/

Web Filters

True Vine Online

This is a Christian Filtered ISP, which removes all porn at the server before it enters your home.

In most cases this is preferable to the software approach but there are many different providers using a variety of different methods. What happens when a user tries to access a blocked site?

The user will be presented with a screen that says they have been blocked from the site they are trying to visit. At this point the user may request a review if they believe the site blocking was in error. Toll Free: 1-877-878-3846 (1-877-TRUEVINE)

http://truevine.net/filterfaq.html http://www.truevine.net

Netmop

For children *and* parents - members will not be allowed to view known pornographic sites on their Netmop protected computers. Their goal is to not only protect your children, but to protect *you*. It blocks not only web pages but chat rooms, email, news, keywords in search engines, and file sharing. "We clean up dirt wherever it is found." What's more, it is tamper-proof – you cannot circumvent the system. http://www.netmop.com/learn_more.html

Sexual Addictions 12-Step Groups

Sex and Love Addicts Anonymous: SLAA National Organization: 781-255-8825; P.O. Box 11910, Norwood, MA 02062-0338; www.slaafws.org

Sexaholics Anonymous: SAA International Central Office: 615-331-6230, fax: 615-331-6901; P.O. Box 111910, Nashville, TN 37222; www.sa.org

Sex Addicts Anonymous: SAA International Service Organization: 713-869-4902; P.O. Box 70949, Houston, TX 77270; www.sexaa.org

Sexual Recovery Anonymous: SRA National Organization: 212-340-4650; P.O. Box 73,Planetarium Station, New York, NY 10024. SRA in Canada: 604-290-9382; P.O. Box 72044, Bumaby, BC V5H4PQ; www.sexualrecovery.org

Treatment Facilities for Clergy:

Bethesda Workshops, Marnie Ferree 615-269-6220
Intensive workshops offered for sexual addiction recovery.

Encouraging sexual wholeness by ministering to those damaged by sexual abuse, sin and addiction. Healing for male and female sexual addicts and spouses. 3710 Franklin Road Nashville, TN 37204
www.bethesdaworkshops.org mferree@whcm.net

Fairhaven Ministries 423-772-4269
Fairhaven offers the opportunity to combine a mountain retreat vacation with the time to explore personal and professional needs. We provide privacy, confidentiality and our commitment to sound Biblical and psychological principles. 2198 Roaring Creek Road Roan Mountain, TN 37687 http://www.fairhaven1.com fhmin@aol.com

Gray Fox Ranch, Dr. Walter Becker 800-336-4405
Christian counseling Retreat designed for individuals and couples in ministry with Walter Becker, Ph.D. and Francoise Becker, M.S. PO Box 434 Alto, NM 88312
http://www.grayfox.org Waltbecker@aol.com

Guest House 810-391-4445
Dedicated to caring for Catholic priests, deacons, brothers, seminarians and women religious suffering from alcoholism, other chemical dependencies and related problems.
PO Box 420 Lake Orion, MI 48361 ghouse@ic.net

Kettering Clergy Care Center, Dr. Robert Peach, Director 800-324-8618
Professional care and support to full-time workers in ministry. Provides counseling, crisis intervention weekend, burnout prevention, marriage enrichment and a two-week training and renewal experience. 1259 E Dorothy Lane Kettering, OH 45419
http://www.ketthealth.com/clergycare

Landing, The, Dave Tarpley 501-225-7255
Brief and intensive (up to 12 days) counseling for pastors, missionaries and their spouses. Crisis and growth oriented counseling for couples and individuals. The director is a former missionary with extensive clinical training. P.O. Box 56556 Little Rock, AK 72215 dbt88@aol.com

Leadership Center, The, David Morgan, Director 603-569-3922
Facilities, staff and environment that provide encouragement to those

in ministry, with focus on pastor/spouse relationships. 112 Lakeview Terrace Wolfeboro, NH 03894

Marble Retreat, Dr. Louis McBurney 970-963-2499, 888-216-2725
Two week intensives limited to clergy and other religious professionals. 139 Bannockburn Marble, CO 81623 http://www.marbleretreat.org/ 72040.1367@compuserve.com

Meadows, The 1-800-MEADOWS
An addiction treatment center with extensive experience in treatment of sexually addicted clergy. 1655 N Tegner St Wickenburg, AZ 85390 http://www.themeadows.org/

Ministry Renewal Center, Joanne Oppelt, M.H.A. 888-299-6732
We offer a continuum of services including Two-Week Intensive Counseling Retreats and Clergy and Family Counseling. One unique aspect of our program is our affiliation with Ramapo Ridge Psychiatric Hospital, where clergy can access care in the safety and intensity of a hospital environment from anywhere around the country (depending on clinical and logistical considerations). 3 Sicomac Road Suite 301 North Haledon, NJ 07508 http://www.ministryrenewal.com info@ministryrenewal.com

New Life Clinics 800-522-5174
The services of New Life Clinics includes assessment and evaluation, inpatient, outpatient, day hospital, eating disorder treatment, alcohol & drug rehabilitation, and Christian resources. The 800 number above is for the personal and professional needs of ministers. They have 80 clinics in the USA and Canada. 820 W. Spring Creek Parkway Plano, TX 75023 http://www.newlife.com

Psychological Counseling Services, Ltd., Dr. Ralph Earle, Marilyn Murray, et. al.
The PCS offers short term, customized outpatient therapy for individuals and couples. They also maintain the New Hope Foundation offering a safe, therapeutic setting where psychological and spiritual healing from inappropriate and destructive behaviors can be attained. Sexual recovery is one of their specialties. 7530 E. Angus Drive Scottsdale, Arizona 85251 Phone: 602-947-5739

RAPHA 800-383-4673

In patient and out patient professional treatment for clergy and others. They have affiliate locations throughout the USA. 8876 Gulf Freeway, Suite 340 Houston, TX 77017 http://rapha-hope.com

Saint Louis Behavioral Medicine Institute, Paul N. Duckro, Ph.D. 314-534-0200

The Program for Psychology and Religion provides an intensive outpatient program (2-6 months) for clergy and religious. Specializations include programs for sexual boundary violators and addictions. 1129 Macklind St. Louis, MO 63110

St. John Vianney Hospital 610-269-2600

A treatment and education center sponsored by the Catholic Archdiocese of Philadelphia. Offers spiritually based, holistic, professional care for religious and clergy from many denominations. Has a specialized program for men with a history of violating personal and professional boundaries. 151 Woodbine Rd. Downingtown, PA 19335-3057

Stonegate Resources, Harry W. Schaumburg

Dr. Schaumburg offers retreats and intensives for Pastors. His specialty is sexual misconduct and sexual addiction. He has written a book on the subject titled, "False Intimacy". P.O. Box 26015 Colorado Springs, CO 80936

Tuscarora Resource Center, Dr. Timothy Boyd, Executive Director 717-897-6077 A residentially-based, short-term facility that offers intensive psychological, pastoral and consultation services. 870 Sunrise Blvd Mt. Bethel, PA 18343

http://tuscarora.org/trc/first.htm

Wounded Brothers Project, The: RECON 314-285-1733

The RECON program provides long-term residential treatment for Catholic clergy and religious in recovery from ministry limiting circumstances. PO Box 220 Dittmer, MO 63023

Other Inpatient/Residential Treatment Facilities

Del Amo Hospital (Torrance, CA) 1 800 533-5266
De Amo has both a Sexual Addictions program as well as a Trauma/Dissociative Disorders program. They also accept clients on Medicare disability.

Keystone Extended Care Unit (Chester, PA) 1-800-733-6840
Keystone is a residential unit specializing in sexual addiction treatment in both men and women.

Sante Center (Argyle, TX) 1-800-258-4250
Sante Center is a residential unit that deals with addictions to alcohol, drugs, eating disorders, sexual addictions, and trauma recovery.

Sierra Tucson (Tucson, AZ)
Sierra has a 4-week multi-addiction program, including a track dealing with sexual trauma and eating disorders.

Other Available Resources

Arizona Counseling, sex addiction - Psychological Counseling Services (Scottsdale, AZ) Psychological Counseling Services, Ltd. is a group practice specializing in intensive outpatient treatment. http://www.pcsearle.com

Bay Area Sex Addiction & Compulsion Site (San Francisco)
Specializing in sexual addiction issues, resources, and a listing of therapists in the San Francisco Bay Area. http://www.sexaddicthelp.com

Breaking Pornography Addiction
A personal guide to overcoming pornography addiction. Some helpful suggestions for recovery. http://www.no-porn.com

Christians in Recovery, Inc. (Tequesta, FL)
A group of recovering Christians dedicated to personal one-on-one sharing of faith, strength and hope through each day in recovery. http://www.christians-in-recovery.com

Clergy Recovery Network (Joplin, MT)
Mentoring Ministry Professionals Through Personal Crisis and Early
Recovery Email: dalew@clergyrecovery.com

Counseling For Sexual Addicts (Pittsburgh, PA)
COUNSELING FOR SEXUAL ADDICTS Private, confidential,
Christian counseling in the Pittsburgh area. http://www.city-
net.com/~impavido

Cybersex Addiction Help Site
CybersexualAddiction.com is a resource and referral information site
for people seeking help with cybersex addiction or compulsive computer-
based sexual activity and cyber-infidelity problems. http://
www.cybersexualaddiction.com

Fires of Darkness
Reaching out to pornography addicts and the people who love them.
Forums and other resources for porn and sex addicts. http://
www.firesofdarkness.com

Free In Christ
FREE IN CHRIST is a group for men who wish to become free from
all sexual sin, pornography in particular. http://freeinchrist.truepath.com

KAVOD Recovery
KAVOD is an outpatient program for people with sexual addictions
and compulsions. http://www.kavodrecovery.com

Life Strategies Christian Counseling - (Memphis, TN)
Life Strategies Christian Counseling Center Helps. Men Struggling
With Sexual Addiction Workshop Topics: *Sexual Addiction Is There
Hope*? http://www.life-strategies.org

NCSAC Home Page
NATIONAL COUNCIL ON SEXUAL ADDICTION AND
COMPULSIVITY. The National Council on Sexual Addiction and
Compulsivity is a Sex Addiction WebRing Site. http://www.ncsac.org

NewHeartBooks.com
Books and other recovery resources for people whose lives have been negatively impacted by addictions to pornography or sex. http://www.newheartbooks.com

Porn-Free.org
Help and hope for people affected by sex addiction. From a Christian perspective, site provides info, prayer, and more… http://www.porn-free.org

Pure Restoration: Purity Workshop for Men
The Pure Restoration workshop helps men of all ages better understand and recover from pornography addiction (including Internet pornography) and other forms of infidelity. http://www.purerestoration.com

S-Anon International Family Groups
Twelve step program for the families of sex addicts. http://www.sanon.org

Setting Captives Free - sex addiction, recovery from pornography addiction!
Free online, interactive 60 Day course to find freedom from pornography and sexual addiction. Lose the guilt, the shame, and the habit. http://www.settingcaptivesfree.com

Sex Addiction Recovery Resources
SEX ADDICTION RECOVERY RESOURCES: provides telephone counseling with national sex addiction expert Douglas Weiss Ph.D. as well as the leading books and videos in the field of sex addiction to date. http://www.sexaddict.com

SexHelp.com - Dr. Carnes' Online Resources for Sex Addiction & Recovery
SexHelp.com offers addiction and recovery resources from international sex addiction expert Patrick Carnes, Ph.D. http://www.sexhelp.com

Sexual Recovery Institute - (Los Angeles)
The Sexual Recovery Institute has offices in LA and Orange County. Outpatient treatment of men or women engaged in compulsive sexual behaviors. http://www.sexualrecovery.com

The Official COSA NSO Website
For friends and family members whose lives have been affected by another person's compulsive sexual behavior. http://www.cosa-recovery.org

Understanding Sexual Addiction
A confidential site for identifying, treating and understanding Sex and Love Addiction. http://www.understandingsexualaddiction.org

Retreat Centers for Clergy

Come away with me by yourselves to a quiet place and get some rest.

Mark 6:31

The following sites provide a place of refuge for pastors and (in some cases) their families free of charge or discounted rates.

Fairhaven Ministries Phone: 423-772-4269 FAX: 423-772-0017
Located in the beautiful Blue Ridge Mountains of East Tennessee. Retreat and Counseling Center. Lovely individual chalets and cottages are situated on 100 acres surrounded by US Forest Service land. Reduced rates available to full time ministry personnel or missionaries. 2198 Roaring Creek Road, Roan Mountain TN 37687 fhmin@aol.com www.fairhaven1.com/index.html

Faith Mountain Phone and Fax: (304) 364.4019
Located in the Central Lakes Region of West Virginia. Faith Mountain is an inter-denominational retreat ministry consisting of 250 beautiful wooded acres, a newly built four-bedroom cabin and three newly built two-bedroom guest cottages. Special rates are available for full time Christian workers, as well as a scholarship fund for full-time Christian workers with limited funds and an immediate need for a get away or counseling. Contact Herb or Kathy Miller at Faith Mountain - HC 73 Box 18 C, Rosedale, WV 26636 faithmtn@mountain.net www.faithmountain.org/

Hidden Hollow Retreat Center (704) 392-7594
In the heart of the Mountains of North Carolina near Wilkesboro. An

affordable haven where personal ministry, retreat, renewed vision and quiet meditation would be the agenda of the day. The 50 mile views are breathtaking (located on a mountain top). Rates start at $45 per night for an apartment all to yourself.

Info@RetreatCabin.com www.retreatcabin.com

Methow Valley Ranch Ministries Phone: (509) 996-3635 Fax: (509) 996-3578
Located in north central Washington State near Winthrop and Lake Pearrygin State Park. The ranch is set in 60 acres of rolling pasture and wetlands, ideal for walks and quiet meditation. As an expression of faith in God's provision, there is no charge for guests to use the facilities. Free will offerings and gifts toward upkeep and expenses are gratefully accepted. blakeney@methow.com, info@mvministries.com, www.mvministries.com

Rancho de la Paz Phone: (909) 245-4082
Located in the rural high desert of Southern California Rancho de la Paz is a place for ministers and missionaries in need of shelter and counseling. Self-serve kitchen is available. Air conditioned. This is a faith ministry with a recommended donation. P.O. Box 1388, Lake Elsinore, CA 92532 USA, admin@across2u.com www.across2u.com/rancho.html

Allison Ranch Ministries Foundation 208-377-3005.
Located on the beautiful Salmon River deep in Idaho's Wilderness. Private Spiritual Retreat for God's Servants. THE TOTAL COST FOR YOUR FAMILY'S 4 DAY STAY IS $200. thomasfoundation@juno.com http://replace.com/allison

Marble Retreat 1-888-216-2725
Located on the River near Marble, CO. This peaceful refuge in the Rockies has been set aside for solace, healing and gentle restoration. It is an interdenominational psychotherapy center serving Christian ministers in crisis that offers a blend of spiritual and emotional approaches to touch the whole person. Scholarships may be available to certain areas of ministry.

139 Bannockburn, Marble, Colorado 8162
MinistryCare@marbleretreat.org.

www.marbleretreat.org/

Mountain Top Retreat 1-406-763-4566 Located south of Bozeman, Montana bordering the Gallatin National Forest, retreat has six houses available. Numerous paths and open space. Pastors and full time Christian workers are offered a $15 per day discount off daily rates. Mountain Top Retreat, 13705 Cottonwood Canyon Road, Bozeman, MT 59718 info@mountaintopretreat.org www.mountaintopretreat.org/

Rancho Mira Sol (815) 858-2435 Fax: (815) 858-2270
Locations: Triple Creek Ranch in northwestern IL and Rancho Mira Sol inSouthwest CO. Their ministry in two distinct locations provides vacation homes for full-time evangelical pastors and missionaries and their families. Their goal is to provide a place of refreshment and relaxation for those who are in so much need of rest. All reservations handled in Illinois. 348 N. Snipe Hollow Rd., Elizabeth, IL 61028 info@triplecreekranch.org www.triplecreekranch.org/

Windmill Meadow Ranch (719) 687-5072, 1-(877) 434-2224
Located in Red Rocks Valley, Pike National Forest, near Woodland Park, Colorado. This 50 acre ranch is nested in a unique meadow valley surrounded by the Rocky Mountains of Pike National Forest. Bed & Breakfast cabin getaway. Contact them directly for current prices and specials for missionaries, Christian workers on support and pastors. 28556 Highway 67, Woodland Park, CO, 80863 Ranch carolyn@operatorservices.com Gary@Global-D.BIZ www.ranchbnb.com

Country Place (336) 786-6857
Provides a comfortable two-bedroom, country cabin in a quiet, rural setting or rest, renewal and reflection to ministers and their families (on a donation basis). 2079 S. Main St. Mt. Airy, NC 27030 darscruggs@surry.net www.countryplaceretreat.org

Genesee Home (530) 284-1082, (530) 284-1083
A safe haven where pastors and their spouses can rediscover the rest God designed for them, be refreshed in a peaceful setting, rekindle their relationship with each other and renew their pastoral hearts 7202 Genesee Road Taylorsville, CA 95983 ghinforequest@geneseehome.org-www.geneseehome.org

188

Hidden Manna Christian Retreat Center (936) 291-7401
A place for those in full-time Christian ministry to find a haven of peace,strengthen their marriages and find freedom from the pas. 35A Hidden Manna New Waverly, TX 77358 (936) 295-9413 info@hiddenmanna.org www.hiddenmanna.org

The Leadership Center (603) 569-4773
Strengthening and encouraging couples in full-time ministry by providing an environment of grace and rest. Offers a four-day pastors and wives retreat twice a year. P.O. Box 2009 Wolfeboro, NH 03894 (603) 569-4004 info@tlcretreats.org www.tlcretreats.org

The Lodge (Life Action Ministries) (269) 695-2474
Helps pastors and spouses refocus on the core issues in their personal, family and ministry lives by creating an environment where they can meet with God and hear His heart and voice, leading them to personal renewal, revival and restoration. P.O. Box 151 Buchanan, MI 49107 (877) 775-6343 info@RetreatAtTheLodge.org www.RetreatAtTheLodge.org

Mountain Top Retreat (406) 763-4566
A quiet, private mountain setting for pastors, vocational Christian workers and their families to find rest and renewal. Light counseling provided. 13705 Cottonwood Canyon Road Bozeman, MT 59718 mtroffice@mcn.net www.mountaintopretreat.org

The Rekindling (505) 286-6111, (505) 286-6111
An ideal setting to gain a fresh perspective, whether "on fire" and just needing a place away from the distractions of daily life and ministry, or "burned out" by the demands and expectations of others. 136 Gonzales Rd. Edgewood, NM 87015 dalton@onfireorburnedout.com www.therekindling.com or www.onfireorburnedout.org

Rock of Refuge Hospitality Ministry (303) 816-2680, (303) 816-2681
A private suite in a log home located in the beautiful Rocky Mountains that provides peace, relaxation, refuge, and supportive counseling by a professional Christian counselor for the purpose of ministering to pastors, missionaries, and Christian laborers who are wounded and weary of soul. 717 Rim Rock Road Bailey, CO 80421 billmarla_kelly@yahoo.com

Standing Stone Ranch (970) 264-9329, (800) 280-0073, (970) 264-9329
Provides pastors, missionaries, Christian leaders and their spouses a peaceful experience to help them lead effective lives as they establish a relationship of trust and support with the hosts. P.O. 145 Chromo, CO 81128 jdhogan@standingstoneranch.org www.standingstoneranch.org

Timber Bay Camp and Retreat Center (320) 532-3200, (320) 532-3199
Provides an environment for rest, renewal and refocus for people in ministry who are overextended in their ministry and personal lives. Light counseling to help refocus is available upon request. 18955 Woodland Road Onamia, MN 56359 tbcamp@timberbay.org www.timberbay.org

Pastors Retreat Network "Strengthening Pastors for Spiritual Revival"

We invite you into the presence of God through carefully selected retreat locations. Upscale bed and breakfast style facilities. The Pastors Retreat Network exists to enrich the lives and ministry of individuals and couples engaged in fulltime pastoral Christian ministry. No Fees, No Agenda, No Schedule, Just time with Him. Cedarly Pastors Retreat (Delafield, WI), Texas Stagecoach Inn (Vanderpool, TX), Valley View Inn (New Bedford, OH). http://www.pastorsretreatnetwork.org

Anchor Missionary and Pastor's Retreat (417) 739-9017, (417) 739-9017
Provides accommodations along with an understanding and listening ear. 170 Deckard Lane Kimberling City, MO 65686 drhlgoodman@tri-lakes.net www.anchor-retreat.org

Beulah Beach Corp. (440) 967-4861, Fax: (440) 967-4783
A place where pastors and their families can be refreshed, restored and revived in the presence of God. Located on the beautiful shores of Lake Erie. 6101 West Lake Road Vermilion, OH 44089 registrations@beulahbeach.org www.beulahbeach.org

Camp Berachah Ministries (253) 939-0488, (253) 833-7027
Offers personal retreat time for pastors, their families and others in full-time Christian ministry. Facilities also available for church planning. Recreation available, as well as space for personal quiet time. 19830 SE 328th Place Auburn, WA 98092 staff@berachahcamp.org www.berachahcamp.org

Camp Victory (334) 898-7948, (334) 898-7947
Offering retreat facilities for pastors, missionaries and their families
"where memories are made where lives are changed" 363 Victory Circle
Samson, AL 36477 campvictory@alaweb.com www.campvictoryal.org

The Carriage House (303) 838-0183
A retreat for pastors nestled in the Rocky Mountains on the North Fork
of the South Platte River in Shawnee, Colorado. Available September
through May only. P.O. Box 115 Shawnee, CO 80475

Diamond T Ranch (970) 663-4183, (970) 663-4183
Provides affordable, comfortable and restful accommodations with
Christian hospitality in a beautiful guest ranch setting for the general
public, but particularly for pastors and missionaries at a greatly reduced
cost. 5361 River Road Clark Fork, ID 83811 TBWagoner@juno.com
www.diamondtranch.com

Eagle Mountain Lodge (505) 377-3682, (505) 377-1390
A luxury mountain retreat specifically designed to provide "rest and
restoration" for Christian ministers and missionaries. Lodge open from
May15 to October 31. HC 71 Box 23 A Eagle Nest, NM 87718
eaglemnt@afweb.com www.eaglemountainlodge.com

Faith Mountain Ministries, Inc. (304) 364-4019, (304) 364-5638
Two-bedroom cottages on 250 beautiful, wooded acres in the
Mountain Lakes region of West Virginia provide an ideal setting for
Christian leaders to experience rest, relaxation and spiritual renewal.
HC 73 Box 18 C Rosedale, WV 26636 faithmtn@mountain.net
www.faithmountain.org

Harvest Prayer Center (812) 443-5703, (812) 443-5505
A nondenominational ministry providing a place for ministers,
missionaries andChristian leaders and their families to come for
relaxation, prayer and spiritual renewal. 11991 E. Davis Avenue Brazil,
IN 47834 prayercenter@harvestprayer.com www.harvestprayer.com

Hidden Hollow Retreat Center (704) 392-7594
A retreat center in the foothills of the Blue Ridge Mountains set aside
specifically for pastors and those in Christian ministry who want to spend

time alone with God. 6800 Tuckaseegee Rd. Charlotte, NC 28214
info@retreatcabin.com www.retreatcabin.com

The Hosanna Way Station Christian Retreat Center (509) 775-2967
*A place free of charge where overworked and underpaid shepherds
can come to find "refuge under His wings" and spend time with their
families.* 8 Hosanna Way Republic, WA 9916 hosanna@cuonlinenow.com

LakeView Heights Way (660) 668-2051, (660) 668-4350
*A quiet, secluded, private suite with kitchenette for a single pastor or a
pastoral couple to get away for rest and spiritual renewal.* RR 2, Box 230-
G Lincoln, MO 65338 bsiebert@iland.net

Makahiki Ministries (209) 966-2988, (209) 966-2988
*A network of hospitality homes in the U.S. and abroad for Christian
workers seeking spiritual and physical renewal.* P.O. Box 415 Mariposa,
CA 95338 makahiki@sti.net www.hospitalityhomes.org

The Marie House (308) 269-2015, (308) 269-2106
*Provides comfortable accommodations to pastoral couples or families
in a private, non-structured setting, giving them opportunity for rest,
renewal and reflection.* 202 Broadway, P.O. Box 193 Naponee, NE 68960-
0193 duanlauber@gtmc.net

Painted Pony Inn (208) 286-0225
*Offers a place of solitude, spiritual guidance and ministry
encouragement* 6926 Highway 44 Star, ID 83669
innkeeper@paintedponyinn.com www.paintedponyinn.com

Pastors Retreat Network (888) 622-3809, (262) 646-7773
*Five-day retreats in secluded locations across the country that provide
an environment for prayer, reflection and fellowship to refocus one's
commitment and relationship to God and spouse. Self-directed programs;
no counseling* P.O. Box 180455 Delafield, WI 53018m
info@pastorsretreatnetwork.org www.pastorsretreatnetwork.org

Peaceful Mountain (800) 893-3695
A comfortable, quiet place to rest, reflect and gather one's wits

175 CR 1270 Kopperl, TX 76652 michaelpoteet@peacefulmountain.org
www.peacefulmountain.org

Railroad House of Prayer (618) 327-4292
A quiet place for an individual to get alone with God. 687 East Maple
Nashville, IL 62263

The Retreat (208) 623-4402, (208) 623-4402
*A place where pastors, missionaries and their families can spend
time alone with the Lord for rest, relaxation and spiritual renewal in
an isolated, peaceful forest setting.* 29961 N. Highway 41 Spirit Lake,
ID 83869

Serenity's Promise (719) 487-1221, (719) 487-1222
*A quiet hospitality haven nestled in the woods where pastors,
missionaries or full-time Christian workers and their spouses may come to
fortify their souls* 1207 Carnahan Court Monument, CO 80132-1222
sherryllp@msn.com www.serenitys-promise.org

Shining Mountain Ranch (719) 783-2627
*Guest houses in a mountain setting of scenic beauty and quiet are
provided for pastors and church workers and their families* P.O. Box 926
Westcliffe, CO 81252

Triple Creek Ranch (Illinois) & Rancho Mira Sol (Colorado)
*Private vacation homes on ranches in Illinois and Colorado are
provided free of charge to full-time evangelical Christian pastors and
missionaries and their families. Please contact ministry coordinators for
more information.*
348 N. Snipe Hollow Road Elizabeth, IL 61028 (815) 858-2435,
(815) 858-2270 info@triplecreekranch.org www.triplecreekranch.org

Beside Still Waters (877) 608-0999, FAX 941-744-9755
A ministry that wishes to bless God's servants from all areas of the
globe, by providing, free of charge, a place of rest, restoration and refocus.
The ministry is coordinated under the umbrella of Manatee Religious
Services, Inc., a Love INC, affiliate, located in Bradenton, Florida.
Manatee Religious Services 3111 29th Avenue East Bradenton, FL 34208
app@beside-stillwaters.org

Nehemiah Ministries

Situated on 130 acres, nestled on the Maple River Valley, 5 miles south of Owosso, MI. Gently rolling terrain surrounds 40 acres of woods; a pond is well stocked with fish and also provides a wonderful summertime play/swimming area. Trails, both completed and under development, wind their way through the wood and along the river, providing tranquil places for private time and nature walks. A beautiful outdoor gazebo seats over 25 people and is used for quiet reflection and group meetings. Nehemiah Ministries, Inc. P.O. Box 397 Owosso, MI 48867 dehaas@michonline.net

Bibliography

a'Kempis, Thomas. *The Imitation of Christ*, trans. L. Sherley-Price. Harmondsworth: Penguin, 1952.

Amandus, Jim. "A Wounded Pastor's Rescue." *Leadership,* Winter 1993.

"The American Institute for Cognitive Therapy – Problems Addressed" http://www.cognitivetherapynyc.com/problemsaddresses.html

Anonymous. "Flirting Was a Real High for Me," in *Member Stories,* vol. 1, 2001. Nashville: Sexaholics Anonymous Incorporated.

_____. *From Shame to Grace: Stories of Recovery from Sex Addicts Anonymous.* Nashville: SA Literature, 1994.

_____. *Sexaholics Anonymous.* Nashville: SA Literature, 1989-2002.

Armstrong, John, H. *Can Fallen Pastors be Restored? The Church's Response to Clergy Misconduct.* Chicago: Moody Press, 1995.

Arterburn, Steven. 2003. "Marks of Addictive Sex," [journal on-line]; available from   http://www.pureintimacy.org/online1/essays/ a0000003.html

Arterburn, Steven. 2003. "Ten Steps to Overcoming Pornography Addiction," [journal on-line]; available from http:/www.pureintimacy.org/online1/essays/a0000003.html

Arterburn, Steven, Stoeker, Fred, Yorkey, Mike, *Preparing Your Son for Every Man's Battle: Honest Conversations about Sexual Integrity.* Colorado Springs: Waterbrook Press, 2003.

Avis, Paul. *Eros and the Sacred.* Harrisburg, PA: Morehouse Publishing, 1989.

Bagster, London, S. *The Analytical Greek Lexicon.* Grand Rapids: Zondervan Publishing House, 1967.

Banks, S., *A Manual of Christian Doctrine.* New York: Eaton and Mains Publishers, 1897.

Barna, George. *Today's Pastors.* Ventura, CA: Regal Books, 1993.

Barna Research Ltd., "Church Attendance" March 1, 2004 www.barna.org/lcgi-bin/Home.asp.

Bartram, Ann. "A Response to Pastor-Client Sexual Relations," in *Pastoral Care and Liberation Praxis,* ed. Perry LeFevre and W. Widdick Schroeder (Chicago: Exploration Press, 1996.

Jeanette Batz, Jeanette. "Strung Out On Sex." *The St. Louis Riverfront Times*, 23 June, 1998.

Beattie, Melody. *Beyond Codependency.* San Francisco: Harper/ Hazelden, 1989.

Benyei, Candace. R., *Understanding Clergy Misconduct in Religious Systems.* New York: The Haworth Press, Inc. 1998.

Berkley, James, D. *Making the Most of Mistakes.* Carol Stream, IL: Word Books, 1987.

Birch, George, A., *The Deliverance Ministry.* Camp Hill, PA: Horizon House Publishers, 1988.

David C. Bissette, David, C. "The Nature of Recovery," 1996 http://www.healthymind.com/s-theory.html

Broadbooks, Bob. *From Pastor to Pastor: Letters of Encouragement and Wisdom.* Kansas City: Beacon Hill Press, 2003.

Boardman, Henry, A. *The Scripture Doctrine of Original Sin Explained and Enforced.* Philadelphia: William S. Martien, 1839.

Bonhoeffer, Dietrich. *The Cost of Discipleship,* revised ed. New York: Collier Books,1963.

Bromily, G.W. *International Standard Bible Encyclopedia,* vol. 1. Grand Rapids:William B Eerdmans Publishing Co., 1988.

Budziszewski, J. *Virtual Unfaithfulness: Pornography Use in a Marriage.* Copyright 2000 J. Budziszewski 7/22/03

Burns, David, D. *The Feeling Good Handbook, Revised Edition.* New York: Plume, a member of Penguin Putnam, Inc., 1999.

Carnes, Patrick, J. *Don't Call it Love.* New York: Bantam, 1991.

Chaudhuri, Haridas. "Wisdom in Human Relations" ed. Scott Miners, A *Spiritual Approach to Male/Female Relations.* Wheaton: The Theosophical Publishing House, 1984.

Cloud, Henry, John Townsend. *Boundaries.* Grand Rapids: Zondervan Publishing, 1993.

Coate, Mary Ann. *Clergy Stress: The Hidden Conflicts in Ministry.* London: SPCK Holy Trinity Church, 1989.

Cochini, Christian, S.J. *Apostolic Origins of Priestly Celibacy,* trans. Nelly Marans. San Francisco: Ignatius Press, 1990.

Curtis Brent, Eldridge, John. "Behind Sex Addiction is a Hunger for God." [journal on-line]; available from http://www.pureintimacy.org/online1/essays/a0000005.html.

Douglas, J.D., ed. *New Bible Dictionary,* 3d ed. Downers Grove, IL: Inter-Varsity Press, 1962.

Earle, Ralph. "Overcoming Sexual Addiction." [cassette] (Colorado Springs: Focus on the Family, 2001).

Earl, Ralph, Laaser, Mark. *The Pornography Trap.* Kansas City: Beacon Hill Press, 2002.

Ecclestone, Alen. *Yes to God.* London: Darton, Longman and Todd, 1975.

Evans, Donald. *Struggle and Fulfillment.* London: Collins, 1980.

Farber, Leslie, H. "Sex in Bondage to Modern Will: 'I'm Sorry Dear'" ed. David Holbrook, *The Case Against Pornography.* LaSalle, Ill: Library Press Book, 1972.

Field, David, H. *Baker Encyclopedia of the Bible,* gen. ed. Walter A. Elwell. Grand Rapids: Baker Books, 1988.

Final Report of the Attorney General's Commission on Pornography. Nashville: Rutledge Hill Press, 1986.

Freedman, David, Noel, ed. *The Anchor Bible Dictionary* vol. 2. New York: Doubleday, 1992.

Frymer-Kensky, Tikva. *The Anchor Bible Dictionary,* vol. 5. New York: Doubleday, 1992.

Garber, P.L. *The International Standard Bible Encyclopedia,* vol. 2. Grand Rapids: William B. Eerdmans Publishing, 1982.

Good, E.M. *The Interpreter's Dictionary of the Bible: An Illustrated*

Encyclopedia, vol. 3, ed., George Arthur Buttrick. Nashville: Abingdon Press, 1962.

Grenz Stanley, J., Roy D. Bell. *Betrayal of Trust: Confronting and Preventing Clergy Sexual Misconduct.* Grand Rapids, MI: Baker Books, 1995.

Grider, Kenneth, J. "A Wesleyan Holiness Theology." Kansas City: Beacon Hill Press, 1994.

Handley, Paul and others. *The English Spirit: The Little Gidding Anthology of English Spirituality.* Nashville: Abingdon Press, 1987.

Hands Donald, R., Fehr, Way, L. *Spiritual Wholeness for Clergy.* New York: The Alban Institute, 1993.

Hanson, Paul, D. *Interpretation: A Bible Commentary for Teaching and Preaching. Isaiah 40-66.* Louisville, KY: John Knox Press, 1995.

Harvey Donald, Gene Williams. *Living in a Glass House: Surviving the Scrutiny of Ministry and Marriage.* Kansas City: Beacon Hill Press, 2002.

Hayford, Jack, W. *Restoring Fallen Leaders.* Ventura, CA: Regal Books, 1988.

Hayman, A.P. *Evangelical Dictionary of Biblical Theology*, ed. Walter A. Elwell. Grand Rapids: Baker Book, 1996.

Holbrook, David. "The Pollution of Culture: Pornography and Philosophical Anthropology." *The Case Against Pornography.* ed. David Holbrook. LaSalle, Ill: Library Press Book, 1972.

Hopkins, Julie, M., *Towards a Feminist Christology.* Grand Rapids: William B. Eerdmans Publishing Co., 1994.

Hopkins, Nancy, Myer. *The Congregational Response to Clergy Betrayals of Trust.* Collegeville, MN: The Liturgical Press, 1998.

"How Pure Must a Pastor Be?" *Leadership*, Spring 1988.

Jackson, Walter, C. *Codependence and the Christian Faith.* Nashville: Broadman Press, 1990.

Johnson, T.F. *The International Standard Bible Encyclopedia*, Vol. 4. gen. ed. Geoffrey W. Bromily. Grand Rapids: William B. Eerdmans Publishing, 1988.

Joy, Donald. *Unfinished Business: How a Man Can Make Peace With His Past.* Wheaton, IL: Victor Books, 1989.

Jud, Gerald, J. and others. *Ex-Pastors: Why Men Leave the Parish Ministry.* Philadelphia: Pilgrim Press, 1970.

Kantzer, Kenneth. "The Road to Restoration." *Christianity Today,* 20 November, 1987.

Khan, Masund, R. "Pornography and the Politics of Anger and Subversion." David Holbrook, ed, *The case Against Pornography.* LaSalle, Ill: Library Press Book, 1972).

Kushel, Casi. "Sexuality: A Consideration of Context." in *A Spiritual Approach to Male/Female Relations.* ed. Scott Miners. Wheaton: The Theosophical Publishing House, 1984.

Laaser, Mark and Nils Friberg. *Before the Fall: Preventing Pastoral Sexual Abuse.* Collegeville, MN: Liturgical Press, 1998.

Laaser, Mark. "Recovery for Couples" *Clinical Management of Sex Addiction.* eds.

Patrick J. Carnes and Kenneth M. Adams. New York: Brunner-Rutledge, 2002.

Lane, William L. *Word Biblical Commentary*, Vol. 47a: Hebrew 1-8. Dallas: Word Books, 1991.

Larson, Craig, ed. *Illustrations for Preaching and Teaching.* Grand Rapids: Baker Books, 1993.

Lewis, C.S. *The Problem of Pain.* London: Geoffrey Bles, 1952.

London, H. B. and Neil B. Wiseman. *Pastors at Risk.* Wheaton, IL: Victor Books, 1993.

Your Pastor is an Endangered Species. Wheaton, IL: Victor Books, 1996.

Lowe, Walter, *Evil and the Unconscious.* Chico, CA: Scholars Press, 1983.

Lowen, Alexander. *Narcissism: Denial of the True Self.* New York: Collier Books, 1985.

Luck, Kenny. "Hazardous Material: The Pitfalls of Handling the Pornography Problem with Kid Gloves." *Christian Camp and Conference Journal* March/April 2003, vol.7 – no. 3

Lundberg, Marilyn, J. *Eerdman's Dictionary of the Bible.* ed. David Noel Freedman. Grand Rapids: William B. Eerdmans Publishing Company, 2000.

MacDonald, Gordon, *Rebuilding Your Broken World.* Nashville: Thomas Nelson Publishers, 1988.

Mayes, James, L., ed. *The HarperCollins Bible Commentary.* New York: HarperCollins Publishers, 1988.

McIntosh, Gary, L., Rima, Samuel, D., Sr. *Overcoming the Dark Side of Leadership: The Paradox of Personal Dysfunction.* Grand Rapids: Baker Books, 1997.

Millon, Theodore. *Disorders of Personality.* New York: John Wiley and Sons, 1981.

Moon, Gary. *Homesick for Eden: A Soul's Journey to Joy.* Ann Arbor, MI: ServantPublications, 1997.

Moore, Beth. *Praying God's Word: Breaking Free from Spiritual Strongholds.* Nashville: Broadman and Holman Publishers, 2000.

Moore, Beth. *When Godly People Do Ungodly Things.* Nashville: Broadman and Holman Publishers, 2002.

Moore, Thomas. *Care of the Soul: A Guide for Cultivating Depth and Sacredness in Everyday Life.* New York: Harper Perennial, 1992.

Mulholland, Robert, M., Jr. *Invitation to a Journey: A Road Map for Spiritual Formation.* Downers Grove, IL: InterVaristy Press, 1993.

Muck, Terry, ed. *Sins of the Body.* Dallas: Word Publishing, 1989.

Nakken, Craig. *The Addictive Personality,* 2d ed. Center City, Minnesota: Hazelden, 1996.

Nay, Robert, W. *Taking Charge of Anger.* New York: The Guilford Press, 2004.

Nelson, James. *Body Theology.* Louisville, KY: Westminster Press, 1992.

Norton, W.W. "Man's Search for Himself" 1953 ed. David Holbrook. *The Case Against Pornography.* LaSalle, Ill: Library Press Book, 1972.

Odelain, O., R. Sequineau. *Dictionary of Proper Names and Places in the Bible.* Garden City, NY: Doubleday & Company, Inc, 1981.

Oswald, Roy and M., Otto Kroeger. *Personality Type and Religious Leadership.* New York: The Alban Institute, 1996.

Pastor's and Counselor' Reference Guide: "Stats and Facts." *Prodigals International* [journal on-line]; available from http://www.prodigals.com/dox/prg_stats.htm.

Pedigo, Thomas, L. *Restoration Manual: A Workbook for Restoring Fallen Ministers and Religious Leaders, 4th ed.* Colorado Springs: Thomas L. Pedigo, 2002.

Playfair, William, L. *The Useful Lie.* Wheaton, IL: Crossway Books, 1991.

Price, Richard, M. "The Distinctiveness of Early Christian Sexual Ethics," in *Sexuality and Gender,* eds. Adrian Thatcher and Elizabeth Stuart. Grand Rapids: William B. Eerdmans Pub., 1996.

"Questions About Sex/Love Addiction Sexaholics Anonymous FAQ 7/7/03,4-5. http://www.understandingsexualaddiction.org/safaq.htm

Ramey, Robert H., Jr. *Thriving in Ministry.* St. Louis, MO: Chalice Press, 2000.

Rediger, Lloyd, G. *Clergy killers: Guidance for Pastors and Congregations Under Attack.* Louisville, KY: Westminster John Knox Press, 1997.

Richards, Ramona. "Dirty Little Secret," *Today's Christian Woman* magazine, September/October, 2003.

Robech, CM, Jr., *The International Standard Bible Encyclopedia* Vol. 4, gen. ed.

Bromily, Geoffrey, W. Grand Rapids: William B. Eerdmans Publishing Company, 1988, 587.

Sandford, John and Mark, *Deliverance and Inner Healing* Grand Rapids: Chosen Books, 1992.

Schuchardt, Read, Mercer. "Hugh Hefner's Hollow Victory," *Christianity Today*, Dec.2003.

Scruton, R. *Sexual Desire: A Philosophical Investigation.* London: Weidenfeld and Nicolson.

Shaw, Theresa, M. *The Burden of the Flesh: Fasting and Sexuality in Early Christianity.* Minneapolis: Fortress Press, 1998.

William Smith, William. *Smith's Bible Dictionary,* revised edition. Philadelphia: A.J.Holman Company.

Toynbee, Phillip. *Toward the Holy Spirit.* London: SCM, 1982.

Unger, Merrill, F. *Demons in the World Today.* Wheaton, Ill: Tyndale House Publishers, 1971.

Uzma, Mazhar. "Cognitive Therapy and Anxiety. [journal on-line]; available from http://www.crescentlife.com/articles cognitive_therapy_ and_anxiety.htm.

Veyne, P., ed. *From Pagan Rome to Byzantium.* Harvard/Cambridge University Press, 1987.

Vine, W.E. *An Expository Dictionary of New Testament Words.* Westwood, NJ: Revell, 1952.

Von Rad, Gerhard. *Genesis: A Commentary,* rev. ed. Philadelphia: The Westminster Press, 1972.

Wallace, R.S., Bromiley, G.W. *The International Standard Bible Encyclopedia* vol. 4, gen. ed. Bromily, Geoffrey, W. Grand Rapids: William B. Eerdmans Publishing Company, 1988.

Walzer, R. *Galen on Jews and Christians.* Oxford: University Press, 1949.

Watters, Steve. "I Know What You Did Last Night" *Boundless Webzine,* 10 January, 2001.

Webster's New Collegiate Dictionary (1973).

Westbrook, Raymond. *The Anchor Bible Dictionary,* vol. 5. New York: Doubleday, 1992.

Westermann, Claus. *Isaiah 40-66: A Commentary.* Philadelphia: Westminster Press, 1969.

Wilson, Earl and Sandy, Paul and Virginia, Larry and Nancy Paulson. *Restoring the Fallen: A Team Approach to Caring, Confronting and Reconciliation.* Downers Grove, IL: InterVarsity Press, 1997.

Wimmer, Joseph, F. *Eerdman's Dictionary of the Bible.* ed. David Noel Freedman. Grand Rapids, MI: William B. Eerdmans Publishing Company.

Wiseman, Neil B., ed. *Architects of the Enduring: Classic Writings from the Builders of our Faith.* Kansas City: Beacon Hill Press, 2001.

Wyman, June, R., "Promising Advances Toward Understanding the Genetic Rots of Addiction" NIDA Supported Research, Vol 12, Number 4, July/August 1997.

End Notes

[1] Ralph Earl, "Overcoming Sexual Addiction," [cassette] (Colorado Springs: Focus on the Family, 2001).

[2] Kenny Luck, "Hazardous Material: The Pitfalls of Handling the Pornography Problem with Kid Gloves" *Christian Camp and Conference Journal* March/April 2003, vol. 7 – no. 3.

[3] Borrowed from a subtitle in book by Donald Joy, "Unfinished Business: How a Man Can Make Peace With His Past." Wheaton, IL: Victor Books, 1989

[4] Ibid., 24.

[5] O. Odelain and R. Sequineau, *Dictionary of Proper Names and Places in the Bible* (Garden City, NY: Doubleday & Company, Inc, 1981), 11-12.

G. W. Bromily, *The International Standard Bible Encyclopedia,* vol. 1 (Grand Rapids: William B. Eerdmans, 1979), 133.

[7] Joy, *Unfinished Business: How a Man Can Make Peace With His Past,* 22.

[8] Ibid, 22-23.

[9] Gerhard Von Rad, *Genesis: A Commentary,* rev. ed. (Philadelphia: The Westminster Press, 1972), 57.

[10] This is not to say that those who choose to live unmarried and chaste are, somehow, incomplete as a human being, but rather has chosen to experience life curtailed from sexual expression.

[11] Paul Avis, *Eros and the Sacred.* (Harrisburg, PA: Morehouse Publishing, 1989), 81.

[12] Title borrowed from Paul Avis' book, *Eros and the Sacred,* 81.

[13] C.M. Robech Jr., *The International Standard Bible Encyclopedia* Vol. 4, gen. ed. Bromily, Geoffrey, W. (Grand Rapids: William B. Eerdmans Publishing Company, 1988), 587.

[14] E.M. Good, *The Interpreter's Dictionary of the Bible: An Illustrated Encyclopedia*, vol. 3, ed. George Arthur Buttrick (Nashville: Abingdon Press, 1962), 165.

[15] Likewise, the soul (*nepes*) is considered the seat of the human emotions, both the center of joy in God (Ps. 86:4; 62:1) and desire of evil in the wicked (Prov. 21:10). Transducianism is the theological understanding that the soul is carried on through childbirth, a significant argument to consider in regard to sin's propensity to be passed on through generational lines.

[16] David Noel Freedman, ed, *The Anchor Bible Dictionary* vol. 2 (New York: Doubleday, 1992), 375-76. Interestingly, the same term, *eros*, is used to describe God's love for Israel in Deut 7:7 and 10:15.

[17] Ibid., 385.

[18] P. Veyne, ed., *From Pagan Rome to Byzantium* (Harvard/Cambridge University Press, 1987), 263.

[19] *parousia* (Gk.): The second coming of Christ.

[20] Richard M. Price, "The Distinctiveness of Early Christian Sexual Ethics," in *Sexuality and Gender*, eds. Adrian Thatcher and Elizabeth Stuart (Grand Rapids: William B. Eerdmans Pub., 1996), 23.

[21] Bromily, *The International Standard Bible Encyclopedia*, vol. 4, 436-437.

[22] Christian Cochini, S.J., *Apostolic Origins of Priestly Celibacy*, trans. Nelly Marans (San Francisco: Ignatius Press, 1990), 3.

[23] Ibid., 3.

[24] A reasonable notion considering the monastics writing these documents were themselves celibate.

[25] Theresa M. Shaw, *The Burden of the Flesh: Fasting and Sexuality in Early Christianity* (Minneapolis: Fortress Press, 1998), 159.

[26] R. Walzer, *Galen on Jews and Christians* (Oxford: University Press, 1949), p. 65.

[27] Thomas a'Kempis, *The Imitation of Christ*, trans. L. Sherley-Price (Harmondsworth: Penguin, 1952), 75.

[28] Avis, *Eros and the Sacred*, 97.

[29] Ibid., 142.

[30] Phillip Toynbee, *Toward the Holy Spirit* (London: SCM, 1982a.), 41.

[31] Donald Evans, *Struggle and Fulfillment* (London: Collins, 1980), 104.

[32] R.S. Wallace and G.W. Bromiley, *The International Standard Bible Encyclopedia* Vol. 4, gen. ed. Bromily, Geoffrey, W. (Grand Rapids: William B. Eerdmans Publishing Company, 1988), 256-58.

[33] Alen Ecclestone, *Yes to God* (London: Darton, Longman and Todd, 1975), 88

[34] Avis, *Eros and the Sacred*, 125.

[35] Von Rad, *Genesis: A Commentary*, 60.

[36] James Nelson, *Body Theology* (Louisville, KY: Westminster Press, 1992), 22.

[37] Quoted by R. Scruton, *Sexual Desire: A Philosophical Investigation* (London: Weidenfeld and Nicolson.), 83.

[38] S. Banks, *A Manual of Christian Doctrine.* (New York: Eaton and Mains Publishers, 1897), 237.

[39] Marilyn J. Lundberg, *Eerdman's Dictionary of the Bible,* ed. David Noel Freedman (Grand Rapids: William B. Eerdmans Publishing Company, 2000), 1224.

[40] J. Kenneth Grider, "A Wesleyan Holiness Theology" (Kansas City: Beacon Hill Press, 1994), 230-231.

[41] Joseph F. Wimmer, *Eerdman's Dictionary of the Bible,* ed. David Noel Freedman (Grand Rapids, MI: William B. Eerdmans Publishing Company, 2000), 993.

[42] Henry A. Boardman, *The Scripture Doctrine of Original Sin Explained and Enforced* (Philadelphia: William S. Martien, 1839), 2.

[43] Ibid, 14.

[44] Tikva Frymer-Kensky, *The Anchor Bible Dictionary,* vol. 5 (New York: Doubleday, 1992), 1146.

[45] Raymond Westbrook, *The Anchor Bible Dictionary,* vol. 5 (New York: Doubleday, 1992), 552.

[46] Ibid, 550.

[47] Anonymous, "Flirting Was a Real High for Me," in *Member Stories*, vol. 1, 2001. Nashville: Sexaholics Anonymous Incorporated, 10.

[48] Mark Laaser, Nils Friberg, *Before the Fall: Preventing Pastoral Sexual Abuse* (Collegeville, MN: Liturgical Press, 1998), 32-33.

[49] Anonymous, *Sexaholics Anonymous* (Nashville: SA Literature, 1989-2002), 15.

[50] Terry Muck, ed., *Sins of the Body* (Dallas: Word Publishing, 1989), 24.

[51] Anonymous, *Sexaholics Anonymous*, 12.

[52] Anonymous, *Sexaholics Anonymous*, 202.

[13] "Questions About Sex/Love Addiction Sexaholics Anonymous FAQ 7/7/03,4-5. http://www.understandingsexualaddiction.org/safaq.htm

[54] *Webster's New Collegiate Dictionary* (1973).

[55] Craig Nakken, *The Addictive Personality,* 2d ed. (Center City, Minnesota: Hazelden, 1996), 2.

[56] Ramona Richards, "Dirty Little Secret," *Today's Christian Woman* magazine, September/October, 2003, 60.

[57] Jeanette Batz, "Strung Out On Sex," *The St. Louis Riverfront Times*, 23 June, 1998. Http://www.healthymind.com/s-strung-out.html 7/30/03,1.

[58] Nakken, *The Addictive Personality, 2nd ed.*, 5.

[59] Steve Watters, "I Know What You Did Last Night" Boundless Webzine,January 10,2001, 4 Copyright Focus on the Family.

[60]Information based on study conducted by Patrick J. Carnes, documented in his book, *Don't Call it Love* (New York, Bantam Books, 1991), 38.

[61] According to numerous surveys, those persons seeking help for pornography addiction are a very small percentage compared to those who still suffer privately.

[62] *Final Report of the Attorney General's Commission on Pornography* (Nashville: Rutledge Hill Press, 1986), 291-301

[63] Carnes, *Don't Call it Love*, 34.

[64] Steven Arterburn, "Marks of Addictive Sex," 2003 [journal on-line]; available from http://www.pureintimacy.org/online1/essays/a0000003.html ; Internet ; accessed on 13 August 2003.

[65]P.L. Garber, *The International Standard Bible Encyclopedia*, vol. 2, (Grand Rapids: William B. Eerdmans Publishing, 1982),796.

[6] Ibid., 3.

[67] J. Budziszewski, *Virtual Unfaithfulness: Pornography Use in a Marriage.* Copyright 2000 J. Budziszewski 7/22/03, 1.

[68] Anonymous, *Sexaholics Anonymous*, 27.

[69] Batz, "Strung Out on Sex," 3-4.

[70]Patrick J. Carnes, *Don't Call it Love* (New York: Bantam, 1991), 30.

[71] Ibid., 25.

[72] Batz, "Strung Out on Sex," 7.

[73]David Holbrook, "The Pollution of Culture: Pornography and Philosophical Anthropology" *The Case Against Pornography*, ed. David Holbrook (LaSalle, Ill: Library Press Book, 1972), 3.

[74] Kenny Luck, "Hazardous Material: The Pitfalls of Handling the Pornography Problem with Kid Gloves," 3.

[75] Budziszewski, *Virtual Unfaithfulness: Pornography Use in a Marriage*, 1.

[76]Read Mercer Schuchardt, "Hugh Hefner's Hollow Victory," *Christianity Today*, Dec. 2003, 50-52.

[77] Leslie H. Farber, "Sex in Bondage to Modern Will: 'I'm Sorry Dear'" ed. David Holbrook, *The Case Against Pornography* (LaSalle, Ill: Library Press Book, 1972).

[78] W.W. Norton, "Man's Search for Himself" 1953 ed. David Holbrook, *The Case Against Pornography* (LaSalle, Ill: Library Press Book, 1972).

[79] Haridas Chaudhuri, "Wisdom in Human Relations" ed. Scott Miners, *A Spiritual Approach to Male/Female Relations* (Wheaton: The Theosophical Publishing House, 1984), 21.

[80] Anonymous, *Sexaholics Anonymous,* 13-14.

[81] Brent Curtis and John Eldridge, "Behind Sex Addiction is a Hunger for God" [journal on-line]; available from http://www.pureintimacy.org/online1/essays/a0000005.html ; Internet ; accessed on 13 August 2003.

[82] David H. Field, *Baker Encyclopedia of the Bible,* gen. ed. Walter A. Elwell (Grand Rapids: Baker Books, 1988), 33-34.

[83] See description of idolatry at beginning of chapter two.

[84] Anonymous, *From Shame to Grace: Stories of Recovery from Sex Addicts Anonymous* Nashville: SA Literature, 1994), 7.

[85] Laaser, Friberg, *Before the Fall: Preventing Pastoral Sexual Abuse,* 32.

[86] Pastor's and Counselor' Reference Guide: "Stats and Facts," *Prodigals International* [journal on-line]; available from http://www.prodigals.com/dox/prg_stats.htm; Internet; accessed 2 July 2003.

[87] Ralph Earle, "Overcoming Sexual Addiction", [cassette] (Colorado Springs: Focus on the Family, 2001).

[88] Nancy Myer Hopkins, *The Congregational Response to Clergy Betrayals of Trust* (Collegeville, MN: The Liturgical Press, 1998), 21-22.

[89] H.B. London and Neil B. Wiseman, *Pastors at Risk* (Wheaton, IL: Victor Books, 1993), 54.

[90] H.B. London and Neil B. Wiseman, *Your Pastor is an Endangered Species* (Wheaton, IL: Victor Books, 1996), 30.

[91] First appeared in the *Toronto Star* (Canada), Friday, March 26, 1999.

[12] Ibid.

[93] June R. Wyman, "Promising Advances Toward Understanding the Genetic Rots of Addiction" NIDA Supported Research, Vol 12, Number 4, July/August 1997,1-5.

[14] Julie M. Hopkins, *Towards a Feminist Christology* (Grand Rapids: William B. Eerdmans Publishing Co., 1994)

[95] Casi Kushel, "Sexuality: A Consideration of Context" in A *Spiritual Approach to Male/Female Relations,* ed. Scott Miners (Wheaton: The Theosophical Publishing House, 1984.), 17-18.

[16] Ibid, 19.

[97] Batz, "Strung Out On Sex," 5.

[98] Avis, *Eros and the Sacred*, viii

[99] Ralph Earle and Mark Laaser, *The Pornography Trap* (Kansas City: Beacon Hill Press, 2002), 25-26.

[100] Candace R. Benyei, *Understanding Clergy Misconduct in Religious Systems* (New York: The Haworth Press, Inc. 1998), 37-38.

[101] Earle, Laaser, *The Pornography Trap*, 34.

[102] Roy M. Oswald, Otto Kroeger, *Personality Type and Religious Leadership* (New York: The Alban Institute, 1996), 24-25.

[103] Ibid., 129.

[104] M. Robert Mulholland Jr., *Invitation to a Journey: A Road Map for Spiritual Formation* (Downers Grove, IL: InterVarsity Press, 1993), 57-77.

[105] Oswald, Kroeger, *Personality Type and Religious Leadership*, 128-129.

[106] Ibid, 133.

[107] There is compelling scientific research being done currently, linking genetic predisposition with addictions.

[108] London, Wiseman, *Pastors at Risk*, 22.

[109] George Barna, *Today's Pastors* (Ventura, CA: Regal Books, 1993), 49.

[110] London, Wiseman, *Pastors at Risk*, 22.

[111] Ibid, 25.

[112] Alexander Lowen, *Narcissism: Denial of the True Self* (New York: Collier Books, 1985), 25.

[113] Benyei, *Understanding Clergy Misconduct in Religious Systems*, 53-54.

[114] Earl, *Overcoming Sexual Addiction*, 134.

[115] Barna Research Ltd., "Church Attendance" March 1, 2004 www.barna.org/lcgi-bin/Home.asp

[116] London, Wiseman, *Pastors at Risk*, 113.

[117] Ibid, 114.

[118] Henry Cloud, John Townsend, *Boundaries* (Grand Rapids: Zondervan Publishing, 1993), 30.

[119] Mark R. Laaser, "Recovery for Couples" *Clinical Management of Sex Addiction*, eds. Patrick J. Carnes and Kenneth M. Adams (New York: Brunner-Rutledge, 2002), 129.

[120] There are a large number of issues involving pornography that are unique to each of the genders; far too many than can be looked at in this paper.

[121] Oswald, Kroeger, *Personality Type and Religious Leadership*, 130.

[122] Ann Bartram, "A Response to Pastor-Client Sexual Relations," in *Pastoral Care and Liberation Praxis*, ed. Perry LeFevre and W. Widdick Schroeder (Chicago: Exploration Press, 1996), 37-50.

[123] Adapted from the SA Manual: "The Spiritual Basis of Addiction," (Nashville: SA Literature, 1989-2002), 45-58)

[124] W. Robert Nay, *Taking Charge of Anger* (New York: The Guilford Press, 2004), 33-35.

[125] Anonymous, *Sexaholics Anonymous* (Nashville: SA Literature, 1989-2002), 51.

[126] Ibid, 52.

[127] Muck, *Sins of the Body*, 64.

[128] Anonymous, *Sexaholics Anonymous*, 52.

[129] Ibid., 53.

[130] Masund R. Khan, "Pornography and the Politics of Anger and Subversion" David Holbrook, ed, *The case Against Pornography*. (LaSalle, Ill: Library Press Book, 1972), 140.

[131] Anonymous, *Sexaholics Anonymous*, 55.

[132] Craig Larson, Ed, *Illustrations for Preaching and Teaching* (Grand Rapids: Baker Books, 1993),146.

[133] Ibid, 56.

[134] London, Wiseman, *Pastors at Risk*, 166.

[135] David D. Burns, MD., *The Feeling Good Handbook, Revised Edition* (New York: Plume, a member of Penguin Putnam, Inc., 1999), 93.

[136] Theodore Millon, *Disorders of Personality* (New York: John Wiley and Sons, 1981), 159.

[137] "The American Institute for Cognitive Therapy – Problems Addressed" http://www.cognitivetherapynyc.com/problemsaddresses.html

[138] Benyei, "Understanding Clergy Misconduct in Religious Systems", 57.

[139] Thomas Moore, *Care of the Soul: A Guide for Cultivating Depth and Sacredness in Everyday Life* (New York: Harper Perennial, 1992), 57-73.

[140] Gary L. McIntosh and Samuel D. Rima, Sr., *Overcoming the Dark Side of Leadership: The Paradox of Personal Dysfunction* (Grand Rapids: Baker Books, 1997), 98-99.

[141] Moore, *Care of the Soul: A Guide for Cultivating Depth and Sacredness in Everyday Life*, 71.

[142] McIntosh, Rima, *Overcoming the Dark Side of Leadership: The Paradox of Personal Dysfunction*, 100.

[143] Moore, *Care of the Soul: A Guide for Cultivating Depth and Sacredness in Everyday Life*, 65.

[144] McIntosh, Rima, *Overcoming the Dark Side of Leadership: The Paradox of Personal Dysfunction*, 101-103.

[145] Laaser, Mark, "Recovery for Couples", *Clinical Management of Sex Addiction* Patrick J. Carnes and Kenneth M. Adams, ed. (New York: Brunner-Rutledge, 2002), 129.

[146] Melody Beattie, *Beyond Codependency* (San Francisco: Harper/Hazelden, 1989), 11.

[147] Walter C. Jackson, *Codependence and the Christian Faith* (Nashville: Broadman Press, 1990), 136.

[148] Ibid, 90.

[149] Gary Moon, *Homesick for Eden: A Soul's Journey to Joy* (Ann Arbor, MI: Servant Publications, 1997), 43.

[150] McIntosh, Rima, *Overcoming the Dark Side of Leadership: The Paradox of Personal Dysfunction*, 122.

[151] Adopted from Melody Beattie, *Beyond Codependency*, 37-38

[152] William L. Playfair, *The Useful Lie* (Wheaton, IL: Crossway Books, 1991),119.

[153] Cloud, Townsend, *Boundaries*, 50-51.

[154] Beth Moore, *When Godly People Do Ungodly Things* (Nashville: Broadman and Holman Publishers, 2002), 40.

[155] Ibid., 34.

[156] Mark Laaser, Nils Friberg, "Before the Fall," 32

[157] William Smith, *Smith's Bible Dictionary*, revised edition Philadelphia: A.J. Holman Company), 260.

[158] Anonymous, *SA Manual*, 208.

[159] Borrowed from chapter one of *The Cost of Discipleship*, by Dietrich Bonhoeffer.

[160] Dietrich Bonhoeffer, *The Cost of Discipleship*, revised ed. (New York: Collier Books, 1963), 45-47.

[161] Ibid., 47-48

[162] Jeanette Batz, "Strung Out on Sex", 11

[163] Adapted from *Steve Arterburn's "Ten Steps to Overcoming Pornography Addiction,"* 3/26/03, http://www.newlife.com/10tips/BT327_overcoming_pornography_p

[164] Adapted from Dr. David C. Bissette, "The Nature of Recovery," 1996 http://www.healthymind.com/s-theory.html

[165] Walter Lowe, *Evil and the Unconscious* (Chico, CA: Scholars Press, 1983), 29.

[166] John and Mark Sandford, *Deliverance and Inner Healing* (Grand Rapids: Chosen Books, 1992), 28-29, 37.

[167]George A. Birch, *The Deliverance Ministry* (Camp Hill, PA: Horizon House Publishers, 1988), 89-90.

[168] Ibid., 90.

[169] Merrill F. Unger, *Demons in the World Today*, (Wheaton: Ill: Tyndale House Pulishers, 1971), 183.

[170] Sandford, *Deliverance and Inner Healing*, 92-93.

[171] Ibid., 41

[172] *Bible Encyclopedia*, Vol. 4, 55.

[173] C.S. Lewis, *The Problem of Pain* (London: Geoffrey Bles, 1952), 110.

[174] Beth Moore, *Praying God's Word: Breaking Free from Spiritual Strongholds* (Nashville: Broadman and Holman Publishers, 2000), 31.

[175]Clergy caught in sexual addiction will argue whether they are lost in sin or not, but if not, they are certainly treading close to the line and can slip at any point.

[176]James D. Berkley, *Making the Most of Mistakes* (Carol Stream, IL: Word Books, 1987), 113.

[177]Jim Amandus, "A Wounded Pastor's Rescue" *Leadership Magazine* Winter, 1993, 2.

[178] Neil B. Wiseman, ed., *Architects of the Enduring: Classic Writings from the Builders of our Faith* (Kansas City: Beacon Hill Press, 2001), 26.

[179]Barna Research Ltd., "Church Attendance."

[180]Barna Research Ltd., "Grow Your Church From the Outside In" March 1, 2004 www.barna.org/lcgi-bin/Home.asp

[181]James L. Mayes, ed, *The HarperCollins Bible Commentary*, (New York: HarperCollins Publishers, 1988), 1173.

[182]John H. Armstrong, *Can Fallen Pastors be Restored? The Church's Response to Clergy Misconduct*, 27.

[183]T. F. Johnson, *The International Standard Bible Encyclopedia*, Vol. 4, gen. ed. Geoffrey W. Bromiley (Grand Rapids: William B. Eerdmans Publishing, 1988), 144.

[184]William L. Lane, *Word Biblical Commentary*, Vol. 47a: Hebrew 1-8 (Dallas: Word Books, 1991), 141-42.

[185] W.E. Vine, *Expository Dictionary of the New Testament (Greek) Words* (Westwood, NJ: Revell, 1952), 220.

[186] Ibid, 220.

[187]London S. Bagster, *The Analytical Greek Lexicon* (Grand Rapids: Zondervan Publishing House, 1967), 220.

[188] Armstrong, *Can Fallen Pastors be Restored? The Church's Response to Sexual Misconduct*, 33-37.

[189] Moore, *Praying God's Word: Breaking Free from Spiritual Strongholds*, 53.

[190] Benyei, "Understanding Clergy Misconduct in Religious Systems", 83.

[191] Earl and Sandy Wilson, Paul and Virginia Friesen, Larry and Nancy Paulson, *Restoring the Fallen: A Team Approach to Caring, Confronting and Reconciliation* (Downers Grove, IL: InterVarsity Press, 1997), 137.

[192] Jack W. Hayford, *Restoring Fallen Leaders* (Ventura, CA: Regal Books, 1988), 26-27.

[193] Chapter two of Donald R. Hands and Way L Fehr's book, *Spiritual Wholeness for Clergy* offer a wonderful three-fold approach to the recovery process, involving "uncovery," "discovery," and "recovery" (New York: The Alban Institute, 1993), 15-26.

[194] Berkley, *Making the Most of Mistakes*, 123-24.

[19] Ibid, 131.

[196] Armstrong, *Can Fallen Pastors Be Restored? The Church's Response to Sexual Misconduct*, 105.

[197] "How Pure Must a Pastor Be?" *Leadership*, 9 (Spring 1988): 16. The roundtable discussion featuring Christian leaders Eugene Peterson, Charles Swindoll, G. Raymond Carlson, and Donald Njaa.

[198] Benyei, *Understanding Clergy Misconduct in Religious Systems*, 145-49.

[199] Steven Arterburn, Fred Stoeker, Mike Yorkey, *Preparing Your Son for Every Man's Battle: Honest Conversations about Sexual Integrity*, (Colorado Springs: Waterbrook Press, 2003.

[200] Hopkins, *The Congregational Response to Clergy Betrayals of Trust*, 33.

[201] Kenneth Kantzer, "The Road to Restoration." *Christianity Today*, 20 November, 1987.

[202] Thomas L. Pedigo, *Restoration Manual: A Workbook for Restoring Fallen Ministers and Religious Leaders,* 4th ed. (Colorado Springs: Thomas L. Pedigo, 2002), 86-87.

[203] Hayford, *Restoring Fallen Leaders*, 42.

[204] Pedigo, *Restoration Manual: A Workbook for Restoring Fallen Ministers and Religious Leaders*, 4th ed., 88-89.

[205] Hayford, *Restoring Fallen Leaders*, 35.

[206] Wiseman, *Architects of the Enduring: Classic Writings from the Builders of our Faith*, 16.

[207] Berkley, *Making the Most of Mistakes,* 141.

[208] J.D. Douglas, ed. *New Bible Dictionary*, 3d ed. (Downers Grove, IL: Inter-Varsity Press, 1962), 1003-04.

[209] Douglas, *New Bible Dictionary,* third ed., 1004.

[210] Claus Westermann, *Isaiah 40-66: A Commentary* (Philadelphia: Westminster Press, 1969), 132-33.

[211] Paul D. Hanson, *Interpretation: A Bible Commentary for Teaching and Preaching, Isaiah 40-66* (Louisville, KY: John Knox Press, 1995), 79.

[212] Hawthorn, Nathanial, *The Scarlet Letter.* (New York: Bartleby, 1999.

[213] Bob Broadbooks, *From Pastor to Pastor: Letters of Encouragement and Wisdom* (Kansas City: Beacon Hill Press, 2003), 53-56.

[214] Donald Harvey and Gene Williams, *Living in a Glass House: Surviving the Scrutiny of Ministry and Marriage* (Kansas City: Beacon Hill Press, 2002), 113.

[215] Gerald J. Jud, and others, *Ex-Pastors: Why Men Leave the Parish Ministry* (Philadelphia: Pilgrim Press, 1970), 2.

[216] Robert H. Ramey, Jr., *Thriving in Ministry* (St. Louis, MO: Chalice Press, 2000), 61.

[217] Jud, and others, *Ex-Pastors: Why Men Leave the Parish Ministry,* 25.

[218] Ibid, 30.

[219] Mary Ann Coate, *Clergy Stress: The Hidden Conflicts in Ministry* (London: SPCK Holy Trinity Church, 1989), 193.

[220] Stanley J. Grenz and Roy D. Bell, *Betrayal of Trust: Confronting and Preventing Clergy Sexual Misconduct* (Grand Rapids, MI: Baker Books, 1995), 133-137.

[221] Coate, *Clergy Stress: The Hidden Conflicts in Ministry,* 193-94.

[222] G Lloyd Rediger, *Clergy killers: Guidance for Pastors and Congregations Under Attack* (Louisville, KY: Westminster John Knox Press, 1997),198-199.

[223] From the ACA Communicator, - March 1990 - Omaha, Council Bluffs Area Intergroup

[224] Paul Handley and others, *The English Spirit: The Little Gidding Anthology of English Spirituality* (Nashville: Abingdon Press, 1987), 16-17.

[225] Published by Covenant Eyes Internet Accountability.

[226] "The porn addict...Accountability," Promise Keepers [on-line]

[227] Questions adapted from Gordon MacDonald, *Rebuilding Your Broken World,* (Nashville: Thomas Nelson Publishers, 1988), 203.

Printed in the United States
60230LVS00004B/39

9 781424 119110